RANGE AND VISION

RANGE
AND
VISION

THE FIRST HUNDRED YEARS OF
BARR & STROUD

MICHAEL MOSS

AND

IAIN RUSSELL

FOREWORD BY SIR ALWYN WILLIAMS

MAINSTREAM
PUBLISHING

First published in Great Britain in 1988 by
MAINSTREAM PUBLISHING COMPANY (EDINBURGH) LTD.
7 Albany Street, Edinburgh EH1 3UG

British Library Cataloguing in Publication Data.
Moss, Michael
    Range and Vision : the first 100 years of Barr & Stroud.
    1. Great Britain. Optical equipment industries. Barr & Stroud (Firm) to
    1987
    I. Title II. Russell, Iain
    338.4'76814'0941

ISBN 1-85158-128-6 (cloth)

Typeset in 12 on 13pt Baskerville by Bureau-Graphics Ltd., Glasgow.
Printed in Great Britain by Butler & Tanner Ltd, Frome and London

TABLE OF CONTENTS

Foreword
7

Preface
Calibrating the Sights
9

Chapter 1
Professors in Business: 1888-1900
13

Chapter 2
'Our Rangefinders have Proved the Most Accurate ...': 1900-1914
41

Chapter 3
Anniesland at War: 1914-1919
73

Chapter 4
Departures: 1919-1939
103

Chapter 5
'That Little Toyshop in Anniesland ...': 1939-1954
133

Chapter 6
New Objectives: 1954-1960
161

Chapter 7
Through a Glass Darkly: 1964-1977
195

Chapter 8
Sighting the Future: 1977-1988
227

Appendices
235

Bibliography
250

Index
251

FOREWORD

by

Sir Alwyn Williams
Principal, University of Glasgow

At a time when British Universities are being criticised for their failure to build close links with the business community, I am delighted to write a foreword to a history of a company that has its origins so firmly in the involvement of scientists in this University in industrial innovation.

From the beginning of the Barr and Stroud partnership in 1888, Professor Barr provided the commercial drive, taking his lead from his university mentor, Professor Sir William Thomson, Lord Kelvin. The outstanding natural scientist of the late-nineteenth century, Kelvin applied his theoretical knowledge to the invention of useful devices manufactured by his own firm.

Throughout the last hundred years Barr & Stroud and this university have maintained close links, feeding off each others' expertise and experience. The company has drawn successive generations of directors and managers from universities and in return has contributed to the development of scientific and management training in the West of Scotland. Such partnerships are not unusual in Glasgow; it is just that as academics we have taken them for granted.

It is, therefore, particularly satisfying for me to congratulate Barr & Stroud on its centenary. The company's recent achievements demonstrate vividly how the results of scientific enquiry, both pure and applied, benefit product development and production techniques. This book should be required reading for policy-makers who doubt the relevance of university-based research, for those businessmen who attach little importance to building bridges with universities, and for academics who believe themselves to be part of a cloistered community.

I wish Barr & Stroud well in the future, working as it is at the very boundaries of scientific knowledge in the complex field of opto-electronics. There is no doubt in my mind that this area of expertise offers exciting potential for the development of advanced innovative products in a number of markets. The continuing success of Barr & Stroud in meeting the challenge of new technology is essential for higher education and research in the West of Scotland.

March 1988
Gilmorehill
Glasgow.

CALIBRATING THE SIGHTS

The year 1888 was an eventful one. In London, Jack the Ripper stalked the streets, the *Financial Times* was established, and the Prime Minister, Lord Salisbury, looked on as the House of Commons rejected the Channel Tunnel Bill. Gustave Eiffel's huge tower was under construction in Paris and work on the Forth Railway Bridge near Edinburgh was well under way. In Glasgow, the City Chambers were inaugurated by Queen Victoria, the International Exhibition was held in Kelvingrove Park, and Renton defeated Clydesdale by six goals to one to win the Scottish Football Association Challenge Cup. It was a year of significant advances in science and technology, when John Boyd Dunlop fitted his first pneumatic tyres to his son's tricycle, the first motion pictures were made by Louis le Prince in a garden in Leeds, Karl Benz began to manufacture the first petrol-driven motor-cars and Sir David Solomons designed the first electric switch socket. It was also the year in which the firm of Barr & Stroud was born.

There is a commonly held view that British universities have contributed little to the development of industrial enterprise. The universities have been perceived as ivory towers in which professors turned their back on trade and confined their studies to purely academic research, while seeking to train their students for careers in the professions. This view does not hold true for the University of Glasgow. As the shipbuilding and engineering industries developed in the West of Scotland during the nineteenth century, professors at the University such as MacQuorn Rankin, Sir William Thomson and his brother, Lord Kelvin, contributed their scientific insight and expertise to the advance of technology. Their close relationship with industry attracted students from countries as far apart as the USA, India and Japan, who were eager to learn and to introduce new skills into their own industries. Lord Kelvin, not content purely to advise others, became an industrialist himself, and his former student, Archibald Barr, followed his example.

Dr Barr was appointed Professor of Civil and Mechanical Engineering at the University of Glasgow in 1889, having already invented an optical rangefinder and other optical instruments in collaboration with Dr William Stroud. Building on the traditions of the University and the example of his predecessors, the new professor was determined to deepen the relationship between his department and industry in the belief that 'the teacher and the research student should both be in intimate contact with the conditions and requirements of the industry to which their work had reference.' With Dr Stroud he formed his own company to develop and manufacture the products of their collaborative work in the invention of advanced optical and mechanical instruments. In shaping their enterprise the two inventors set great store by the recruitment of men with academic training, most of them from Dr Barr's own classes, and by the application of their skills to product development. This commitment has been a characteristic of the business of Barr & Stroud ever since.

Soon after setting up their first workshop in Byres Road, in Glasgow, Dr Barr and Dr Stroud employed three engineering students, five tradesmen and an apprentice. Today, over one quarter of their 1,300 employees have degree or standard technical qualifications. The close links with local institutions of higher education have remained since the deaths of Dr Barr and

Dr Stroud, Sir James French serving as chairman of the board of governors of the Royal Technical College (the predecessor of the University of Strathclyde) until his death in 1954, Dr J. Martin Strang acting as an assessor of the General Council of the University of Glasgow between 1953 and 1969, and Tom Johnston, the current managing director, as a member of the Court of the University of Strathclyde.

The case of Barr & Stroud provides a counter to the argument that British universities were biased against careers in business, and that industrialists were generally unwilling to employ the talents of science graduates and exploit the technological breakthroughs achieved by British scientists and inventors. The company was founded by two academics with the drive and initiative to apply their talents to commercial enterprise, and Barr & Stroud quickly established a world-wide reputation for innovation and for the quality craftmanship and reliability of their instruments. That reputation survives today, and Barr & Stroud are acknowledged world leaders in many areas of modern technology. With so many books being written about the history of once-great companies in the West of Scotland, which have stagnated and gone into decline, it is a pleasure to recount the story of a Glasgow firm which has not only survived, but gone from strength to strength. We know that the directors, staff and employees of Barr & Stroud have no illusions about the difficult challenges they face in the future, in the highly competitive markets in which they compete. However, we have sensed also a determination to do everything possible to ensure that the firm goes into its second century enjoying the high reputation and success it gained during the first.

In calibrating our sights we would like to thank Tom Johnston and his fellow directors for inviting us to undertake the task. We owe a special debt of gratitude to Charles Lindsay, the assistant managing director, for his guidance and his assistance in tracking down old photographs and missing pieces in the jigsaw of the story. David Ritchie, formerly the firm's technical director, offered encouragement and took a great deal of time to explain to us, in simple language, the intricacies of the most complex scientific instruments and techniques. Hugh Kelly, formerly the company's secretary and financial director, helped us to interpret the financial records of Barr & Stroud and compiled for us, in tabular form, a useful summary of the firm's performance during the private partnership years, 1895-1954.

The full examination of Barr & Stroud's extensive archive of business correspondence, technical papers and legal documents would provide full employment over many years for a team of researchers. We were lucky to have guides to lead us to the most fruitful sources of information, and to enlighten us on aspects of the company's history which were not recorded at the time. Our first guide was Dr J. Martin Strang himself, who compiled a manuscript history of the company shortly before his death in 1970. It provided us with his recollections of 65 years with the firm, and a host of leads to follow up in the company's archives. This volume was annotated and extended by Montague Timbury, and then taken up to 1977 by Guthrie Strang. The second was Archie Walker, who joined Barr & Stroud as an apprentice in 1919, was in charge of Dr Barr's private laboratory at Anniesland between 1927 and 1931, and went on to pursue a highly successful career with the firm, most notably in the development of optical cements. Mr Walker's detailed knowledge of the Barr & Stroud archives, and his vivid memories of events in the factory stretching back over 69 years, were made freely available to us. His painstaking attention to detail proved equally valuable when he read and offered his comments on the text. Tom Johnston, Charles Lindsay and David Ritchie also provided us with useful comments on early drafts of the chapters.

We are grateful to others from Barr & Stroud for their help and advice. Gordon Hamilton, Dr Alexander Hope, Stanley Pratt, and Ian Fischbacher offered expert advice on the story of the development of Barr & Stroud equipments. Ian Foster and Lynn Mathieson in the photographic department dealt cheerfully with requests for hundreds of photographs, many of them printed from the firm's vast collection of glass negatives, from the period c.1900 to 1945. Ann MacDonald helped us track down various items in the company library, and Kate Murchison provided additional material. Charles Lindsay's secretary, Joyce Gallagher, helped us to gain access to the many men and women in the factory whose assistance we required, whether it was to give advice on technical matters, to produce keys for long-unopened cupboards and storerooms, to provide assistance in transporting records or boxfuls of old glass negatives around the works, or to decipher her boss's handwriting!

We have been very fortunate in obtaining sound guidance and great assistance in our research, from many individuals and institutions from the world beyond Anniesland. John Campbell answered our many inquiries relating to naval history, Jon Sumida shared with us the results of his meticulous research in the history of naval fire-control, Alan Mackinlay offered notes on the company's labour relations 1914-39, Mari Williams provided information on Barr & Stroud's competitors in Britain and France, and R. Wallace Clarke's notes on aircraft gunsights proved to be fascinating and very helpful. Mrs Louise Harper, W.S. Murray and the Archivists of Oxford, Leeds, and London Universities, and of the City of Bristol, helped to obtain a clearer picture of the lives and careers of Dr Barr and Dr Stroud.

Staff in the Glasgow Room of the Mitchell Library, Glasgow University Library, the British Library newspaper annexe, the Public Record Office at Kew, the National Library and Scottish Record Office in Edinburgh, and the Imperial War Museum's Department of Photographs, were unfailingly helpful. Our written enquiries were answered promptly and fully by James Insley, William Reid, V. A. Tarrant, Professor Sami Kita, Robert Bell, Ewan Small, and the libraries of the Ministry of Defence, Science Museum, Royal Artillery Institution, RAF Museum, and Naval Historical Library.

Mrs Rita Hemphill exhibited great patience and skill in typing and correcting numerous drafts of the chapters, and the final manuscript of the book.

PROFESSORS IN BUSINESS: 1888-1900

Early on the morning of 26 May 1888 a 32-year-old Scotsman named Archibald Barr paid an unexpected visit to his next-door neighbour, William Stroud, at his home in Ashwood Villas in Leeds. Barr was the Professor of Engineering at the Yorkshire College of Science, and his 28-year-old neighbour was the Cavendish Professor of Physics there. The two young men had been collaborating on a scientific research project, hoping that they might be able to publish their findings and establish their reputations in the world of academic science. However, after three months of hard work they had begun to tire of their worthy investigations, and Professor Barr made his early morning visit to suggest to his colleague that they embark on a more exciting project. He had been reading the previous day's edition of the journal *Engineering* and noticed an advertisement placed by the War Office, inviting inventors to submit designs for a military rangefinder suitable for service in the field with the British Army. The two professors had worked together a year earlier to devise a teaching aid, a photographic machine which could produce lantern slides from book illustrations, and they had discovered that the mechanical engineer with a talent for design and the scientist with a flair for invention made an excellent team. With this in mind, Dr Stroud readily agreed to his colleague's suggestion that they abandon their academic research for the time being, and concentrate on the potentially lucrative task of devising an optical rangefinder. Thus began a distinguished partnership, and a leading firm of optical instrument makers was born.

Archibald Barr and William Stroud were two remarkable Victorian men of science.

The Secretary of State for War, on behalf of the Lords Commissioners of the Admiralty, is prepared to receive PRO-POSALS from persons desirous of SUBMITTING, for competitive trial, RANGE-FINDERS for NAVAL USE, which shall fulfil the following conditions:—

1. The instrument should be dependent on one observer, but consideration will be given to any two-observer instrument that shows exceptional merit, and is found workable on ship-board.

2. It must be capable of recording the ranges in yards, either continuously or at least ten times a minute.

3. The instrument should be capable of having its records transmitted to the gun or guns through some system of instantaneous communication.

4. The instrument should be capable of measuring the range from the ship to any vessel or object, irrespective of the course steered by, or the speed of, either vessel.

5. The instrument should be such that, irrespective of the motion of the ship, it should be possible for the observer to follow the object, and (without calculation) to take continuous records of its distance.

6. It should be capable of standing the usage which it would receive in actual service, and should be as simple in construction as possible.

7. It should be uninfluenced by any ordinary changes in temperature or weather.

8. The instrument should be capable of measuring ranges up to at least 3000 yards, with a maximum error of 3 per cent.

9. Preference will be given to a range-finder that can be used at night.

_____

The advertisement which led to the founding of Barr & Stroud: from Engineering, *25 May 1888.*

Archibald Barr was born on 18 November 1855 in Glenfield, near Paisley in the West of Scotland, the son of a yarn merchant.[1] He was educated at Paisley Grammar School, which he left at the age of fifteen to begin an apprenticeship in the workshops of a local firm of boilermakers and engineers, A. F. Craig & Co.[2] Two years later, in 1873, he matriculated at Glasgow University to study for a degree of Bachelor of Science, specialising in engineering.[3] The Department of Civil Engineering and Mechanics, founded in 1840, had pioneered 'sandwich' courses, whereby students were expected to spend their summer holidays, from late March until early October, gaining practical experience by working in engineering workshops. Some firms encouraged their apprentices to attend a few science and engineering classes in order to further their education, but BSc courses were only introduced at the University in 1872, and Barr was one of the first students to study for the degree while serving his apprenticeship.[4]

Archibald Barr was a gregarious young man, and he enjoyed the social life of a student. Although he was only about five feet five inches tall, he was well-built and physically strong, and he was a keen sportsman. He became a fine lacrosse player during his university days, and was selected to play for his country against Ireland during the 1870s.[5] Nevertheless, social and sporting pursuits took second place to Barr's studies, and his academic record was an impressive one. He was rarely to be found outwith the top three in his class when examination results were published, and at the end of his second year he won two class prizes for engineering subjects, as well as the George Harvey Prize of £20 for showing 'the greatest proficiency in the Department of Applied Mechanics and Shipbuilding'.[6] James Thomson, Regius Professor of Civil Engineering and Mechanics, was impressed by his talented student's enthusiasm for experimental work and by his ability to find practical solutions to theoretical problems set before him in the classroom. Soon after Barr completed his apprenticeship in 1876 the professor offered him a position in his department.

The widow of the Reverend Black of the Barony Church in Glasgow bequeathed £15,000 to the University in 1876, stipulating that part of the bequest be used to create a new post for an assistant to the Professor of Civil Engineering and Mechanics. The post was to be called the Young Assistantship, in memory of her late father, and the salary was to be '£140 or thereby'.[7] Barr completed his degree course in March 1877, in the same month that the University Court approved his appointment as the first Young Assistant.[8] He took up the post in November, and delayed sitting his final examinations until 1878, when he graduated with a BSc in Engineering Science.[9]

Barr's duties involved assisting the professor with lecturing and giving laboratory demonstrations to the students. He also helped Thomson, the foremost engineering scientist of the day, with the latter's private consultancy work and other projects. Some of this private research was undertaken in collaboration with Thomson's brother, Sir William, whose classes in Natural Philosophy at Glasgow University Barr had attended for one session as a student.

The two inventors deep in discussion in Dr Stroud's garden in Leeds, c. 1890. Dr Barr is on the left.

Sir V...   Kelvin of Largs in
189...   eatest physicist of
his   also a successful
inv...   ...netic, electrical,
o...   ...ruments, which he
p...   ...ured and marketed
...   ...nstrument makers,
James ...   ...s Thomson and his
young assistant ...ped ...ir William with his
experimental work and also suggested ways in
which his inventions could be designed to
simplify the process of manufacture and to
ensure the greatest ease of use for the customer.
Barr found the experience of working with the
two famous brothers an exhilarating one, and
he wrote later of his mentors that:

> No one who has studied under these masters and
> worked in close association with them for many
> years could fail to find that the whole of his
> subsequent work and his every thought regarding
> the methods and results of physical science were
> not only founded upon the principles which they
> taught, but conditioned and controlled by the
> punctilious regard for strictness of proof and
> exactitude of expression which characterised all
> their investigations and writings.[11]

Sir William exerted a particularly strong
influence on Barr's subsequent career. He
believed strongly in the importance of
providing well-equipped laboratories in
universities, to offer students a practical
education in scientific subjects, and Barr never
forgot the importance of demonstration work
in his later career as a teacher. In addition, Sir
William impressed the young assistant with his
view that 'the life and soul of science is its
practical application', and that academic

research could and should be put to
commercial uses.[12] Barr left the University in
1884 to become Professor of Engineering at the
Yorkshire College of Science in Leeds, and set to
work immediately to raise money from local
industrialists to build a new laboratory for his
department. When he met William Stroud one
year later, he found a man willing to join him in
applying science to industrial enterprise.

William Stroud was born in Bristol on
2 February 1860, the son of a dispensing
chemist who was the proprietor of 'Stroud's
Pectoral Oxymel of Horehound', a shop in the
city's Wine Street.[13] Young Stroud was troubled
by ill-health, but he was an excellent pupil at the
local grammar school, Clifton College, and won
a scholarship in 1878 to study at University
College Bristol. Despite the advice of his
teacher, that he should pursue his studies in
Latin and Greek, Stroud chose to study
chemistry. He showed a great talent for what he
liked to call 'stinks', and in 1879 he gained
another scholarship, to study at Owen's College
in Manchester for a BSc awarded by London
University. He graduated with a first in
Chemistry in 1882.[14]

Stroud left Manchester before sitting his final
examinations, after winning yet another
scholarship in 1881 to study at Balliol College,
Oxford. According to family tradition, he
intended to enter the Church after completing
his university education and he went to Oxford
intending finally to study classics. However,
soon after he arrived at Balliol he attended a
lecture given by the famous physicist Professor
Tyndall, and he was so enthralled that he
decided to study natural science instead.[15]

Stroud's health improved during his teens,
and while he was not keen on team sports he led

an active social life, possessing a whimsical sense of humour and a keenly expressed sense of the ridiculous which endeared him to most of his fellow students. At Balliol, however, he felt that he was snubbed by the offspring of the rich and titled. He remembered in later years that the future Lord Curzon and his 'set' were contemptuous of a mere chemist's son, with his unsophisticated manner, unfashionable clothes and provincial accent, and they looked down upon a student who required a scholarship to enable him to meet his university fees and living expenses. Stroud never forgot the experience, and in later years he showed a marked lack of interest in climbing social ladders or in acquiring the trappings of wealth and status which his success made available to him.[16]

The snobbery which he encountered at Balliol did not prevent Stroud from performing brilliantly as a student there. He graduated in 1884 with a double first in Mathematics and Natural Sciences, and in July he set off for Germany to continue his studies. His mother, Mary Stroud, had a small private income, and she had helped William and his younger brother, Henry, to complete their university educations by giving them each a small monthly allowance to help pay for books and lodgings.[17] She gave her elder son £66.10s to help meet the cost of the trip to Germany, and the remaining part of his expenses was met by one of his professors, who sponsored him in the belief that further study abroad would help him in gaining his doctorate. Stroud went to the University of Wurzburg, where he experimented with electricity in Professor Kohlransch's celebrated laboratory, and also attended Professor Quincke's lectures at the University of Heidelberg. It was on a visit to Heidelberger

Schloss in 1884 that he smoked his first cigar, thus acquiring a habit for life. He returned to England in April 1885 to sit examinations at London University in static and dynamic electricity, electro-chemistry, heat, and magnetism for his doctorate, and he was awarded a DSc some months later.[18]

Soon after his return from Germany, Dr Stroud was told that the Cavendish Chair of Physics at the Yorkshire College of Science in Leeds had fallen vacant. He was pressed by his former tutors to apply for the post and one of the testimonials he presented in support of his candidacy, written by Harold B. Dixon, the lecturer and tutor in Natural Science at Balliol, reveals that Dr Stroud was already recognised as an exceptionally able young scientist:

My pupil William Stroud...in standing for a Professorship at the close of his University course may perhaps lay himself open to the charge of presumption. Mr Stroud has come forward as a candidate...only under strong pressure from those who know him intimately.

Of Mr Stroud's special knowledge of Electricity it is not my place to speak, but of his wide study of chemistry and chemical physics, of his rapidity and manipulative skill in experiment, of his indomitable energy and power of work I can speak by reason of my close association with him in our College laboratory. But Mr Stroud is much more than a quick learner and successful student; his cleverness and ingenuity in device are remarkable. In the application of principles to practice Mr Stroud seems to me to possess a real genius.

I have had several opportunities of hearing him speak before the University Scientific Club, and have been struck by the cleverness of his exposition and the enthusiasm of his style.[19]

Any doubts about the suitability of so young a man for the chair at the Yorkshire College of Science were dispelled when Dr Stroud presented his glowing testimonials and the evidence of his brilliant academic record. He was appointed in July and travelled north immediately to prepare for his first term as a professor. Dr Stroud soon discovered that the equipment in his small departmental laboratory was old and obsolete, and that the College could not afford to replace it. He began the laborious task of writing out descriptions of experiments to hand out to his thirty-seven students, and began to paint diagrams on black cloth of the apparatus which would be suitable for conducting these experiments. He found the job of illustrating his lectures particularly tedious, and in his spare time he and his assistant began to design a magic lantern which could magnify small apparatus on a screen. Archibald Barr, the new Professor of Engineering at the College, had already raised the large sum of the money required to build and equip his new engineering laboratory, and was looking around for suitable equipment to install there. When he met Dr Stroud for the first time in August 1885 the conversation probably turned to the Professor of Physics' magic lantern, and Barr may have offered advice on the problems involved in designing mechanical parts which would best serve Dr Stroud's requirements. The two men struck up a friendship, but they were too busy with their professorial duties at first to devote time to devising other teaching aids together. They also took on greater domestic responsibilities in 1885, Barr marrying Isabella Young, the

daughter of a Paisley timber merchant, and Dr Stroud marrying the 17-year-old Louisa Emett, whose family lived near the Stroud family home in Bristol.[20]

When the Strouds moved to a semi-villa next door to the Barrs, the professors' friendship deepened. During 1887 they started to work together on devising the lantern-slide camera, which they patented two years later and which soon became a standard item of equipment in

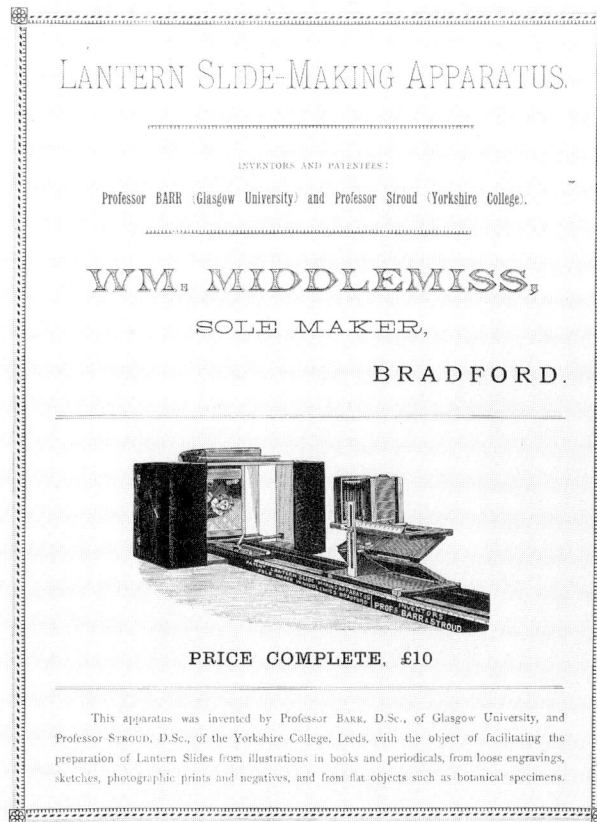

The first product of Dr Barr's collaboration with Dr Stroud, manufactured by William Middlemiss under licence. In 1892, the two inventors were paid £23.10s in royalties for sales of the laintern-slide camera: their first earnings as partners in scientific enterprise.

British colleges and universities. Their desire to further their reputations and careers in academia then led them to start work on their own research project, an investigation of means of determining the numerical value of the mechanical equivalent of heat, before Barr suggested that they turn instead to devising an optical rangefinder to the specifications laid down in the War Office's advertisement in *Engineering*. Although they had no specialist knowledge of optics, they felt sure that Dr Stroud's wide knowledge of theoretical science and Barr's experience in assisting Lord Kelvin in the design of scientific instruments would enable them to overcome the problems involved in making a new rangefinder. At this early stage of enthusiastic commitment to their joint project, they were unaware of the problems which had beset other inventors in the development of military rangefinders.[21]

The Royal Artillery had been equipped with its first optical rangefinders in the late 1870s, to assist officers to find the ranges of distant targets. These instruments operated on the principle that a triangle is determined by a side and two angles. The standard British Army rangefinder was a two-observer instrument, the Watkin Mekometer, which consisted of an instrument similar to a box sextant, attached by a cord of 25 or 30 yards in length to an optical square. The observer carrying the optical square manoeuvred, keeping the cord taut, until the instrument showed that the angle subtended by the line of sight to the target, and the other to his comrade, was one of 90°. The second observer then measured the second base angle in the right-angled triangle of known base length. The scale on the second observer's instrument was calibrated to give a reading of the range of the target when the right-angled triangle had been set out.[22]

The Mekometer, like the other two-and three-observer instruments available, could measure distances with great accuracy in good conditions. However, the delicate optical parts were liable to become damaged and the calibrating screw deranged by rough handling in the field, while the observers sometimes found difficulty in communicating with each other, and with the gunlayers, in the noise and confusion of battle. Moreover, the system was too cumbersome to provide a sufficiently swift series of readings when a target was on the move and the range was changing rapidly.[23]

During the 1870s and 1880s the British infantry fought several campaigns in distant parts of the empire, nearly all against tribesmen with primitive weapons and, by European standards, using primitive tactics. Despite some spectacular reverses, British troops were usually successful in holding off frontal attacks by massed ranks of hostile natives. However, it was discovered that vast quantities of ammunition were wasted as the troops were unable to estimate ranges accurately, particularly when an enemy advanced at speed. The inferior marksmanship of British Tommies was highlighted at the Battle of Majuba Hill in South Africa in 1882, when Boer riflemen found little difficulty in picking off their targets, forcing the British to retreat in disarray from a strong tactical position.[24] The War Office responded in 1888 by placing the advertisement in *Engineering* for an infantry rangefinder which could withstand rough usage in the field, which could provide a range at 1,000 yards to within an error of 4 per cent (40 yards), and with which a man of average intelligence could take four

Two observers using a Steward Telemeter, one of several instruments advertised during the 1880s and 1890s which worked on the same principles as the Watkin Mekometer.

readings per minute. Their advertisement noted that single-observer instruments would be preferred to others, and so Barr and Dr Stroud concentrated on devising just such an instrument.[25]

The first British single-observer rangefinder of note had been invented by Patrick Adie, a scientific instrument maker, who patented it in 1860. It consisted of a metal tube, with an eye-piece at the centre and mirrors set at each end, 3 feet 6 inches apart. The observer held the instrument horizontally, and an image of the object was reflected by each of the end mirrors along the tube to two mirrors at the centre, which reflected the images to the eye-piece.

One end mirror was fixed at an angle of 135° to the line of the tube, which formed the base of the triangle, and so the beam of light from the object was reflected through an angle of 90° to the centre mirror. The other end mirror was attached to an arm, and by turning a micrometer screw it could be manipulated to the angle required to make the two images of the object appear as one at the eye-piece. Once the images coincided, the observer knew that he had set out a right-angled triangle, and the micrometer screw was calibrated to give a reading of the range according to the angle at which the adjustable mirror was set. Adie's instrument was ingeniously simple in conception, but like the Mekometer it featured too many delicate parts to be entirely suited to the needs of the infantry or artillery. The base length of the triangle was so short that the slightest error in determining the angular motion of the end reflector gave great errors in the readings of ranges. As the reflectors could not be fixed firmly, and as any want of truth in the micrometer screw which moved the arm, or any bending of the arm itself, affected the accuracy of the rangefinder, a hard knock was sufficient to render the instrument practically useless. Rangefinders developed by Arnulf Mallock, the Astronomer Royal W.H.M. Christie, and other inventors, featured minor improvements on Adie's design, but they too were considered too fragile and too bulky for military service.[26]

The War Office required that a rangefinder design had to be submitted to them by 1 August 1888, and a completed instrument by 31 December, so Barr and Dr Stroud had to work quickly. Dr Stroud recalled later that their first, hastily assembled model, was 'a ghastly failure',

but they persevered.[27] Encouraged by Lord Kelvin, to whom Barr wrote seeking comments on their first rough sketches, they were able to produce a practical design by the end of June, and complete a working model rangefinder in time to meet the War Office's deadline at the end of the year.[28]

Although the design which Barr and Dr Stroud presented to the War Office in 1888 bore similarities to earlier instruments, it incorporated important innovations. The rangefinder had a base length of 3 feet, with reflectors at the ends, but featured two eye-pieces rather than one. The left eye-piece formed part of a Galileo's telescope of small magnifying power and a wide field of view, and the observer used it to 'find' the target and fix it at the centre of the field. He could then observe the target, under greater magnification, in the more restricted field of view of the right eye-piece. Other instruments embodied mirrors as the end reflectors, but Barr and Dr Stroud found that they were difficult to fix securely. They decided instead to use totally reflecting glass prisms, forming grooves on the upper and lower surfaces and clamping them lightly between the top and bottom members of the framework of the instrument, where they were fixed with a hard dental cement. The college professors provided a novel arrangement for the central mirrors, which transmitted the images from the end reflectors to the right eye-piece, by placing one over the other and inclining each one at 45° to the axis of the rangefinder. Part of each mirror was blocked off, so that a partial image from the right-hand reflector appeared below and the partial image from the left appeared above a horizontal line of separation. To find the range, the observer had

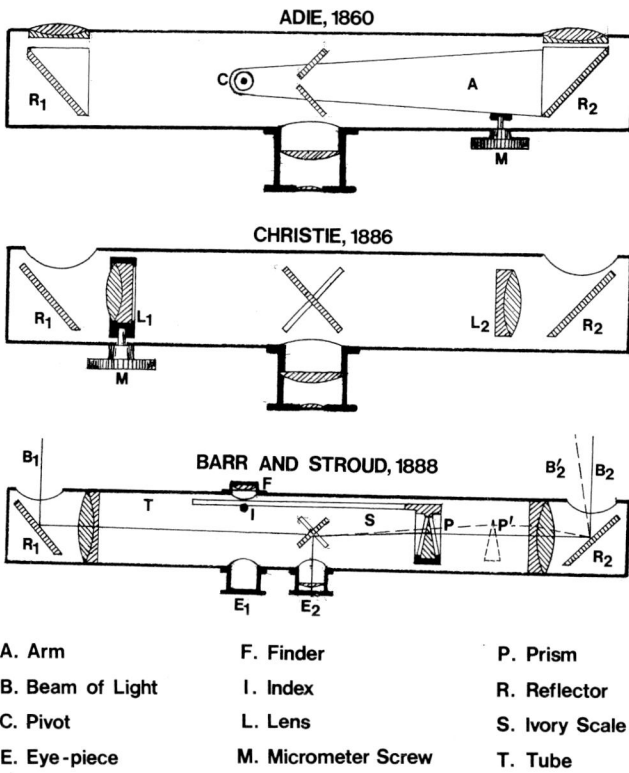

A. Arm

B. Beam of Light

C. Pivot

E. Eye-piece

F. Finder

I. Index

L. Lens

M. Micrometer Screw

P. Prism

R. Reflector

S. Ivory Scale

T. Tube

The internal arrangements of early single-observer rangefinders. The Barr & Stroud was more practical in design and mechanically more reliable than earlier inventions.

to bring the partial images into coincidence at the line of separation — in other words, he had to make the two halves of an image of the object appear as one whole.

The professors' most important innovation lay in their method of bringing the partial images into coincidence. 'Drunken' screws, faulty micrometers and deranged reflectors had adversely affected earlier instruments. In the Barr & Stroud instrument, however, both end reflectors were fixed securely in place to translate the rays of light from the target through 90° and transmit them along the

instrument. The displacement of the image from the right-hand reflector was effected by moving an achromatic refracting prism of small angle along the path of the beam of light. This was done by turning a screw. A scale was attached to the prism and was calibrated to translate the position of the prism into a reading of the range, when the partial images coincided at the right eye-piece and the right-angled triangle was thereby set out with the target. The scale appeared in the upper field of view in the left eye-piece.

As the range of the distant object was found by the relatively open scale movement of the prism, rather than by making minute alterations to the angle at which a reflector was set, the rangefinder invented by Barr and Dr Stroud was less prone to derangement than other single-observer instruments. Mechanical imperfections, such as drunken screws, did not affect the readings, because the scale was attached to the prism itself and moved with it. The professors guarded against damage to the optical parts by mounting them on a special frame, protected by an inner tube to which they were attached at only two points by a gimbal-ring arrangement and by three struts. The inner tube was protected in turn by an outer tube, and a wide space separated the two so that even a considerable blow causing damage to the latter would not harm the inner tube or the frame enclosed within it. The space between the outer and inner tubes also helped protect the frame from the effects of sudden changes of temperature, as when bright sunshine fell upon only one side of the instrument.[29]

In the invention of the rangefinder, as in the lantern-slide camera, the partnership of the scientist and the mechanical engineer proved highly successful. Dr Stroud's inventive mind produced the ideas for overcoming problems which arose in making a reliable single-observer rangefinder, and he was able to test his theoretical solutions by setting up experimental models in his laboratory. When Dr Stroud was satisfied that his ideas were practicable, Barr took over. Barr believed that 'the skill of the inventor and designer...should be directed towards the elimination, as far as possible, of the need for accurate and difficult craftsmanship, the effects of the qualities of materials available, and the wear and tear in the finished product.'[30] He took Dr Stroud's inventions and incorporated them in the design of an instrument which was relatively simple to manufacture and assemble, which contained as few delicate parts as possible, and which was simple to use, maintain and repair. The two men worked as a team, and did not stick rigidly to their own areas of expertise. Barr criticised Dr Stroud's ideas and theoretical drawings when they seemed impractical or over-elaborate, and the inventor offered suggestions to the designer on how best to turn his plans into a working model. However, each man worked to his strengths, and respected the genius of the other in his field. When the time came to manufacture the new instrument, Dr Stroud drew up the specifications for the lenses and prisms they required, and sent them off to the optical instrument makers, Thomas Cooke & Sons of York. Barr returned to Glasgow to obtain the mechanical parts they required. James White & Co, with whom Barr would have had dealings during the days when he worked with Sir William Thomson, were asked to manufacture the frame, tubes, screws and other metallic parts of the rangefinder. Barr then

BOTTOMLEY & LIDDLE,
CHARTERED PATENT AGENTS,
154 St. Vincent Street, GLASGOW.

N° 9520   A.D. 1888

Date of Application, 30th June, 1888
Complete Specification Left, 30th Apr., 1889—Accepted. 29th June, 1889
PROVISIONAL SPECIFICATION.

Improvements in Instruments for Measuring Distances and Angles, Specially Applicable to Telemeters or Range Finders and other Analogous Instruments.

We Archibald Barr professor of Engineering and William Stroud professor of Physics both of the Yorkshire College Leeds in the County of York do hereby declare the nature of this invention to be as follows :—

The object of our Invention is to provide an instrument whereby the distance of moving or stationary objects or the size of the same may be easily and rapidly indicated or ascertained, with a considerable degree of accuracy ; whilst the base line from which such observation or observations are made may be of very limited length : such instrument being also capable of measuring or indicating with like facility and accuracy the angle included by lines of direction, which have but an exceedingly slight inclination with regard to each other ; and also the direction and the rate of the motion of moving bodies.

Our Invention further relates to the means for mounting such instrument for the special purpose for or to which it may be applied, and for avoiding any liability to derangement or damage during use or transport :—to means for correctly adjusting the same either during construction or for the correction of any derangement it may have suffered during use or transport :—and lastly to the combination with it of means for levelling or contouring, and ascertaining the dip and azimuth of objects observed by the instrument.

Our principal improvements are specially applicable to Range Finders for Military and Surveying purposes, and are hereunder described chiefly with reference to the former ; but it will be evident that they can be readily applied for other purposes, where it is requisite to measure distances or angles.

An instrument constructed in accordance with our Invention, consists of a pair of mirrors or reflecting prisms, placed at or near the ends of a tube (or frame piece) the optical length of which forms, so to say. the base of the triangulation or observation used for ascertaining the distance of the object observed. Near to each of these outer mirrors (or prisms) either in or about the line joining the same, or in the lines of sight from the object to the outer mirrors (or prisms) respectively, is placed an object glass or lens. Between the mirrors (or prisms), preferably midway and in or about the line joining the same are provided two small reflecting mirrors (or prisms), placed the one above the other, and facing the one, one of the outer mirrors (or prisms) and the other the other outer mirror (or prism). A small eye-piece is placed in front of these two centre reflecting mirrors (or prisms) to receive and magnify the images. In the path of the rays between one of the object glasses, and the corresponding reflecting mirror or prism, is introduced a deflecting prism, generally of very small angle ; which is moveable longitudinally along the path of the rays traversing it from the outer to the inner mirror (or prism). This deflecting prism is placed or mounted on or in a guide or slide ; and connected with the prism, or the mechanism by which it is moved, is a scale for the purpose of indicating the distance of the object being observed, or the angle being measured.

The rays of light from the distant object are received first by the outer reflecting mirrors (or prisms) and object glasses at the two ends of the instrument, and are reflected inwards and towards the centre reflecting mirrors (or prisms) ; which latter are so placed as to receive the corresponding rays and to reflect them to the eye-piece.

This arrangement just described is such, that an object viewed is partly seen by reflection from one of the centre mirrors (or prisms), and partly by reflection from

[Price] 8d.

The first page of the patent for the original Barr and Stroud rangefinder. Dr Barr and Dr Stroud were co-inventors of 108 British patents between 1888 and 1931. In all, Barr & Stroud have been granted over 420 patents in Great Britain during their first century, and hundreds of corresponding patents in countries around the world.

took the components back to Leeds, and he assembled them in Dr Stroud's laboratory, with the assistance of a mechanic named J. Watkinson who was employed there. The professors mounted the optical parts themselves, and carried the completed instrument to a quiet lane near the College, where they calibrated the rangefinder by observing on objects at carefully measured distances. Barr took the finished instrument to London in December, delivering it to the War Office just in time to meet the deadline.[31]

Dr Stroud travelled to Aldershot in March 1889 to attend the first trials of the rangefinders submitted by British inventors.[32] The Army's representatives were sufficiently impressed by the professors' instrument to recommend that it be accepted for further trials in the autumn, and it was the only single-observer rangefinder to be given a second opportunity to impress the authorities. Barr and Dr Stroud did not submit their original instrument at the second trials, however, as they feared that the high cost of its manufacture, compared with the cost of some two-observer rangefinders, might prejudice its chances of being adopted by the Army. The professors built a second model rangefinder with a base of 2 feet 9 inches, and replaced the reflecting prisms at the ends with plane-parallel silvered reflectors, effecting a substantial saving on the cost of the instrument.[33] Dr Stroud returned to Aldershot with the new rangefinder in August, and it performed well on the morning of the trials, when the weather was cloudy. In the afternoon, however, the clouds cleared and, to Dr Stroud's dismay, the rays of the sun heated and distorted the mirrors, and the rangefinder's readings became wildly inaccurate. It came as no surprise to the

inventors, therefore, when the War Office announced that their rangefinder had been rejected, and that the Army would adopt the Watkin Mekometer as standard equipment for the infantry. The professors were left to agonise over their mistake in substituting a cheaper design for the one best suited to the purpose for which it was intended.[34]

Despite the disappointment of having their rangefinder rejected, Barr and Dr Stroud continued to work on developing their invention. They produced a model for

The rangefinder submitted for the second series of trials at Aldershot in August 1889.

surveying purposes, and several two-observer military rangefinders similar to the Mekometer in which, ironically, they replaced mirrors with prisms in order to eliminate the risks of derangement in the optical parts of the instrument.[35] The expense of manufacturing and patenting their inventions was high, and they found it impossible to meet the costs from their modest professors' salaries. In 1888 they spent just £21.11s 6d on their rangefinder project, a sum which included £3.12s 6d to register the patent. During the following year, however, their expenditure rose to £200.18s 11d and they had to find a similar sum in 1890, for although they manufactured only a few instruments they patented all their inventions in Britain and in European countries and spent

£245. 9s 4d on registration fees during these two years alone. Between 1888 and 1892 the professors spent £742.17s 2d on the rangefinder project, a large sum of money for young men with salaries of only a few hundred pounds.[36] There is a tradition that Mrs Barr's family was able to help them with their expensive 'hobby' by lending them £300, and it is difficult to imagine how they could have continued without such assistance.

Archibald Barr left Leeds in 1889, when he was appointed to succeed James Thomson as Regius Professor of Civil Engineering and Mechanics at Glasgow University. Thomson was probably consulted on the choice of his successor, and there is little doubt that his recommendation, and Barr's achievements in trebling the number of students studying engineering at the Yorkshire College of Science and in raising £10,000 from local industrialists to build and equip what was recognised as Britain's finest engineering laboratory, must have impressed the Crown Commissioners responsible for making the appointment.[37] The new professor was awarded a Doctorate of Science by the University the following year. Dr Stroud was concerned that Dr Barr's departure from Leeds heralded the end of their association in developing their rangefinder, and became so dispirited at the lack of success in finding a market for their inventions that he offered to sell his share in their patents to Dr Barr, for half the cost of registration plus sixpence. However, Dr Barr was able to assure his colleague that Glasgow University imposed no restrictions on the amount of private research work which could be undertaken by a professor, and he persuaded Dr Stroud against ending their association.[38] The two men

continued to collaborate, albeit mostly by post, and devised a number of two-observer rangefinders of their own. They earned their first reward in 1890, when they were invited to appear in Leeds to deliver a lecture to the British Association for the Advancement of Science, 'On Some New Telemeters, or Rangefinders', in which they discussed the Watkin Mekometer and other rangefinders, as well as three of their own inventions. Their paper was published in the prestigious *Report of the British Association* later that year, and it aroused a great deal of interest in both academic and military circles.

The professors' faith in their rangefinders was tested once more in 1891. The Admiralty had become concerned about the poor results obtained by Royal Navy gunners in sea trials. British ships were being equipped with more powerful and more accurate guns. It was no longer enough, as in Admiral Nelson's day of close-quarter engagements, to simply point a gun at the enemy and fire - modern gunners had to 'lob' the shells on to the target from ever-greater distances and had therefore to find the range more accurately. Foreign navies were also acquiring bigger and better guns, and it was considered essential that British ships be provided with the means to find the range of an enemy before themselves coming under fire.[39] A system of 'bracketing' the target was evolved, the gunners firing off a series of ranging shots and then adjusting the elevation of the guns according to whether the shots fell short of or beyond the target, but this was a slow process. Consequently, the Admiralty advertised through the War Office for inventors to submit designs for a rangefinder accurate to within 3 per cent (90 yards) at 3,000 yards, to provide information on ranges more speedily.[40] As the naval authorities had heard of the initial success of the Barr and Stroud instrument at Aldershot in 1889, the Secretary of the Admiralty wrote to the professors personally to invite them to submit a modified instrument for the trials.[41]

Like the War Office, the Admiralty did not offer financial assistance to inventors to develop a rangefinder for the competition, and Dr Barr and Dr Stroud had to spend still more of their own money with no guarantee that the rangefinder they produced would find a market. Nevertheless, with the benefit of their experiences at the Army trials and in the knowledge that they had made significant improvements to their single-observer rangefinder design since 1889, the professors believed they had a good chance of winning the competition. They devised a new instrument with a base of 5 feet, and substituted speculum-metal reflectors for the plane-parallel silvered reflectors at the ends because the former could be fixed by screwed and soldered connections. The most important new feature of their rangefinder was an astigmatiser. Dr Barr and Dr Stroud were aware that the naval rangefinder could prove useful for station-keeping and navigation, but that there were times, especially at night, when it was impossible to find a well-defined object such as a ship's mast upon which to observe. Partial images of specks of light such as those from a lighthouse or ship lamp, could not be brought into coincidence on either side of a line of separation, and so the professors devised a means of altering the images of single points of this kind. The astigmatiser consisted of small cylindrical lenses, one of which was placed in the path of light from each end reflector. The lens had the axis of the cylinder horizontal and transverse to

the direction of the beam, and it transformed a speck of light into a vertical streak in both fields at the right eye-piece. The streak could be brought into alignment on either side of the line of separation by altering the position of the prism, as was done when ranging on any clearly

The naval rangefinder submitted by Dr Barr and Dr Stroud for trials in April 1892.

defined vertical object.[42]

The frame and inner tube of the naval rangefinder were made of copper, and the outer tube of brass, because magnetic metals might upset the ship's compass on the bridge. James White & Co built a special stand which was fixed to the ship's deck and allowed the rangefinder to turn freely in azimuth about a vertical axis, and to be held fast on the target as the ship pitched and rolled. A rubber face-mask was provided at the eye-piece, to prevent external light and draughts from disturbing the rangetaker and to protect him from bumping

Naval Rangefinder No 3, on an early mounting manufactured by James White & Co.

his forehead against the outer tube when the ship pitched in heavy seas. The new instrument was designated the FA Mark 1, 'F' standing for rangefinder, 'A' signifying that it was the first model, and 'Mark 1' referring to the fact that it was the first design of this type.[43]

The Admiralty held preliminary trials of three rangefinders on board HMS *Arethusa* at Chatham in April 1892. Arnulf Mallock submitted a single-observer instrument of 8-foot base, mounted vertically, and Major Watkin a two-observer rangefinder adapted from the design of his Mekometer, to compete with the FA Mark 1.[44] The professors' instrument produced the most accurate readings of the three, and impressed naval officers who subjected it to further trials at HMS *Excellent*, the Royal Navy's gunnery school, in June.[45] The Admiralty then asked Dr Barr and

Dr Stroud to offer their patents to the Crown, but Dr Barr, realising the enormous commercial potential of their invention, set a price of £75,000 on the patent rights. The Crown decided not to accept the offer of purchase, which would have given the Admiralty the right to put manufacturing contracts out to tender. However, the two professors intimated that they could supply any instruments required by the armed forces.[46] Consequently, they were invited in November to provide the Admiralty with an estimate of the time and cost of manufacturing six rangefinders, and early in 1893 they received an order for five.[47]

Dr Barr and Dr Stroud began to order parts for new rangefinders at the end of 1892, in anticipation of the Admiralty order. James White & Co made the mechanical components, and a workman named Sinclair Reid was assigned to carry out most of the work under Dr Barr's supervision. Prisms, lenses and reflectors were ordered from Adam Hilger & Co of London, and Dr Stroud was responsible for drawing up the specifications and for checking the optical components when they were delivered to Leeds.[48] Dr Barr and Sinclair Reid assembled the bodies of the rangefinders, and Dr Stroud spent much of his holidays at Dr Barr's new home, 'Royston' in Dowanhill, Glasgow, helping his friend to mount the optical parts he brought north with him. The professors adjusted the rangefinders for infinity by observing features on the moon while lying on their backs on a flat part of the roof at 'Royston', and then calibrated and tested each instrument by observing on local landmarks from the roof of James White & Co's premises in Cambridge Street.[49] The calibration work nearly cost Dr Stroud his life. While descending

A photo of HMS Iron Duke, *altered to illustrate the field of view in the right eye-piece of the Barr & Stroud rangefinder. The observer's task was to bring the two images of the target into coincidence — in the naval rangefinder, this was most easily achieved by bringing the upper and the lower images of the ship's mast into alignment.*

'Royston', Dr Barr's Glasgow home. The two professors lay on their backs on the roof of the house, and adjusted their first rangefinder for infinity by observing on the moon.

from the roof one day, he felt the ladder collapse beneath him, and he told later of how he fell to the ground 'plump upon the providentially padded posterior of the end of the spinal column'. Had he fallen only inches to one side, he would have landed on a lathe and even his 'padded posterior' would have offered little protection. As it was, he suffered injuries which led to his confinement to bed for several months.[50] The partnership-by-post arrangement of earlier days was resumed during the period of his convalescence.

Dr Stroud's enforced withdrawal from a fully active role in the rangefinder project led Dr Barr to suggest that they take on an assistant, and Harold Drinkwater Jackson joined them in April 1893.[51] Harold Jackson was the son of a bank manager from the Isle of Man, and the nephew of one of Glasgow's leading printers and bookbinders, Robert MacLehose. He came to Glasgow to serve an apprenticeship in the Fairfield Shipyard in Govan, and in 1892 he matriculated at Glasgow University to study for an engineering degree.[52] Dr Barr was impressed by the 21-year-old student, and Jackson assisted him in some of his private consultancy work, testing engine and boiler plants.[53] When Dr Barr invited him to join the embryo rangefinder business as a salaried assistant, to help deal with the growing volume of their business correspondence and assist with the supervision of the manufacture of the rangefinders, he made it clear that he could offer no guarantee of employment should further orders for their instruments fail to materialise. However, as the Admiralty seemed set to adopt the rangefinder for naval service, Jackson was happy to abandon his university course and to throw in his lot with Dr Barr and Dr Stroud.[54]

The first rangefinder for the Admiralty's order was completed during the summer of 1893. It was an improved version of the model submitted for the *Arethusa* trials, with the base length shortened to 4 feet 6 inches (1.37 m), and Dr Barr took it to Torbay on 22 July to join HMS *Blenheim* for a week of trials at sea.[55] The Royal Navy's rangefinder gave highly accurate readings and impressed the officers who were given demonstrations of its capabilities, and word of its potential spread quickly. Vice-Admiral Sir Reginald Tryon, Commander-in-Chief of the Mediterranean Fleet, heard of the instrument's triumph at the *Arethusa* trials and wrote to the inventors in the spring of 1893. The Vice-Admiral, who had a reputation for being 'an able, energetic and extremely scientific officer', invited Dr Barr and Dr Stroud to join him on his flagship, HMS *Victoria*, and to demonstrate the instrument's uses to his officers during fleet manoeuvres in June. As the inventors were unable to complete their first new naval rangefinder before the fleet sailed from Marseilles they were obliged to decline Tryon's invitation, and in consequence they missed an eventful voyage. The Mediterranean Fleet sailed to Beirut, and on 22 June the ships weighed anchor and made for Tripoli. They were sailing in two columns, six chains apart, when Tryon gave the order to invert course in succession, by turning six points inwards. It was generally accepted that this dangerous manoeuvre, known as a grid iron, could be carried out safely only if the two columns were separated by a distance of at least eight cables, but Tryon ignored the doubts expressed by the officers on the bridge of the *Victoria* and repeated the order. As soon as the *Victoria* and

Dr Barr with naval rangefinder No 3, on board HMS Blenheim in July 1893.

rangefinder obviously had great potential as a navigational aid, and he wondered whether, had they been able to complete their first naval instrument a month or two earlier, they might have been able to avert the Royal Navy's worst peacetime disaster of the century.[56]

The five rangefinders were completed and delivered to the Royal Navy by the beginning of 1894, for a special discounted price of £200 apiece.[57] The sixth instrument, on which work had begun before the Admiralty's order arrived, was sold to the professors' first foreign customer. In April 1893 Dr Barr wrote to W.G. Armstrong, Mitchell & Co, to ask if they would consider becoming sole agents for the sale of rangefinders to foreign navies.[58] Armstrong, Mitchell & Co were the world's leading naval construction and armaments company and had built up a network of contacts in foreign governments and navies. Dr Barr and Dr Stroud were delighted when the Tyneside company agreed to accept the agency for the sale of the naval rangefinder to all foreign countries except Germany, for a commission of 15 per cent of the standard retail price of £250 on each instrument sold abroad. Armstrong, Mitchell earned their first commission soon after the agreement was signed.[59]

the leading ship in the other column, HMS *Camperdown*, began to turn, it became obvious that they would collide. There was no time to reverse or alter course before the *Camperdown* rammed the flagship, and the *Victoria* went to the bottom taking Tryon, twenty-two officers and 336 men with her. Dr Stroud wrote later that the Vice-Admiral 'might have been convinced by the RF readings that the manoeuvre he was contemplating was impractical, owing to the want of room'. The

The Japanese took the Royal Navy as their model when they set out to improve and expand their fleet during the 1890s. It was inevitable that their naval officers would show an interest in the new rangefinder once the Admiralty began to place orders with Dr Barr and Dr Stroud. Armstrong, Mitchell were building the *Yoshino*, a new protected cruiser for the Imperial Japanese Navy, at their Elswick yard and they were asked to obtain a rangefinder for the vessel. Naval Rangefinder No 8 was sent from

Glasgow to Elswick in November 1893.[60]   The *Yoshino* saw action during the Sino-Japanese War of 1894-95, as the flagship of Rear-Admiral Tsuboi at the Battle of Yalu on 17 September 1894, and as the flagship of Admiral Togo during the attack on the Pescadores Islands in March of the following year.[61]   Although Armstrong, Mitchell received a favourable report from Japan of the rangefinder's performance, no further orders were forthcoming.   Dr Barr and Dr Stroud were not unduly concerned, as they were kept very busy during 1894 meeting orders from other navies.

Two new rangefinders were sent to Elswick, where Armstrong, Mitchell were building the first-class ironclads *Blanco Encelada* and *Buenos Aires* for the Chilean and Argentinian navies respectively.   The Germans, Swedes, Turks, Italians and Brazilians each purchased an instrument to submit to trials, and in June 1894 the Admiralty placed an order for six more rangefinders, confirming later that large orders would follow.[62]   It seemed clear to Dr Barr that he and Dr Stroud could no longer manufacture rangefinders as a cottage industry, and that they must establish their business on a more formal basis.   They set up a company, Barr & Stroud's Patents, with the professors as equal partners, and Dr Barr began to look for suitable premises in which to house their expanding business.[63]

As James White & Co manufactured the mechanical parts of the rangefinders, Dr Barr asked if he could rent a portion of their Cambridge Street premises and set up an office and a small workshop there.[64]   His request was turned down, but he managed to find other premises even closer to home.   The Glasgow District Subway Co started work on the construction of a new underground railway in

One of the first Barr & Stroud naval rangefinders, on the chart house of HMS Royal Sovereign, *c.1894.*

the city in 1891.   Hillhead Station was built beneath a tenement at No 250 Byres Road, only a few hundred yards from Dr Barr's house and from Glasgow University, and the subway company advertised a room in the building for let.   Dr Barr was able to rent the room for £50 per annum, and set up an office, laboratory and workshop there.   Barr & Stroud's Patents moved to No 250 Byres Road on 1 July 1895.[65]

Most of the 700 square feet of floor space rented by the firm was taken up by the small workshop, in which it was intended to adjust and finish the rangefinders.   It was equipped by Dr Barr with a screw cutting lathe and accessories and a foot lathe.   Sinclair Reid accepted an invitation to leave James White & Co and start work with Barr & Stroud, and a young man named Robert McNab was taken on as an apprentice to assist him.[66] Harold Jackson was in charge of the office, and two young 'draughtsmen or general assistants' were employed to help him and Dr Barr with secretarial and experimental work. James Weir French was the son of a respected local chemist and metallurgist, and matriculated to study engineering at Glasgow University in 1894. John Donald Morrison also began an engineering course at the University in 1894, and both he and French were asked by Dr Barr if they would like to spend the following summer working for Barr & Stroud. Dr Barr wrote to the headmaster of Allan Glen's School in Glasgow in June 1895, to enquire if he could recommend a senior boy who might wish to work for the firm, and when William G. Strang left the school to study engineering at Glasgow University in October, he began to work at number 250 Byres Road during his spare time. James French also continued to work part-time for the firm while studying for his degree, but Morrison left the University and Barr & Stroud in March 1896.[67]

The Byres Road premises were far from satisfactory when Harold Jackson and the others began working there. In September, the secretary wrote to the factors to complain that 'the WC in the workshop has never flushed properly' and 'the damp weather has made three more doors jam'. In October he asked that something be done 'about condensed water on our skylight rooflights being prevented from dripping on the floor' and on 6 November he wrote that 'the heavy rain of last night and today has come through the roof of these premises pretty badly.' Later in November, Jackson added to his catalogue of complaints, noting that 'the ventilation is very bad now that

we have to keep the windows shut' in the laboratory and office, and he asked the factors to fit up some means of aerating the rooms.[68] The premises were obviously unfit to house what Dr Barr proudly described as 'practically the only naval rangefinder manufactory in the world'.[69] However, the factors acted swiftly to deal with the problems, and Jackson found no cause for complaint after November 1895. As the firm took on five new men, an apprentice, and a cashier in 1896, the improvements made to the small factory proved timely.[70]

Barr & Stroud were able to open the new factory in Byres Road and to take on additional staff because of the increase in demand for their rangefinders. The number of rangefinders ordered rose from six in 1893 to fourteen the following year, and to twenty-nine in 1895.[71] Dr Barr and Dr Stroud earned a return on the time and money they had invested in their rangefinder project for the first time in 1893, when the Admiralty paid them £400 for two of the new rangefinders. However, Dr Barr had to find £249.3s 5d and Dr Stroud £240.12s 8d that year to pay for the manufacture of other instruments on order. The business made its first profit in 1894, when receipts of payments for eleven rangefinders, for minor repairs to two instruments, and of £14.16s 6d in commission from the manufacturer of their patented lantern-slide camera, gave them an income of £2,722.9s 2d. Dr Barr took almost £600 from the business that year, part of which may have been withdrawn to repay the £300 loan to his wife's family, the Youngs. The firm remained in debt to Dr Stroud to the tune of £664.15s, representing his capital in the business. In 1895 Barr & Stroud's receipts from sales amounted to £3,025, and the firm recorded a small profit of

£512. The following year, orders for fifty-five rangefinders were placed at Byres Road, sales receipts increased to £13,409 and the profit for distribution was £5,915. Harold Jackson was paid a commission of 5 per cent, and the professors shared the remaining sum of £5,620.[72] The early years of hardship at last began to seem worthwhile.

By November 1895 Barr & Stroud had delivered twenty-seven rangefinders, numbers 3 - 29 to their customers.[73] Subsequent sales were of an improved model of the FA instrument, the Mark 2, in which the most important difference from the FA1 was that the partial images of the object at the right eye-piece did not appear inverted. The re-inversion of the images was achieved by including a new feature in the rangefinder, an eye-piece prism combination in place of the central mirrors, which also gave a more clearly defined line of separation between the partial images.[74] Dr Barr and Dr Stroud felt unable to continue to give the Admiralty large discounts on the FA2 rangefinder and they produced a new standard price list, fixing the price at £250 for one instrument, including the tank pedestal, instrument case, two electric batteries, two lamp leads and a set of discharging leads, a spare face piece and other spare parts. Discounts were offered on orders of over ten instruments, and a customer ordering fifty rangefinders could expect to pay 10 per cent less than the listed price.[75] The Admiralty welcomed the improvements incorporated in the design of the FA2 and ordered twenty of the new rangefinders for £240 apiece.[76] By January 1896 sixteen rangefinders had been supplied to the Royal Navy and a total of thirty-six more were on order from the Admiralty, and when Armstrong, Mitchell asked to increase their order for six instruments by two, Jackson wrote to apologise that the extra pair could not be completed before May because 'the Admiralty has taken the instrument up so strongly that we are unable, at present, to cope with their demands'.[77]

During 1897 Barr & Stroud leased a shop at No 230 Byres Road, which they converted into a workshop in order to be able to meet the growing demand for rangefinders.[78] An Admiralty order for fifty instruments was received in November 1897, and by March 1898 the firm had sold over 150 of their rangefinders around the world.[79] On 22 March they despatched a rangefinder to Elswick to be fitted on board the new Japanese protected cruiser *Takasaga*, and Dr Barr and Harold Jackson sailed with the ship when the rangefinder was tested during sea trials.[80] The Imperial Japanese Navy was to be strengthened under the Naval Programme of 1896, and Barr & Stroud were informed in October 1898 that their rangefinders were to be fitted on the ten powerful new warships on order from British and Continental yards. Four instruments each were sent to the armoured cruisers *Asama* and *Tokiwa* and six each to the battleships *Shikishima* and *Asahi* in 1899. Further orders followed in 1900, for instruments for the armoured cruisers *Izumo*, *Yakumo* and *Azuma* and the battleships *Hatsuse* and *Mikasa*, and later for the armoured cruiser *Iwate*.[81]

The Japanese fitted up to six rangefinders on each vessel, and had purchased forty-seven by February 1901.[82] The manufacture of these instruments posed a novel problem for Barr & Stroud. Harold Jackson wrote tactfully to Armstrong, Whitworth (W.G. Armstrong,

Mitchell & Co became W.G. Armstrong, Whitworth & Co after the acquisition of the Manchester engineering firm Sir Joseph Whitworth & Co in 1897) on 14 October 1898, to say:

> We notice that the height of a Rangefinder as we make it is rather too great for the average height of the Japanese officers. [The rangefinder was 5 feet high, from deck to eye-piece.] This could of course be overcome by placing a platform round the Rangefinder on the deck; but perhaps it would be more convenient if we were to make the Rangefinder rather lower.

Armstrong, Whitworth asked the Japanese for their opinion on the matter, but the Japanese did not reply until June 1900. Barr & Stroud offered to supply them with adjustable stands for the latest batch of four instruments, but Captain Ijichi, the Japanese Chief Inspector, asked instead for stands 6 inches lower than the usual height.[83] The firm was happy to oblige.

The Japanese followed the lead of the Royal Navy in adopting Barr & Stroud rangefinders, but they were the first to place orders for another of the firm's inventions. The original advertisement for naval rangefinders specified that 'the instrument should be capable of having its records transmitted to the gun or guns through some system of instantaneous communications.' The Admiralty reaffirmed its interest in such a system in June 1892, and the firm developed prototypes of range and order transmitters and receivers during 1894.[84] Jackson was able to write in July 1898 that 'we have now worked out our system sufficiently as to put it into practice', but even before the Admiralty could decide whether to fit the fire-

control instruments on British warships, Commander Iwasaki was sent to Byres Road to see the 'Range and Order Indicators'.[85] He reported favourably, and the Imperial Japanese Navy began to place orders for the instruments at the end of July. Range and order indicators were fitted on every Japanese capital ship which carried Barr & Stroud's rangefinders.[86]

The firm's system of relaying ranges and orders was relatively simple in conception. A transmitter was placed on the bridge, charthouse or the fighting top, close to the

Naval rangefinder No 30, the first FA Mark 2 instrument, on display in 1896.

rangefinder, and connected to a receiver in the conning tower. The transmitter was fitted with a handle which could be set to point at any indication of the range on a dial, and the handle was followed automatically by a pointer. The

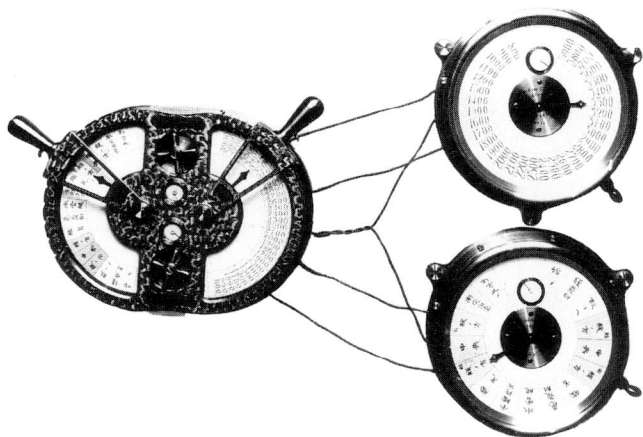

Range and order instruments supplied to the Imperial Japanese Navy, c.1900. The double transmitter is on the left and the range receiver is above the order receiver on the right.

transmitter and receivers contained two trains of clockwork, one for clockwise and the other for anti-clockwise motion of the pointer, and an escapement operated by an electro-magnet was interposed in each train, pointed to run during the passage of a current through the magnetic coils. When the handle on the transmitter was moved to a different indication from the pointer, a current passed to the electro-magnet and started the train, so that the pointer followed the handle until it reached the same indication and the current was shut off. An intermitter in the transmitter made contact as the pointer passed each indication on the dial, and the intermitted current was conveyed to the magnet controlling the train in the receiver, the

pointer on that instrument then moving to the same position on the dial as the pointer on the transmitter. In the conning tower, there were two double transmitters to pass on the ranges and orders to receivers at the guns. One transmitter served the forward barbette and port casements and batteries, the other the after barbette and starboard casements and batteries.[87] A double transmitter sold for £31.10s, a single one for £31, and receivers for £19, with batteries extra. A Japanese battleship was equipped with sixteen order receivers and seventeen range receivers, while a cruiser usually carried two or three less of each. The cost of equipping a ship with the system came to just over £800.[88] By February 1901 Barr & Stroud had sold thirty transmitters and over 200 receivers, one set being installed for trials on board the battleship HMS *Canopus*, another being sent to an Argentinian coastal fortress, and the rest to Japan.[89]

The Admiralty placed an order for one hundred rangefinders in June 1899, as the Royal Navy wanted to have an instrument fitted to the fore and the aft charthouse of every capital ship.[90] The French naval authorities declined to adopt the rangefinder on the grounds that it was too expensive, although they received favourable reports from the trials they conducted, and the Italians and Germans also decided not to purchase instruments.[91] Despite these setbacks, however, Barr & Stroud continued to win valuable orders from overseas. They sent eleven rangefinders to Spain in 1898, when that country went to war with the USA, and supplied dozens to the Chileans and Argentinians.[92] The Dutch, Swedes, Danes, Americans, Austrians, Turks, Russians and Portuguese were carrying out trials with the rangefinder at the turn of the century, and Barr & Stroud were confident that demand would continue to grow after their main rival, the rangefinder developed by Lieutenant Bradley A. Fiske of the US Navy, proved quite unreliable during the naval engagements of the Spanish-American War.[93] The value of the firm's sales during the four years 1897-1900 amounted to £62,316, and Dr Barr and Harold Jackson decided that it was time to invest part of the business's healthy profits in the further expansion of their production capacity.[94]

'The only naval rangefinder manufactory in the world' at 230 and 250 Byres Road was far too small to cope with demand for Barr & Stroud's products at the turn of the century, and Dr Barr began to search for more space. In May 1899 the firm leased a building at 44 Ashton Lane, behind Byres Road, acquiring an additional 3,360 square feet of floor space. More men were

Barr & Stroud's workshops at Ashton Lane, c. 1902, with the workforce of sixty-five men and boys. Note the naval rangefinder on the special roof-top testing platform.

taken on, and new lathes, milling machines and other plant, imported from the USA.[95] Men and machinery were at work in the new factory by June.[96] A machine shop was set up on the ground floor, and a fitting shop on the floor above, while the assembly, adjustment and testing of the rangefinders were carried out in the attic. A platform was built on the roof to provide a vantage point from which to test the instruments by observing on local buildings which were at known distance from the works.[97] In May 1900 Harold Jackson obtained permission to measure out a test area at the Agricultural Showground at Scotstoun, just over two miles to the west of Byres Road.[98] Barr & Stroud acquired more space in January 1901, when they leased a stable in Ashton Lane and converted it into another workshop. The office, drawing office, pattern shop and testing laboratory remained at the old premises above the subway station, but the firm left the workshop at 230 Byres Road in May 1901.[99]

The extension of Barr & Stroud's premises was essential to accommodate the rising number of workmen employed by the firm. Although James White & Co continued to manufacture most of the mechanical parts of the rangefinder, the firm produced an increasing number of components in its own workshops. More men were required to assemble, test and adjust new rangefinders and to repair old ones or to convert FA1s to FA2s. Albert Smith joined the firm in 1896, to cement and mount optical parts sent up by Adam Hilger & Co from London, and a small optical department was created.[100] As Barr & Stroud began to produce short-base rangefinders and range and order indicators, and planned to begin production of vacuum pumps and

electric clocks, more jobs were created at Ashton Lane. George Blair, who graduated with a BSc in Engineering Science from Glasgow University in 1895, was appointed works manager at the new factory, with Sinclair Reid as head foreman, and by 1902 at least sixty-five men were working under them.[101]

As the volume of Barr & Stroud's business grew, Harold Jackson was called upon to visit clients and potential customers in England and abroad. To provide cover during his absences and assist him with his secretarial duties, a man named Oliver Porter was recruited in 1901.[102] Meanwhile, after graduating with a BSc in 1898, James French went to Germany and worked for a year in the workshops of Barr & Stroud's newly appointed agents in Germany, Herren Optische Anstalt C.P. Goerz A.G. Barr & Stroud were

The machine shop at Ashton Lane c.1902. The gas engine which provided the power for the belt-driven machines is on the right.

contemplating setting up a grinding and polishing shop, and it was hoped that French would be able to take charge of the project after studying German methods.[103] William Strang remained at Byres Road until 1903. He had been joined there in 1898 by James B. Henderson, another former pupil of Allan Glen's School. Henderson studied under Dr Barr at Glasgow University, where he won the George Harvey Prize. He graduated in 1892 and in 1894 took a post with Dr Stroud at the

The fitting shop at Ashton Lane, c.1902.

Yorkshire College of Science as lecturer in Electrical Engineering. He returned to Glasgow in 1898 to take charge of Barr & Stroud's scientific department, and worked with Dr Stroud on the design and development of the range and order indicators system and in supervising the installation of the apparatus on Japanese warships. He resigned from the firm in 1901 to become lecturer in Electrical Engineering at Glasgow University, and in 1905 he was appointed the Professor of Applied Mechanics at the Royal Naval College in Greenwich. Henderson became a noted inventor himself and was knighted in 1920 for his work on improving naval gunnery, but he continued to advise Barr & Stroud's scientific department on matters relating to the

development of electrical instruments.[104]

The recruitment of a talented team of engineers and scientists, and the excellent training given to the men on the shop floor, were factors in the success of Barr & Stroud's business during the latter years of the 1890s. The firm continued to rely heavily on the inventive genius of the two founders when a new instrument had to be devised or improvements to existing products had to be made, but Dr Barr and Dr Stroud were able to count on expert assistance from the staff at Byres Road and on a high quality of workmanship from the men working under Sinclair Reid's eagle eye in Ashton Lane. The firm owed much, too, to the administrative talents of Harold Jackson, who believed that 'nothing much can be done in the way of good organisation unless it is to be in the hands of a man who has the time and who is willing to thrash the subject out, and who also has the power of putting his foot down and saying "this must be done", and who acts accordingly.'[105] Jackson was responsible for the administration of the firm's finances as well as the factory, and by keeping tight control of costs and husbanding Barr & Stroud's financial resources he built sound foundations for future growth. He was also skilled in the art of public relations and, like Dr Barr, was adept in dealing with the firm's clients and their representatives and in gaining their trust and confidence. By 1900 he had become commercial manager in all but name, promoting and finding new customers for the instruments developed by the two professors, and was undoubtedly the architect of the business organisation which brought Barr & Stroud's products to the attention of the world.

Perhaps the greatest of the firm's assets were

The fitting, adjusting and testing shop in the top flat at Ashton Lane, c. 1902.

the business principles laid down soon after Dr Barr and Dr Stroud started their venture, principles which were adhered to strictly thereafter. Jackson told Adam Hilger & Co in 1908 that 'we have never considered competitors' prices when computing our own prices but have worked entirely on our own estimates of costs adding such a proportion of the oncost charges as the kind of work may reasonably be expected to bear, and adding a profit also in proportion to the amount of the work that is our own invention.'[106] The failure of their rangefinder at the second Aldershot trials in 1889 had convinced Dr Barr and Dr Stroud that they must never again be tempted to sacrifice quality in order to cut production costs, and Jackson noted in 1907 that 'Professor Barr

Harold Drinkwater Jackson.

will not allow any instrument to leave here (if he can help it) that is not as perfect as he can make it in all respects'.[107] The emphasis placed by the firm on ensuring that their instruments were of the highest quality proved to be a commercial drawback during the 1890s, when many navies shunned the Barr & Stroud rangefinder because of its comparatively high price and conducted extensive trials with cheaper instruments such as Fiske's. However, the Glasgow firm's steadfast commitment to high standards of design and manufacture paid dividends later, when the rangefinder was proven to be the most reliable and accurate on the market.

Harold Jackson justified Barr & Stroud's unwillingness to cut costs by saying that 'we could make cheaper rangefinders, but refuse to do so because we know of the great importance of every detail of an instrument on which a warship depends, and it is attention to these details which makes the instrument costly.'[108] The firm appreciated that ships which had no rangefinder, or poor ones, wasted large numbers of expensive shells trying to 'find' a target with ranging shots. Moreover, a warship cost hundreds of thousands of pounds to build, and no nation could afford to send one into battle against an enemy equipped with superior rangefinders and fire-control instruments, when it might be sunk or severely battered by enemy guns before it could bring its own guns to bear with effect.

Barr & Stroud were always willing to listen and reply to complaints and words of advice from clients, and to give prompt attention to repairs of instruments which were damaged or which failed to live up to the high standards of performance expected of them. They maintained a dignified approach to their business affairs, and did not 'approve of destructive criticism of opponents' instruments [but preferred] to make points on the advantages of our own'.[109] The firm became respected for open, frank and honest dealing, and these attributes were undoubtedly important in persuading clients to send valuable orders to Byres Road. Soon after the turn of the century, the navies of 'every civilised power except Germany' had adopted Barr & Stroud's relatively expensive but superior instruments.

'OUR RANGEFINDERS HAVE PROVED THE MOST ACCURATE...': 1900-1914

The success of their naval rangefinder did not stop Barr & Stroud from continuing with their efforts to produce a light instrument which could be carried in the field by artillery, cavalry and infantry units. Germany's Artillerie Pruefugs Kommission inquired about the availability of such a rangefinder in 1895, and Harold Jackson took the firm's first 3-foot base instrument to Berlin in 1897.[1] The artillery rangefinder was made mostly of aluminium and weighed just 12 pounds, less than one quarter the weight of the brass and copper naval instrument.[2] It was accurate to within 3 per cent (30 yards) at 1,000 yards, and Barr & Stroud offered it for sale at £125.[3] The new instrument impressed the industrialists and officials Jackson met in Berlin, and C.P. Goerz agreed to act as the firm's agents in Germany to promote sales there.[4] However, the Artillerie Pruefugs Kommission were not satisfied with the performance of the rangefinders they tested in 1898 and 1899, and others supplied to the British, Russian and Swiss armies for trials also failed to live up to the inventors' expectations.[5] It became clear that the aluminium frame and tubes were seriously affected by changes in temperature, which in turn upset the working of the optical parts, and that the metal was not sufficiently tough to withstand heavy knocks.[6] Dr Barr and his staff returned to the drawing-board to redesign the instrument.

The firm persevered with the field rangefinder in the knowledge that a vast market existed for a sturdy and reliable instrument, as military experts began to study the lessons learned by the British Army during the disastrous campaigns at the beginning of the Boer War in 1899. Field artillery fired regularly

An early FQ artillery rangefinder on a tripod, c1904. Barr & Stroud employees who joined the Territorial Army were often asked to don their uniforms and 'model' for promotional photographs of military instruments.

at ranges of up to 6,000 yards in Southern Africa, but British gunners experienced difficulty in dropping shells accurately on the well-concealed positions of the enemy. The Boers often subjected British troops to devastating rifle fire from up to 2,000 yards, while poor Tommy Atkins found it virtually impossible at first to estimate distances with accuracy in the particularly clear atmospheric conditions to which he was not accustomed.[7] The optical instruments makers Thomas Cooke & Sons of York supplied over 1,000 Mekometers to the British forces in Southern Africa.[8] Unfortunately, the instruments performed unsatisfactorily in bright sunshine and in conditions of heat haze and were easily damaged by rough usage. Moreover, observers were often unable to find suitable prominent objects close to Boer positions in the veldt upon which to observe.[9]   To make matters even worse, the supposedly unsophisticated Boers soon learned the lengths of the cords which attached the two instruments of the Mekometer, and by measuring the angle subtended by the 'base' set out by the Mekometer operators they were able to calculate the range themselves, and open fire on the British rangetakers before they could complete their own observations and take cover.[10] The British Army's early reverses at the hands of the Boers illustrated the point that superior fire power gave an army an advantage in the field only if it could be brought to bear quickly and accurately.   A better system for finding ranges was required urgently, and Barr & Stroud hoped to replace the Mekometer and similar instruments used by foreign armies with a single-observer rangefinder of their own design and manufacture.

Barr & Stroud's first artillery rangefinder was returned from Germany in 1899, and the firm modified it before lending it to Major Guiness of the 86th Howitzer Battery to take to Southern Africa in February 1900.[11] Another trial instrument was loaned to Major Hervey Scott of the Elswick Ordnance Corps, and the two British officers reported back that the Barr & Stroud rangefinder, although still at the experimental stage, was easier to use, superior in accuracy and less likely to be damaged by hard wear in the field than the Mekometer.[12] Professor George Forbes, a Scottish inventor, took his own folding stereoscopic rangefinder into action with an artillery regiment during the war, and the success of his instrument and of others lent to British officers by the German

firm of Carl Zeiss, received a great deal of publicity in the British press.[13] Harold Jackson and Dr Barr were encouraged by reports of the performance of the field rangefinder to persevere with the development of a short-base instrument for field work, despite Dr Stroud's preference for longer instruments working on the stereoscopic principle.[14]   They were convinced that the days of the Mekometer were numbered, but realised that they would encounter stiff competition from other manufacturers seeking to provide a replacement.

The firm's efforts to find a suitable design for a field rangefinder became more determined when there was a drop in the demand for naval instruments at the turn of the century. With the Admiralty's requirements apparently satisfied for some years to come, the Imperial Japanese Navy almost fully equipped with new rangefinders, and other navies continuing to place only small orders for trial instruments while they searched for a cheaper alternative, Barr & Stroud faced the prospect of having to lay off many of their newly recruited workers. They won orders for just forty-four rangefinders in 1900, twenty-three in 1901 and twenty-six in 1902, and the two professors and their secretary were made acutely aware of the over-reliance of the business on the willingness of the governments of the world to continue to spend vast sums on expanding and modernising their navies.[15]   Dr Stroud was particularly concerned about their failure to devise a field rangefinder acceptable to the War Office, and he persuaded Dr Barr and Harold Jackson that the time had come to diversify the range of products manufactured at Ashton Lane.[16]

In 1899 Barr & Stroud began to sell a small vacuum pump designed by Dr Barr. As it could produce a very high vacuum, the pump was especially suited to the evacuation of electric light bulbs and Rontgen ray tubes, and it sold in respectable numbers to firms such as the Edison, Swan Electric Co.[17] However, profit

The Barr & Stroud vacuum pump.

margins on the pump were relatively slight, and demand never became large enough to establish the pump as anything more than a sideline to the business. The firm also began to manufacture a new electric clock invented and patented in 1890 by Dr Barr, Dr Stroud, and the Professor of Astronomy at Glasgow University, Ludwig Becker. The Becker clocks, as they were called, worked from a master clock which sent out pulses of electricity every 30 seconds to move forward the hands of every subsidiary clock connected in the system. Because the subsidiary clocks had no springs or other mechanisms of their own, they were practically weather and dirt proof, and were ideally suited for outdoor locations and factories.[18] Dr Barr was Vice-Convener of the Machinery and Electric Lighting Committee of the Glasgow International Exhibition, held in Kelvingrove Park near Glasgow University in 1901. He arranged for the firm to install fourteen Becker clocks in the exhibition buildings, wired to a master clock, and this system quickly came to the attention of Glasgow Corporation.[19] The city fathers ordered some clocks and, after a trial period, had them fixed to tramway poles throughout the north-west of Glasgow and operated them from a master clock in the Observatory near Byres Road.[20] Becker clocks were installed at the Wolverhampton Exhibition in 1902 and sold to Sir William Arrol & Co, British Westinghouse, the Bridgewater Trustees, and the Nord Deutscher Lloyd Co, the latter installing them on board the liner *Kaiser Wilhelm.*[21] Like the vacuum pumps, however, the Becker clocks were only marginally profitable. Barr & Stroud patented other inventions which could have been developed for the civilian market, including an internal combustion engine, prismatic field glasses, and a 'map carrier for cycles and other vehicles'.[22] They also accepted small orders from the War Office to supply Mekometer parts and from the Royal Navy for telescope sights but, when demand for rangefinders picked up in 1903, any plans to manufacture these and other products on a large scale were set to one side.

The recovery in rangefinder sales was due almost entirely to the development of an improved FA instrument by Dr Barr, Dr Stroud and their technical staff. The basic design of the first FA rangefinder, delivered to the Royal Navy in 1893, was retained for nearly all the 490 instruments sold by Barr & Stroud during the following ten years. Although the firm

produced fourteen different experimental
types of rangefinders, the FAs remained Barr &
Stroud's staple product.[23] The first short-base
rangefinders designed both for field service
and for use at sea, on torpedo-boats and
destroyers, as well as standard instruments sold
on special fortress mountings, were also FAs.[24]
The firm was determined to increase the
accuracy of the naval instruments, however,
and the ranges at which they could give reliable
information to the bigger and better guns
being supplied to warships. The accuracy of a
single-observer rangefinder increases in direct
proportion to increases in the length of the
base, as well as in magnification, and Barr &
Stroud attempted first to increase the length of
their instruments. The Admiralty ordered a
rangefinder with a base of 6 feet in March 1901,
specifying that it should be accurate to within 3
per cent (180 yards) at 6,000 yards.[25] The Royal
Navy and US Navy each received a model of the
larger instrument for trials, but their reports
were not encouraging. Barr & Stroud were
unable to prevent the copper frame of the 6-
foot rangefinder from bending slightly under
its own weight, and as the end reflectors were
mounted on the frame, so the paths of the
beams of light they transmitted were affected to
the detriment of the accuracy of the
instrument.[26]   While work continued on
finding a means of avoiding this drawback in
instruments of longer base, however, the firm
was able to make improvements in the design of
the 4-foot 6-inch base FA rangefinder which
met, for the moment, the Admiralty's
specifications of accuracy.

The FA Mark 3 naval rangefinder was
introduced in 1903. It featured a stronger eye-
piece to give greater magnification (24

The workforce at Ashton Lane, 1902.

diameters as opposed to 20 diameters in the
FA1 and FA2), and a deflecting prism of smaller
angle to allow the images to be adjusted with
greater delicacy.[27] The FA3 was discovered to
be nearly twice as accurate as the FA2, capable
of giving readings at sea which were within the
3 per cent at 6,000 yards demanded by the
Admiralty, and its appearance on the market
rekindled interest in naval rangefinders.[28] Barr
& Stroud received orders for seventy-seven new
instruments in 1903, and the Admiralty, which
had ordered only eleven FA2s between June
1899 and September 1903, purchased a large
number of FA3s and asked Barr & Stroud to
begin converting the Royal Navy's FA2s to the
improved design.[29]

The slump in rangefinder orders at the turn
of the century proved only a temporary set-back
to Barr & Stroud's business. Sales slipped in
value to £15,070 in 1901 and to £14,522 the
following year, and after-tax profits to £3,365

and £610, as many of the firm's sales were of instruments such as early models of the range and order indicators, or of vacuum pumps and Becker clocks, which were only marginally profitable. In 1903, however, the introduction of the FA3 provided a fillip for rangefinder sales, and the firm's administrative structure was reorganised to ensure that it could expand smoothly and rapidly if the increase in demand was sustained.[30] Harold Jackson, whose management skills and business expertise made him indispensable to the professors, became a junior partner in Barr & Stroud's Patents in May 1903.[31] James French had already become chief scientific assistant after James Henderson left the firm in 1901, and Oliver Porter became secretary in 1903. They were given increased responsibilities as the business expanded, and both were rewarded with an annual bonus of 1 per cent of profits.[32] Sales amounted to £20,889 in 1903, and the firm recorded an excellent profit after tax of £5,630.[33] By then, the three partners had already decided to build a new factory to enable them to increase their production capacity.

The site chosen for Barr & Stroud's new works was on the eastern side of Crow Road at Anniesland on the Scotstoun estate, about two miles to the west of Byres Road. It lay adjacent to Robert MacLehose & Co's new printing works and close to the growing residential and commercial community at Anniesland Cross, but was otherwise surrounded by green fields and was situated far enough from the city's industrial centre to be largely free from the atmospheric pollution which plagued other parts of Glasgow. The area was by no means remote, as Corporation trams ran from Glasgow to a terminus at Anniesland, and the

North British Railway's Great Western Road Station, on the Glasgow, Dumbarton and Helensburgh line which also served the fashionable suburbs of Bearsden and Milngavie, was only a few hundred yards from the factory site.[34] Barr & Stroud purchased the ground at Anniesland for £648 in July 1902, and work began on the construction of the new factory in the autumn of 1903.[35]

The Glasgow architect Alexander Paterson designed the office block for the new factory. It consisted of a three-storey brick building with a frontage of 90 feet, facing on to a private road which, with MacLehose's agreement, Barr & Stroud named Caxton Street after the famous English printer. The building housed the workers' canteen, a kitchen and a strong room on the ground floor and the general office, cloakrooms, waiting room, audit room and Dr Barr's private room on the first floor. The rangefinder adjusting shop was on the top floor.[36] Behind the office complex, the engineering contractors Sir William Arrol & Co, built a workshop designed by their engineer, A. C. Auden. It was a single-storey brick building with a glass roof supported by steel columns, and it accommodated the machine shop, grinding department, a general store and work-in-progress store, a tool and a paint shop and an optical grinding room.[37] The office block and workshop were already near to completion in 1904 when the partners decided that, in the light of the surge in orders for rangefinders, they required still larger premises.[38] A single-storey building was put up on the west side of the machine shop, to house fitting and assembly shops. Another was built to the north, separated from the rest of the works by a lane to reduce the dangers of fire,

Dr Barr's Albion motor-car parked outside the main entrance to the factory in Caxton Street, c.1905. Dr Barr had a love-hate relationship with the temperamental vehicle, and broke his arm while attempting to crank-start the engine in 1904.

and provided accommodation for a foundry, pattern shop, smithy, paint shop and packing case store. A further series of extensions was put in hand in 1906. Two storeys were added to the west bay of the machine shop, at right angles to the office block; the Scientific Department's machine shop was set up on the first floor; and a large rangefinder adjusting shop was installed in the top flat.[39]

When a reporter from *Engineering* visited the new factory in 1906, he was particularly impressed by the airiness and cleanliness of the workshops, and he noted with approval that the glass roofs permitted the maximum amount of natural light into the building. Tools and materials were kept in their proper place, while the floors were cleaned every lunch-time to ensure even greater tidiness and prevent dust and dirt from gathering. Employees were provided with khaki overalls at cost price by the firm, to protect their clothes. Personal hygiene was encouraged, and earthenware sinks were fitted at regular intervals along the walls with ample supplies of soap and towels. While spitting on the floors was forbidden, the management provided spittoons because 'it is much more sensible to recognise that men who chew tobacco have to spit somewhere'. The reporter found the toilet facilities to be remarkably good by the standards of the day, and he commented that 'there is no excuse why the closets in any works should not be fit for the use of a self-respecting workman, as they are at Barr & Stroud.'[40] Another reporter, who visited the works in 1914, suggested one way in which the firm ensured that standards of cleanliness in the toilets were maintained. He noted that:

> For two periods, each of twenty minutes during working hours - one in the morning and one in the afternoon - smoking is permitted in the shops. Like most wise concessions, this arrangement is by no means one-sided. It is a relief and gratification to many of the employees, while, from the firm's point of view, it not only improves the work – people's efficiency by improving their content, but quite remarkably diminishes the load factor of the lavatories.[41]

Most of Glasgow's engineering works opened at 6 a.m., and the men were given a short interval for breakfast later in the morning. Dr Barr, however, believed that this was inefficient, as men had to rise too early for them to give their best to their work at such an early hour,

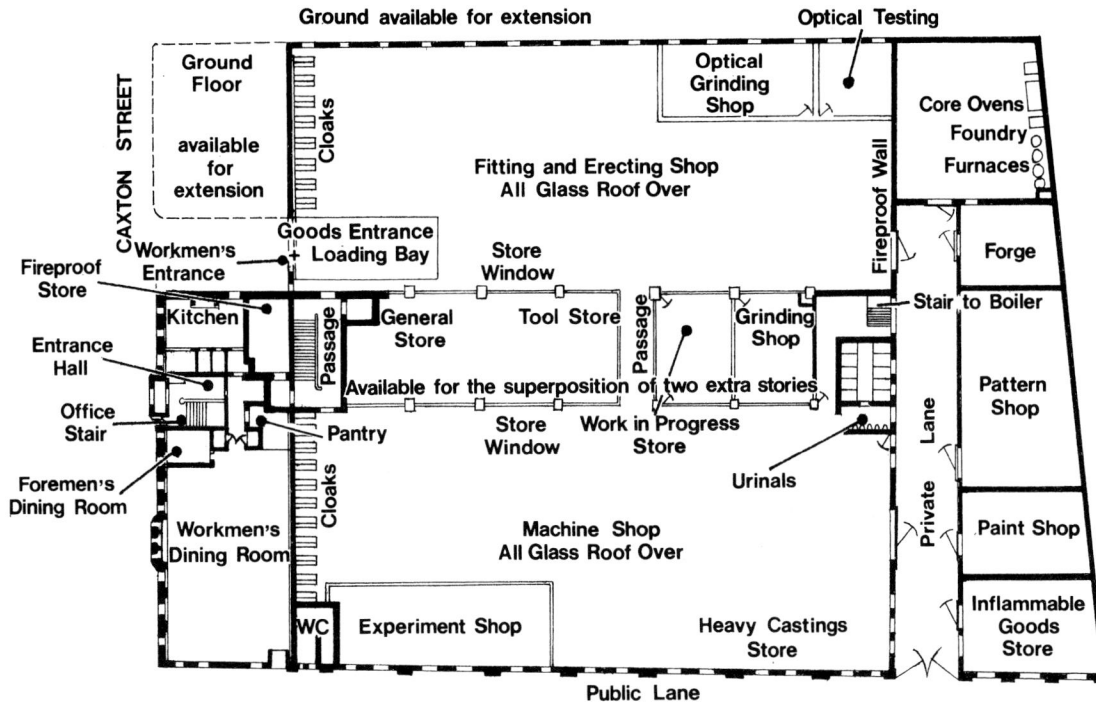

Ground Floor Plan

CAXTON STREET

Ground available for extension

Optical Testing

Ground Floor available for extension

Cloaks

Optical Grinding Shop

Core Ovens
Foundry
Furnaces

Fitting and Erecting Shop
All Glass Roof Over

Fireproof Wall

Workmen's Entrance

Goods Entrance + Loading Bay

Store Window

Forge

Fireproof Store

Kitchen

Passage

General Store

Tool Store

Passage

Grinding Shop

Stair to Boiler

Entrance Hall

Office Stair

Available for the superposition of two extra stories

Pattern Shop

Pantry

Store Window

Work in Progress Store

Lane

Foremen's Dining Room

Cloaks

Private

Urinals

Paint Shop

Workmen's Dining Room

Machine Shop
All Glass Roof Over

WC

Experiment Shop

Heavy Castings Store

Inflammable Goods Store

Public Lane

0 .... feet 100

TOP FLOOR

Fireproof Store

Stairs to Roof

Hoist Well

Fireproof Strong Room

Works Staircase

Urinals

Range Finder Adjustment Shop

Fire Escape Staircase

Optical Store

FIRST FLOOR

Board Room

WC

Works Staircase

Private Room

Waiting Room

Office Stair

Private Office

WC

Cloak Rooms

General Office

Drawing Office

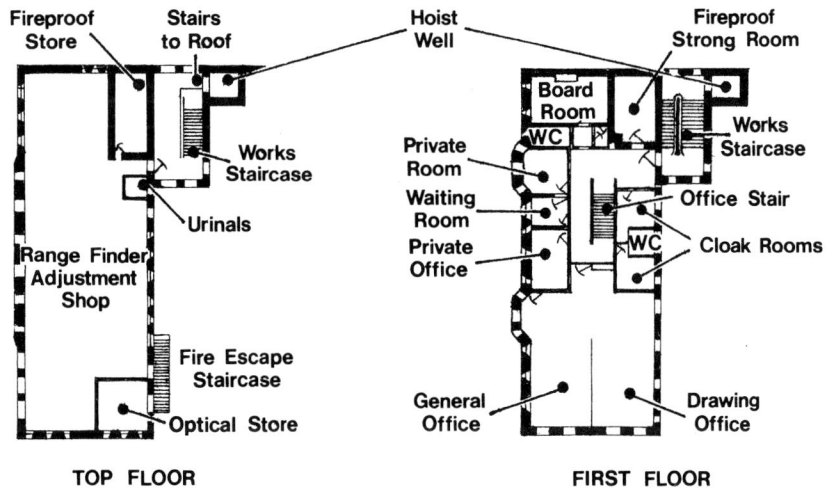

The lay-out of the Anniesland factory, as illustrated in Engineering, *4 May 1906. The factory provided Barr & Stroud with a floor area of 25,000 square feet in 1906.*

DAVID ASHMAN

while there was a greater tendency for them to sleep in or to 'lose time', especially on dark, cold winter mornings. Consequently, Barr & Stroud's workers did not start until 8 a.m. and, although they were given no breakfast interval, their standard working week was of fifty hours, 4 hours less than was normal in other works.[42] The men also worked under a novel bonus scheme, introduced at Ashton Lane in 1901. James Rowan, of the Clydeside firm D. Rowan & Co, adapted the system from American methods in 1898 and introduced it in his family's marine engineering works. The 'Rowan System' was taken up by several engineering firms in the West of Scotland as an incentive to boost productivity, and it appealed to Dr Barr's practical mind. Under the system, a workman received a standard hourly rate of pay, which was supplemented by a bonus for prompt completion of a piece of work. Each job in the workshops was given out with a certain time allotted for its completion, perhaps four hours. If the workman took the allotted time, or longer, to complete the job, then he received only his standard wage. However, if he completed it in half of the allotted time, say two hours instead of four, then he received a bonus of 50 per cent of his standard wage for the two hours. If he completed the same job in three hours, he had saved a quarter of the allotted time and his bonus was a quarter of the standard wage for the three hours taken. The Rowan System was retained by Barr & Stroud until 1932.[43]

The number of Barr & Stroud's employees grew steadily after the opening of the new factory, from 147 in September 1904 to 252 men and boys by November of the following year.[44] Many of the new recruits were apprentices, for it was the firm's policy that 'there cannot be too many highly trained apprentices', and they took on few youngsters for unskilled labour. Although the apprentices were not indentured, they were expected to complete the full five years of a rigorous and sound course of training. That training was the responsibility of the works manager, who had to ensure that the boys were properly supervised while learning their trade, that they were always kept busy, and that they were allowed to move on to more difficult jobs as they improved their skills.[45] Inevitably, given his professional interest in the education of young men, Dr Barr was determined to ensure that every effort was made to develop the scientific talents of those who showed promise. He made arrangements in 1904 for apprentices to attend evening classes in scientific subjects, and the youngsters earned bonuses based on their records of attendance at the classes and their results in tests and examinations. The most promising apprentices were encouraged to pursue their studies further at Glasgow University, just as Dr Barr had done during the 1870s.[46]

Lazy, disruptive or boisterous behaviour involving apprentices in the workshop was reported by the head foreman or works manager to Harold Jackson, and a letter to an errant youngster's parents usually served as sufficient warning to ensure that his conduct improved. The Glaswegian passion for football caused Jackson most cause for complaint. He wrote to the parents of thirty apprentices in February 1908, to inform them that their sons had left the factory without permission during working hours to go to watch a football match.[47] This mass desertion of the works was an unusual event and it was more common for him to write to complain about apprentices playing football themselves in the streets outside the factory, in breach of instructions from the management. Some apprentices proved wanting in the finer skills of the game and, when office windows were broken, the firm began to retaliate by suspending the wrong-doers from work for a few weeks.[48] Eventually, the youngsters and some of their older work-mates moved on to a new lunch-time football pitch in some fields nearby, but Jackson's problems did not end there. The Anniesland UF Church suffered a number of broken windows in 1915, and asked the firm to stop the workmen playing football in the vicinity. Jackson apologised, but said that the firm had tried everything in its power to put an end to the impromptu matches. He suggested that the police might meet with greater success in curbing this particular case of soccer hooliganism.[49]

George Blair did not take charge of the apprentices at the new factory, as he left Barr & Stroud in 1904 to become shop manager at the Arroll-Johnston motor car works in Paisley.[50] His successor was Neil J. Maclean, the son of a Baptist minister from Greenock. Maclean had gained valuable experience working in engineering workshops before he went up to Glasgow University at the age of twenty-one in 1900. When he graduated with a BSc in Engineering three years later, Dr Barr had no hesitation in recruiting him as the new works manager.[51] Maclean helped Dr Barr, Harold Jackson and Charles Macgill, a manager in the optical department, to lay out and equip the workshops at Anniesland in 1904.[52] He proved to be an excellent organiser, and was awarded a commission of 0.5 per cent of profits in 1904, when sales reached a new peak of £49,691. His

A row of vertical milling machines in the new factory, c.1906. A gas engine provided the power for all the belt-driven machinery, until Glasgow Corporation opened a new electricity generating substation at Anniesland in 1915.

commission was raised to 1 per cent, equal to the bonus paid to James French and Oliver Porter, in 1905, when the value of sales rose to £77,512.[53] Profits soared during these years, and came mostly from one source, the manufacture of rangefinders for two nations at war in the Far East.

The Russians, who became embroiled in a war with Japan in 1904, had ordered two naval rangefinders in January 1899, and inquired about the price of 100 more in June.[54] The two rangefinders performed well in trials. Rear-Admiral Zinovy Petrovich Rozhestvensky, Chief of the Naval Gunnery Training Detachment of the Baltic, reported that 'the Telemeters of Messrs Barr & Stroud in use on the vessels of the Detachment have in practice fully justified their reputation as the best of their kind . . . [It] may thus far be considered to be the only reliable Telemeter which can be used with success'. The Gunnery Lieutenant on board the cruiser *Diana*, which carried both rangefinders during sea trials, wrote that he was 'delighted with that excellent instrument'.[55]   Despite these favourable reports, the Russian Ministry of Marine was slow to order more rangefinders. The Russians haggled over prices, gave the impression that they intended to copy the instrument without compensating the inventors, and by the end of 1903 had acquired only twelve new rangefinders.[56]   Meanwhile, the Japanese were busy acquiring large numbers of the instruments as they prepared for war.

Barr & Stroud's agency agreement with Armstrong, Whitworth expired in September 1903, and the Glasgow firm declined to enter into a new arrangement. Relations between the two had become strained, especially as Barr

Apprentices help test naval fire-control instruments, 1913.

& Stroud came to feel that their agents did not devote sufficient time and energy to promoting rangefinder sales abroad. Commissions paid to Armstrong, Whitworth constituted only a minute percentage of the Tyneside firm's income, and Dr Barr and Harold Jackson felt that individuals and smaller foreign firms might make greater efforts to win orders.[57] As a result, Barr & Stroud began to build up a network of contacts across Europe, refusing to appoint a sole agency for a particular country but promising to pay a commission of 10 per cent of the value of any order secured for the firm. One of the new agencies was the Japanese company Takata & Co, whose London office secured an order for 100 of the new FA3 rangefinders for the Imperial Japanese Navy in January 1904.[58]

The Japanese and Russians had been at loggerheads for a number of years over their rival claims to spheres of influence in Korea and Manchuria. In 1904 the Trans-Siberian Railway was nearing completion, and the Russians hoped to use it to rush troops to the east in the event of a military confrontation there. The Russian Pacific Fleet was due to be strengthened with several powerful new battleships, threatening to tilt the balance of naval power in Russia's favour. Fearing Russian intentions in the Far East, the Japanese decided to take pre-emptive action. On 8 February Admiral Togo launched a surprise torpedo-boat attack on the Pacific Fleet as it lay at anchor in the roadstead at Port Arthur in Korea. The attack failed to deliver a 'knock-out blow', and Togo settled down to blockade the port and prevent the Russian fleet from attacking the transport ships which carried troops from Japan to invade Korea. Although the Pacific Fleet made several sorties, and there was a major engagement at the Battle of Round Island in August, when the Russians attempted unsuccessfully to break out for Vladivostok, there was no conclusive fleet action. The warships were scuttled when the Russians surrendered Port Arthur to the Japanese Army in January 1905.[59]

The Russian cruisers *Diana, Pallada, Variag*

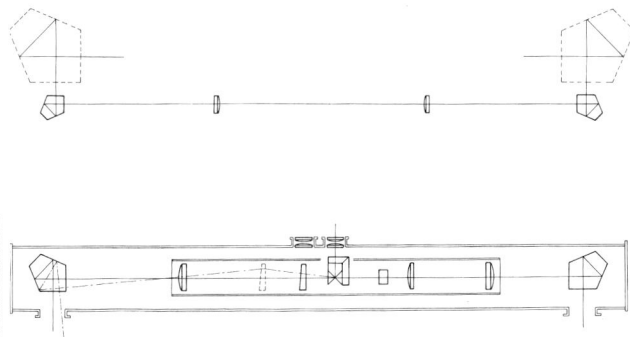

BILL MACFARLANE

The internal arrangements of the FQ2 of 9-foot base and, above, of the internal adjuster.

and *Askold*, were equipped with rangefinders, and it is likely that one or two of the battleships of the Pacific Fleet received some others from the batch of ten delivered to St Petersburg in September 1902.[60] The Japanese battleships and armoured cruisers all carried rangefinders, and Barr & Stroud sent off the 100 FA3s to Japan between January 1904 and the summer of 1905.[61] It is generally agreed that, on the occasions when the Pacific Fleet emerged from Port Arthur to engage Togo's ships, the accuracy of gunfire from both sides left a lot to be desired. However, Togo was rarely prepared to allow his battleships to come within 8,000 yards of the enemy, and the FA2, accurate only to within 6 per cent (360 yards) at 6,000 yards, was not intended by its manufacturers to be used to measure such an extreme range with great accuracy.[62] Moreover, officers on both sides were inexperienced in using the rangefinders in action, and gunnery practice was conducted at far shorter ranges. The true test of the rangefinder was yet to come.

Russia's Baltic Fleet set sail from Libau on 2 October 1904 with instructions to join up with the Pacific Fleet and bring the Japanese to a decisive action. The Vice-Admiral in command of what became known after the fall of Port Arthur as the Second Pacific Fleet, was none other than Zinovy Rozhestvensky, who had been so impressed by the Barr & Stroud rangefinders in 1902. His ships provoked a serious diplomatic incident on the night of 21 October when they mistook some British fishing vessels near the Dogger Bank in the North Sea for Japanese torpedo-boats and opened fire on them. In the noise and chaos the gunners could not hear orders to cease firing and, by the time the shooting stopped, in many cases after gunners were physically torn from their guns, one fishing boat had been sunk and three damaged, while the cruiser *Aurora* had been hit five times by other ships of the fleet.[63] Only Rozhestvensky's flagship, the *Kniaz Suvaroff*, was equipped with Barr & Stroud's range and order indicators, which could relay cease fire and other orders automatically to the gun turrets and casements.[64] In this respect, as in many others, the Russians were more poorly equipped than the enemy which awaited them on the other side of the world.

The Second Pacific Fleet was reinforced by Rear-Admiral Nebogatoff, with an obsolete battleship and a motley collection of coastal defence vessels, just before it set off on the final leg of its epic journey. As Port Arthur had fallen, Rozhestvensky was under new orders to take his ships to Vladivostok, and to do this he decided to pass through the Straits of Tsushima, between the small island of that name and the main Japanese island of Honshu. His eight battleships, three coastal defence vessels and one reconstructed armoured cruiser were formed in two parallel columns and steaming north-east by north through the Straits, when Togo's ships, steaming south-east by south, appeared on the scene in the early afternoon of 27 May. Togo ordered the four battleships and two cruisers of the 1st Division to execute a dangerous 'turn in succession' just within range of the Russian guns (the six cruisers of the 2nd Division turned further north) to bring his ships on to a course roughly parallel to the Russian columns. He knew that his ships could not return enemy fire while they were 'under helm', and that they would present a good target as each one turned at the same point as the one before it in the line, but he did not believe that the Russians would be able to find the range until the manoeuvre was close to completion and most of his ships were able to return fire. It came as a great shock to the Admiral when the first shot from the *Kniaz Suvaroff*, fired from about 7,400 yards, fell only 20 yards astern of his flagship, the *Mikasa*. The *Mikasa* was hit fifteen times, and two other Japanese battleships and most of the cruisers were also damaged during the next half hour, but the Japanese had gained the upper hand by the end of the opening phase of the battle. Togo's ships began to overhaul their slower opponents, and poured broadsides into the leading Russian ships from 4,700 to 6,500 yards, after using rangefinders and ranging shots from the 6-inch guns to ascertain the range. The leading Russian ships veered to starboard under this murderous fire, as the Japanese battle line threatened to cut across their bows to complete the classic naval tactical manoeuvre of 'crossing the T'. The Russian battle lines were thrown into confusion. After two hours, the leading Russian battleships had been pounded until they were incapable of offering even token resistance to the Japanese, and Togo closed for the kill. The Second Pacific Fleet was in total disarray by nightfall, four battleships having been sunk and the others seriously damaged. By the end of the following day, twenty-nine of the thirty-eight Russian warships, including all eight battleships, had been sunk, captured or destroyed.[65]

Rozhestvensky is reported to have said after the battle that his ships 'were not equipped with telemeters', but this is either a misquotation or a deliberately misleading statement. The *Kniaz*

Suvaroff is known to have had a rangefinder on the conning tower, and the battleships *Oslyaba* and *Orel* each had one on their forward bridges.[66] It is highly unlikely that the sister ships of the *Kniaz Suvaroff* and *Orel*, the *Borodino* and *Alexander III*, were not similarly equipped, and there are strong grounds for believing that many more instruments reached the Pacific Fleet before it sailed into the Straits of Tsushima. Rear-Admiral Nebogatoff was court-martialled for surrendering the ships under his command once the battle was lost, and he commented on his squadron's rangefinders during his trial:

Regarding the measurement of distances, whilst the Japanese ships were all supplied with Barr & Stroud Rangefinders and each piece or group of

An FQ2 of 2-metre base. Note the brake handle on the mounting, to 'lock' the instrument in position once the target was found, and the battery which provided the power for light-bulbs which illuminated the range scale in the left eye-piece.

large calibre guns had a rangefinder, on our ships there was in use the Jolg system combined with the Mikaschoff and it was only during the war that the Barr & Stroud were introduced.

According to the calculation of the Japanese from 12 to 13 of such instruments are necessary for each cruiser and some of them had this number whilst to each of our ships were allocated two or three.

My squadron received a small number of Rangefinders in closed cases as they arrived from England when there was no time to verify their quality. The officers and marines did not know how to manage these Rangefinders and made errors of two miles on the same distance. I compiled some rules for the management of the Barr & Stroud and reduced these errors to 600-800 m. When I overtook Rodjestwansky [sic] he asked me to give my rules to his ships also.[67]

The rangefinders received by Nebogatoff, and probably many of those received by Rozhestvensky's ships, were purchased through the agency of Basil Zaharoff, the world's leading arms dealer. Zaharoff placed the first order for Barr & Stroud naval rangefinders for his 'friends' in April 1904, and ordered a total of sixty-six FA3s and sixty short-based instruments by March 1905.[68] Twenty-nine FA3s were sent from Anniesland to St Petersburg before the Second Pacific Fleet sailed from Libau in October 1904, and another fifteen, which were sent off on 15 October, may have been picked up by a fast Russian destroyer at a British port and delivered to the fleet during its voyage.[69] Twenty-five more were completed in time to be sent to Nebogatoff's squadron, although it is not clear just how many it received.[70] Nebogatoff's statement suggests that, on his ships at least, the rangetakers were inexperienced and had not been trained in the use and adjusting of their rangefinders. Nevertheless, the Russians had enough of the instruments to equip each of their battleships with at least one, and Rozhestvensky was well enough acquainted with the instruments to ensure, during the voyage to Tsushima, that the Second Pacific Fleet's rangetakers were trained to use them effectively.

The Russian gunnery at the beginning of the battle was excellent, and they found the range of the Japanese quickly, despite misty conditions and the great distance which separated the two fleets.[71] However, Japanese officers reported later that 'after the first twenty minutes . . . the Russians seemed suddenly to go all to pieces, and their shooting became wild and almost harmless', and it is unlikely that this was due entirely to the gunners' lack of experience in combat.[72] Many Russian ships seem to have had just one rangefinder, and the *Oslyaba*'s was destroyed early in the action, when a shell hit the forward bridge, while the second shot to hit the *Orel* destroyed the rangefinder station.[73] The Japanese had the advantage of carrying up to six rangefinders on each capital ship, so that an unlucky hit did not destroy their capability to find ranges. They also had better shells, filled with a high explosive called shimose. This exploded with great force and gave off clouds of noxious fumes, so that those Russian buglers and signallers who were not wounded by shrapnel, found it difficult to send orders and ranges as they were engulfed in choking yellow smoke.[74] Three of the four Japanese battleships and five of the eight armoured cruisers were fitted with Barr & Stroud's range and order indicators, and their captains could continue to transmit ranges and orders directly to the guns while their ships were under fire.[75] The Russians found the task to be virtually impossible without similar equipment.

The excellent use to which the Japanese put their rangefinders and fire-control instruments at Tsushima was commented upon by many experts when news of the sensational victory flashed around the world. Reuters reported that 'the [US] Navy Department has been informed that the Japanese gunners' long-range aim . . . was due to the rangefinders in the Japanese ships' fighting tops, which gave the range of the Baltic Fleet at a greater distance than the Russians could locate Admiral Togo's fleet.'[76] Harold Jackson wrote:

We are inclined to think that the superiority of the Japanese firing was probably due more to the fact that they had scientifically trained their gunners with the Rangefinder and other appliances than to the mere fact that their ships carried Rangefinders and the Russians did not.

We think probably both fleets carried Rangefinders: in the one case they were properly used during the action, and in the other case probably badly used: but still more that it was owing to the training in peacetime with Rangefinders that the superiority of the Japanese Gunners was obtained.[77]

He told C.P. Goerz, one year after the battle, that:

. . . we have now received information regarding the use of our Rangefinders in the Russo-Japanese War. The opinions of the Japanese Officers regarding our Rangefinders are very enthusiastic, so much so that one of them has remarked that he would rather have three 12" guns and a Rangefinder than four 12" guns. He considers the Rangefinder to be as valuable as a 12" gun.[78]

When naval experts from other countries studied the Battle of Tsushima, they concluded that Barr & Stroud's rangefinders had played a vital part in the Japanese victory. Orders from existing customers increased, the Italian Navy decided to adopt the rangefinder, and the Germans and French decided to conduct further trials.[79]

The pace of the Great Naval Race quickened in 1905, after Britain laid down the battleship HMS *Dreadnought* in 1905 and the first dreadnought battle-cruiser, HMS *Invincible*, in 1906. Dreadnought battleships and battle-cruisers carried ten and eight 12-inch guns respectively, and could outgun and outrun any other ship afloat. The navies of the world had to build their own dreadnoughts, at great expense, or allow their fleets to lapse into obsolence. The consequences of the destruction of a new fleet of dreadnoughts in action would be calamitous for any great maritime power. Just as naval experts were contemplating the implications of the Battle of Tsushima, where a large fleet had been lost to an enemy possessing better techniques in ranging and fire-control, Barr & Stroud brought out their latest improved rangefinder, the FQ2 with a base of 9 feet.

Barr & Stroud were unwilling to increase the magnification in the FA3 beyond 24 diameters. Higher magnification resulted in a proportional loss of brightness and a more restricted field of view. In addition, it increased the difficulty in keeping the partial images of the target in the centre of the field of view, on the line of separation, when the host ship steamed at speed and caused the rangefinder platform to vibrate. To improve the accuracy of their rangefinder, Barr & Stroud had to find some way of increasing the base length while avoiding the problems created by the bending of the frame in the 6-foot experimental instrument in 1901. Dr Stroud's solution was to retain the short frame in a new 9-foot-base rangefinder, the FQ, but to replace the end mirrors with pentagonal prisms and mount these double-reflecting end prisms on the outer tube itself, rather than on the frame with the other optical parts. A small rotation of the pentagonal prism, such as might occur if the tube bent slightly, made no angular change to the beam of light transmitted to the central optical system, as any change in the angle of reflection from one of the prism's two reflecting surfaces was cancelled out by an exactly opposite change in the angle of reflection from the other.[80] This imaginative solution to the problem of increasing the base length proved effective during trials of the FQ instrument conducted by the Japanese in 1903, and by the Royal Navy the following year.[81]

The FQ naval rangefinder included other modifications in design to facilitate manufacture. To increase its ease of use, it featured a patented eye-piece arrangement, inclined at 45° to the plane of the instrument to allow the observer to look down into the instrument without causing the same strain to his neck muscles which resulted from prolonged viewing through the old eye-piece set at 90°. When the FQ2 naval rangefinder went into production in 1906, it was supplied complete with yet another of Dr Stroud's inventions. Prior to the introduction of the FQ, rangefinders were checked for infinity by viewing on a star or, in daylight, on an adjusting board on which were painted two vertical lines separated by the distance between the end reflectors of the rangefinder. The internal adjuster was an ingenious arrangement of lenses and pentagonal prisms which allowed the observer to adjust the instrument without having to wait until the stars came out, or until the opportunity arose to set up the large adjusting board in front of the rangefinder.[82]

The 9-foot FQ2 naval rangefinder had a standard magnifying power of 28 diameters, was accurate to within 0.5 per cent (30 yards) at 6,000 yards, and was priced at £325.[83] By December 1906 a total of eighty-six had been sold or were on order, half of them to the Admiralty, and the FQ2 became the firm's standard model for capital ships.[84] Barr & Stroud's 9-foot FQ2 was adopted by the Royal Navy and Italian Navy in 1906, the French and Japanese in 1907, the American in 1909, the Russian in 1910 and the Austro-Hungarian in 1911.[85] Other countries followed suit with modest orders to equip their smaller navies.[86]

Barr & Stroud had been able to brush aside competition from other rangefinder manufacturers during the nineteenth century, as their rivals seldom possessed the research and production facilities required to perfect their instruments and few could match the combined talents of Dr Stroud and Dr Barr for invention and design. By the turn of the century, however, the famous German optical instrument makers, Carl Zeiss of Jena, had developed a new rangefinder which impressed many of Europe's military leaders. The instrument was invented by an Alsatian engineer, A.H. de Grousilliers, who patented it

in Britain in 1893 and succeeded in having it taken up and developed by Zeiss. It was similar in external appearance to the Barr & Stroud, except that the observer viewed the target through binoculars rather than two telescopes with a common eye-piece. Rays of light from the end reflectors of the Zeiss stereoscopic rangefinder were focused on slides mounted in front of the eye-pieces, and a series of scale graduations, in the form of little arrows, was marked on the slides in such positions that, when viewed simultaneously through the binoculars, they appeared to read back into the distance and to become part of the stereoscopic view of the landscape. As the arrows appeared to be at the same distances as objects in the field of view, a physically suitable and well-trained observer could 'drop' one on or close to the target, and thereby find the range.[87] Initially, Zeiss produced a small rangefinder with a base length of 0.87 metres, and a second model of 1.3 metres which was accurate within 1 per cent at 1,000 metres.[88] The latter was submitted for trials by several European armies at the turn of the century.

Zeiss had an excellent reputation as optical instrument makers, a highly skilled workforce of over 1,000 men and dozens of scientists, and a source of high quality glass from Otto Schott's Jena Glassworks.[89] Barr & Stroud were quick to acknowledge the achievement of their formidable rivals in producing an instrument of great quality, Dr Stroud referring to it as 'highly ingenious and very pretty' and Harold Jackson admitting that it was 'exceedingly beautiful in conception and construction'.[90] Nevertheless, Dr Barr and Harold Jackson were convinced of the superiority of the coincidence method of rangetaking over the stereoscopic, and while they continued to praise Zeiss for the inventive and manufacturing skills so evident in the rival instrument, they took great pains to inform clients of their reservations concerning the potential performance of stereoscopic rangefinders in military or naval warfare.

Good stereoscopic vision is not something with which all men are blessed. Hereditary factors, illness, or the over use of one eye by men involved in a great deal of rifle-shooting or in similar pursuits, can result in vision in one eye being stronger than in the other. Barr & Stroud pointed out that only men with equally good vision in both eyes could obtain accurate readings from a stereoscopic rangefinder. These men had to be given extensive training before they could 'drop' the arrows accurately on to the target, and had to be in good health, because 'since the quality of stereoscopic vision depends on the control of the very sensitive muscles of the eyes, and since this control depends upon the health of the individual, an observer who could take readings one day is perhaps unreliable the next...and the observer cannot refer to another person for corroboration.'[91] Many healthy men suddenly develop stomach upsets in heavy seas, and for this reason Barr & Stroud believed that the stereoscopic instrument was unsuitable for service with warships.[92]

Harold Jackson emphasised to clients that even a man with good vision in only one eye could use the Barr & Stroud rangefinder, after only a few minutes' training. He referred to the firm's own experiments with a stereoscopic rangefinder, when it was discovered that 'Professor Barr has a very good stereoscopic faculty, Professor Stroud not nearly so good, and the undersigned can hardly see

stereoscopically at all. All three of us are equally good at coincidence.'[93] He admitted that the lenses manufactured by Zeiss were superior to any Barr & Stroud could obtain in Britain and that this, coupled with the fact that stereoscopic rangefinders featured fewer optical faces, meant that the Zeiss instruments could give a clearer and brighter definition of the landscape and target in the field of view. He

An experimental FT field rangefinder, c.1904. The observer is demonstrating how to use the instrument to range on a horizontal target such as a hedge or ridge.

also admitted that the stereoscopic rangefinder held an advantage in having no moving parts, and was therefore less prone to needing adjustment and repair, and that it was cheaper than the Barr & Stroud.[94]   It was hardly surprising, though, that Jackson had no qualms in referring to the results of tests which showed the superiority of the Barr & Stroud over the Zeiss rangefinder for military uses.

The Swedish Army was one of the first to test the Barr & Stroud field rangefinders against those of Zeiss in 1902. Although they preferred the optical qualities of the Zeiss rangefinder, and the use of stereoscopy *per se*, the Swedes found the Scottish 4-foot 6-inch FA instrument to be generally superior as a distance measurer.[95] Their findings were confirmed in the first tests conducted in several countries of the Barr & Stroud versus the Zeiss and the instruments of other German manufacturers.[96] For these trials the Glasgow firm was able to submit a number of improved FA and FQ rangefinders of base lengths of up to 4 feet 6 inches. In 1907 the FT rangefinder, specially designed for field work by Dr Barr, went into production at Anniesland, and the firm fixed on 0.8 metres as the standard base length for infantry, and 1.0 metres for artillery. The FT had larger pentagonal prisms and objectives to allow a greater amount of light to be transmitted through the instrument, and featured an internal aperture through which a second observer could view the scale while the first concentrated on keeping the partial images of the targets in coincidence. The scale was brighter than in earlier models, and new optical arrangements made the instrument capable of measuring distances with even greater accuracy.[97] Steel replaced aluminium

An FT1 rangefinder of 0.8 m base, on a belt mounting with shoulder supports. Note the handles and the inclined eye-piece, two features which were patented by Barr & Stroud and which were challenged by German competitors just before the First World War.

in the construction of frames and tubes, and by 1912 the firm was also using the strong light alloy, duralumin, which was considerably cheaper than steel, so that the FTs were not only more accurate and easier to use than the old FA and FQ field rangefinders, but were also able to withstand rougher treatment. Dr Stroud, who had originally favoured the development of a stereoscopic rangefinder for field service, was also able to come up with an idea to improve the performance of the coincidence rangefinders in ranging on objects such as trees, rocks or hedges whose outlines lacked the continuity of a ship's mast or similar target. In what he jokingly referred to as the 'kaleidoscopic rangefinder', which went into production in 1908, the field of view above the line of separation at the eye-piece of the FT instrument was inverted, so that the observer was able to bring the two partial images into coincidence more easily.[98]

Harold Jackson noted in November 1908 that 'we believe in all strictly correct trials our [field] rangefinders have proved the most accurate.'[99] Nevertheless, he had to admit ruefully that 'sometimes we have been told that they are more accurate for infantry than is necessary, and a cheaper instrument with less accuracy stands a good chance of being successful in such cases.'[100] This was certainly

An FT1 of 0.8 m base on a tripod mounting. The provision of an inclined eye-piece made the observer's task of using the instrument while lying down a far more comfortable one.

true in 1906, when the German Army's Gewher Pruefugs Kommission announced that the Barr & Stroud infantry rangefinder had proved to be the best submitted for trials in Germany, but rejected it on the grounds of cost (and because Germany, like most European powers, did not wish to rely on foreign firms for military equipment). A cheaper rangefinder invented by Lieutenant Friedrich Hahn of the German Army was adopted in place of the Barr & Stroud.[101]   The British authorities, too, preferred a cheaper field rangefinder to those sent for trial from Anniesland, and a coincidence instrument invented by Captain A.H. Marindin of the Black Watch was adopted by the British Army in 1907 to replace the obsolete Watkin Mekometer.[102]   Barr & Stroud's field rangefinders were ordered only in ones and twos for trials, until the French Army adopted them for the infantry in 1909 and placed orders for 610 instruments that year.[103]   Zeiss met with just as little commercial success with their stereoscopic field rangefinders prior to 1909. After Barr & Stroud's original patent expired in 1906, they began to manufacture a coincidence rangefinder which, Jackson was amused to hear, was advertised as the 'système Barr & Stroud'.[104] The firms of Zeiss, A. & R. Hahn and Goerz (which acquired a controlling interest in Hahn in 1907) made rapid strides in developing their own coincidence rangefinders in the five years before the outbreak of World War One, and by July 1912 Jackson was forced to admit that 'we have now to recognise that we no longer enjoy a monopoly of the construction of rangefinders, and that the firm of Zeiss, and perhaps also the firm of Goerz, are serious competitors.'[105]

The German firms were able to produce instruments which proved superior only in certain respects to those of Barr & Stroud (for example, Zeiss field rangefinders were usually found to give a better illumination of the field of view, and Hahn's were sometimes considered to be more sturdy), but the Glasgow firm succeeded in keeping one step ahead of its competitors in designing rangefinders which gave the best overall performance in trials.[106] The decision of the French to adopt Barr & Stroud rangefinders for all branches of the Army in 1910 gave greater weight to the partners' claims that theirs were the best instruments available, and further large orders from other nations seemed certain to follow.[107] Then, in 1911, Zeiss and Goerz took concerted action to close the technological gaps which had opened between them and Barr & Stroud in the business of rangefinder manufacture. The Germans began by appealing against two of Barr & Stroud's most important new patents. One of these related to the design of an eye-piece inclined at 45° to the plane of the rangefinder, which allowed the rangetaker to use the instrument for long periods, especially while lying prone, without straining his neck muscles (German Patent No 175896);   the other related to a design for special handles which made it easier to carry and operate hand-held instruments in action (No 228648).[108] Zeiss withdrew their appeal to Germany's Imperial Patent Court in November, when Barr & Stroud agreed to grant them sole rights to the two patents for all rangefinders manufactured for the German authorities. Goerz continued with the action, however, and succeeded in having the eye-piece patent annulled in February 1912.   Barr & Stroud promptly

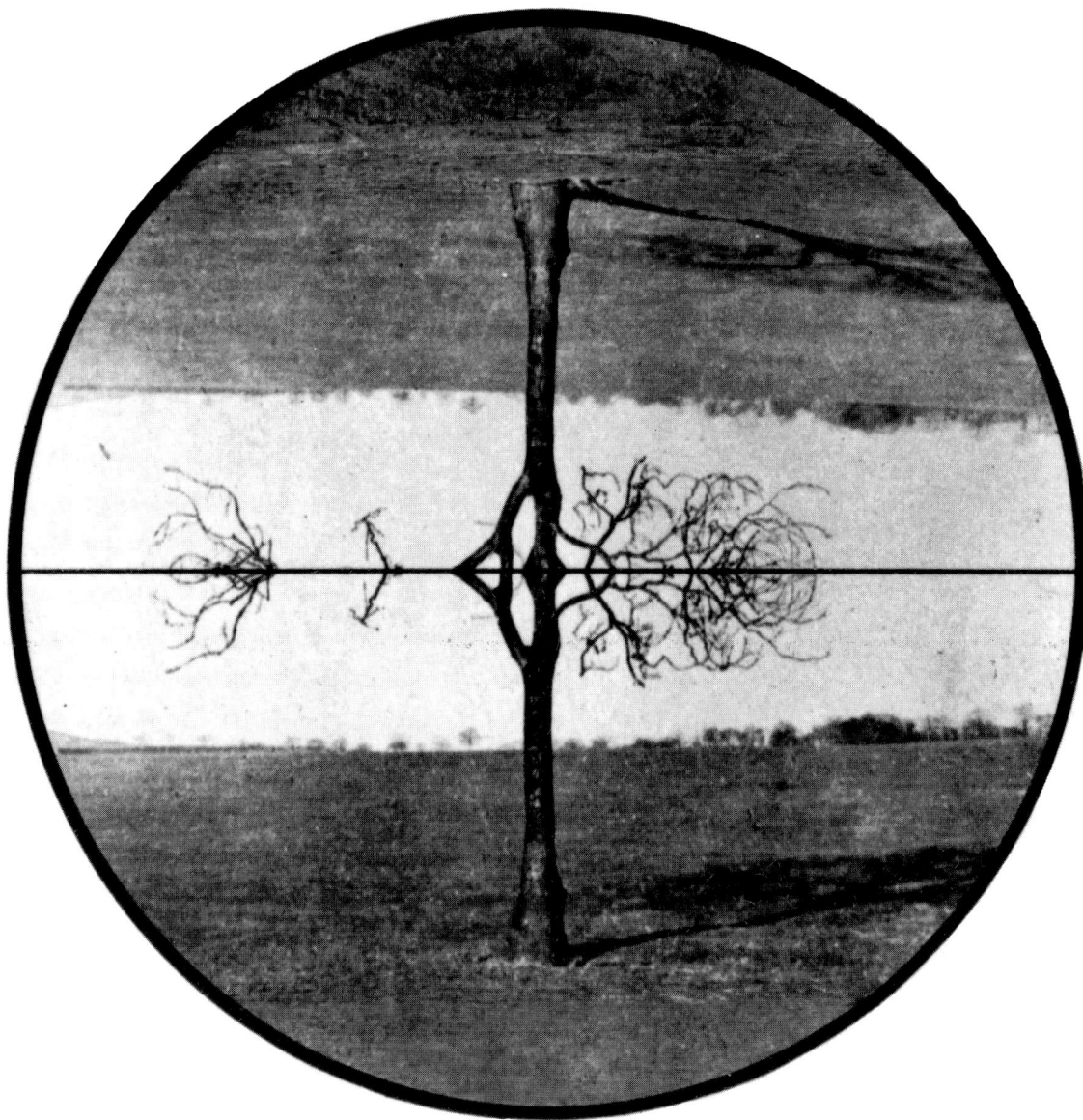

The field of view in a 'kaleidoscopic' rangefinder, with the upper image inverted.

appealed to the Imperial High Court, and the patent remained valid while the appeal was pending.[109]

The prospect of having to pay large sums in legal fees, to defend their patents in Germany and other countries from further attacks by Zeiss or Goerz, and of the German firms embarking on a potentially ruinous price war if Barr & Stroud began to gain too great a share of the market for rangefinders, persuaded Dr Barr, Dr Stroud and Harold Jackson to accede to German requests for a conference of Europe's leading rangefinder manufacturers. Such conferences were popular at the time as a prelude to agreements on the divisions of markets, and sometimes to the formation of large international cartels. Dr Barr and James French met representatives of Zeiss in Berlin in February and Harold Jackson and J. Martin Strang (William Strang's brother, who joined the firm's staff in 1908) met with directors of Goerz in St Petersburg in April, before a conference of all three firms was held in Berlin in June 1912.[110] Jackson and the firm's Glasgow lawyer, William Mckinnon, attended the conference, and agreed to present tentative proposals to Dr Barr and Dr Stroud for the division of Europe into 'spheres of influence'. The proposals involved 'allocating' each country in Europe to either Barr & Stroud or the German firms, and although a firm would be permitted to tender for orders in a country not allocated to it, it would be required to pay a commission on any sales to the firm or firms which had priority there. It was also agreed in principle at the Berlin conference that the three firms should work towards agreements to exchange or pool their rangefinder patents.[111] No sooner had the conference ended, however,

than the firms began to argue over just what had been agreed, tentatively or otherwise, by the representatives who met in Berlin.

Barr & Stroud favoured a long-term arrangement, but Zeiss and Goerz later disputed the Scottish firm's claim that they had declared themselves to be in favour of a ten-year agreement, and demanded instead that any accord should be of only three years' duration. Both German firms began to haggle over Barr & Stroud's proposals for licensing fees for their patents — Zeiss offered only two-thirds and Goerz half of the price settled on by the partners at Anniesland, and Zeiss were not prepared to relinquish their sole right to manufacture rangefinders under the handles patent for the German authorities. Barr & Stroud claimed that they had offered to grant licences to both firms to make rangefinders embodying their patents for the German authorities alone, but the German firms wanted licences to produce rangefinders with Barr & Stroud's handles and inclined eye-pieces in every country in which the Scottish firm had patented these inventions. Dr Barr, Dr Stroud and Harold Jackson met to consider the course of events, and agreed that 'it is the German firms who are much more desirous of coming to an arrangement than the firm of Barr and Stroud.'[112] The Germans had practically admitted that they were negotiating from a position of weakness when they told Jackson in Berlin that 'lately no profit has been made by them from rangefinders in the past [sic]', and the partners were persuaded by renewed German demands that 'the desire appears to be not an arrangement for the mutual benefit of the firms, but a wish to obtain as much as possible at the expense of Barr &

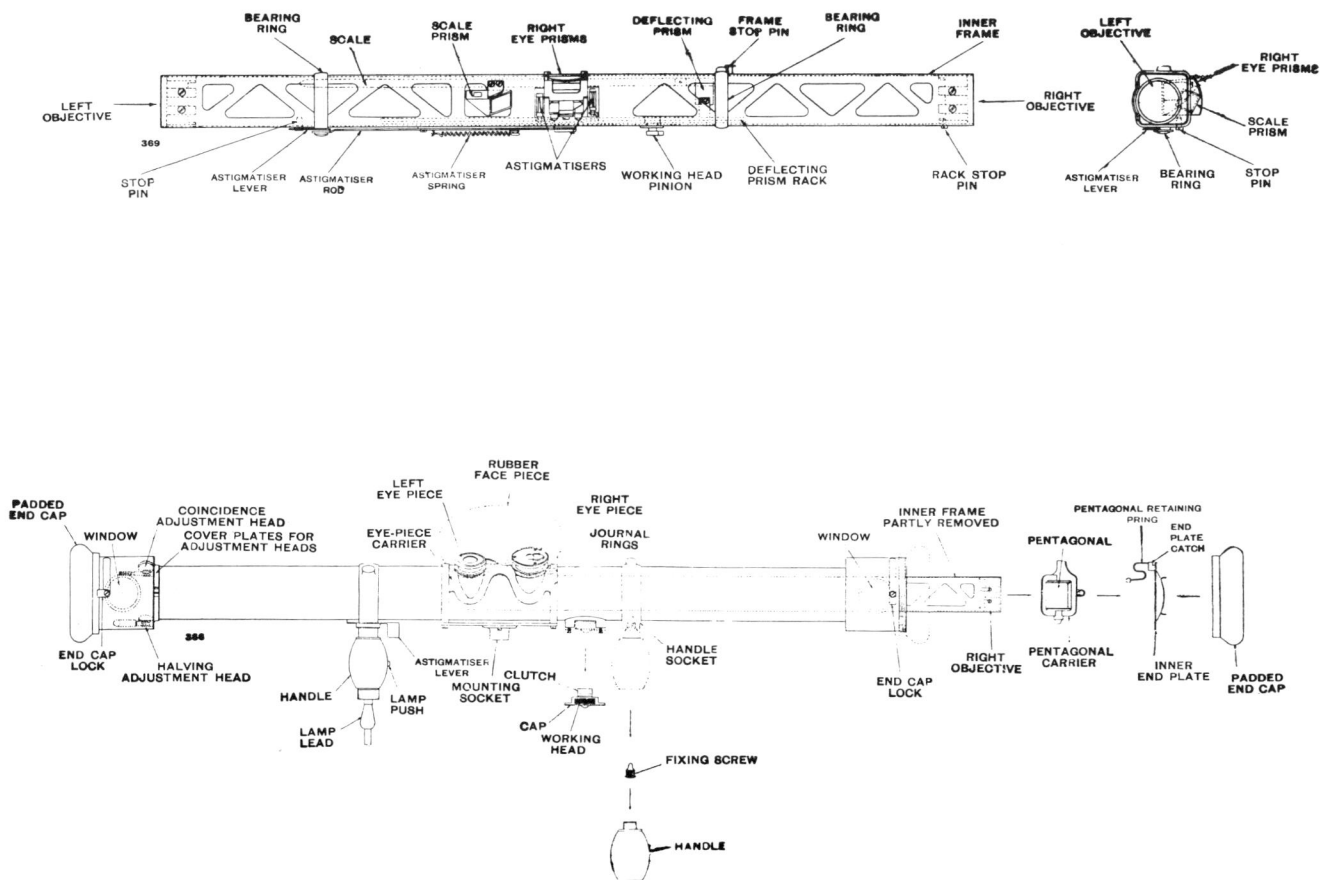

The FT17 field rangefinder. Dr Barr's design for the FT1 was retained with only minor alterations in later field rangefinders, the FT4, 17, 27, 32 and 37. The inner tube was of square section, with the vertical sides cut out in lattice form, in order to keep the weight of the instrument to a minimum.

Stroud.' [113]   Consequently, and with growing evidence of a general preference for their own rangefinders among Europe's army officers, Barr & Stroud broke off negotiations with Zeiss and Goerz in January 1913. [114] Six months later, the Imperial High Court reversed the decision of the Imperial Patent Court, and Goerz were ordered to meet the legal costs incurred by Barr & Stroud in defending their patent. [115]   The decision confirmed the wisdom of Barr & Stroud's resolve to resist the pressures exerted by their powerful and predatory rivals, and to remain free to conduct their business unfettered by restrictive agreements.

Barr & Stroud received orders for a total of 2,900 field rangefinders of various base lengths from France before August 1914, and their 0.8-

Austro-Hungarian soldiers, each with a rangefinder submitted for trials at Brück in 1911. At the beginning of the twentieth century, European inventors devised a host of tiny instruments for measuring distances. While the pocket rangefinders were easy to carry and use, they did not provide sufficiently accurate readings to satisfy the needs of army officers.

metre FT instrument was adopted by the War Office at the end of 1911, once it became clear that the Marindin instrument, although relatively cheap, was not suitable for field service.[116] The War Office was so impressed with the 0.8-metre rangefinder that Barr & Stroud were asked to sell the patents covering the instrument to the nation. The firm replied that it would sell the rights for £150,000 plus a commission of 2 per cent on every 0.8-metre rangefinder made by the War Office contractors, and in February 1914 submitted new terms, offering the rights for £30,000 but asking for a royalty of 6 per cent on the price of each instrument manufactured to their patents. The War Office was unwilling to agree to Barr & Stroud's terms, and the matter was dropped, but orders for large numbers of FT rangefinders for the British Army soon began to arrive at Anniesland.[117] Zeiss and Goerz might have expected the British Army to reject their instruments in favour of domestically manufactured rangefinders, but they suffered other, more surprising, setbacks. It was particularly galling for the German firms to hear of the decision taken by the Austro-Hungarian authorities in November 1912, after nearly four years of trials of various instruments, to follow the French lead and adopt Barr & Stroud rangefinders for all branches of the army.[118] Austria-Hungary was alarmed by the dramatic successes of the Serbian Army at the beginning of the First Balkan War in 1912, successes which might lead the Dual Monarchy into conflict with its upstart neighbour, and asked Barr & Stroud to deliver 1,000 new rangefinders to Vienna by March 1913. Harold Jackson replied that his firm was already committed to delivering 2,000 rangefinders to other countries and that, as the interests of established customers had to be given priority, he could could guarantee to supply only a small quantity of instruments by the deadline.[119] Zeiss and Goerz then stepped in, each offering to supply 200 rangefinders by March, but the Austro-Hungarians insisted that the rangefinders must be of the Barr & Stroud type, and as the Glasgow firm believed that 'the German instruments are copies of our instruments' and infringed Barr & Stroud's handles and eye-piece patents, preparations were made to take legal action.[120] The cases

were never taken to the Austro-Hungarian courts — the First World War broke out before the necessary briefs could be prepared — but Barr & Stroud were grimly satisfied to hear that by March 1914, one year after the deadline set for delivery of the German rangefinders, Zeiss had managed to deliver only fifty instruments to Vienna, and Goerz had failed to deliver even one.[121]

Zeiss began to advertise their first stereoscopic naval rangefinders in 1906.[122] They were adopted by the Imperial German Navy in 1912, and although no other navy followed suit, Barr & Stroud recognised that the German company might well pose a serious threat to their dominance of the market in the future.[123] Barr & Stroud rangefinders also proved more popular than German instruments with the army officers of most of Europe's armies, but the Scottish firm could not afford to relax in the face of increasingly tough competition. The Germans recognised that, in an age of strident nationalism, there was an advantage in setting up factories to produce rangefinders in the client country.[124] Barr & Stroud feared that this might tip the balance in favour of German instruments produced under licence or in subsidiary factories in foreign countries, and the Scottish firm considered it prudent to set up their own multinational organisation.

Negotiations between Goerz, Zeiss and French armaments firms such as Schneider, aimed at joint ventures to manufacture rangefinders in France, had persuaded Barr & Stroud to set up a French subsidiary in 1911. The subsidiary was managed by Robert McNab, who had come to Barr & Stroud as an apprentice in 1895.[125] It occupied a small

Four Barr & Stroud, three Goerz, four Zeiss and five Hahn rangefinders at the Brück trials. Four adjusting boards, each clearly marked with vertical lines, stand in the foreground. The Barr & Stroud instruments are the only ones with inclined eye-pieces and handles.

workshop in Paris in which repairs and some assembly work could be carried out, but Barr & Stroud hoped, eventually, to manufacture complete rangefinders there, to meet French demand.   Other workshops were set up in Calais and Toulon, to adjust and repair military and naval rangefinders respectively.[126] Realising that Goerz and Zeiss were also offering to manufacture rangefinders in Austria-Hungary, and with regular orders coming in from the Austro-Hungarian Navy and the prospect of huge orders from the Army to follow, Barr & Stroud decided in November 1912 to set up another subsidiary in the Dual Monarchy.   G.R. Siebert, the firm's agent, informed the partners that the Hungarians exerted considerable influence in military affairs in the Empire, and so it would be politic to build factories in both Austria and Hungary.[127] Two new companies were formed: Barr und Stroud GmbH was set up in Austria, with a small factory at Katzeldorf, and Barr es Stroud es Tarsa in Hungary, with a small factory across the border from Katzeldorf, at Lajtaszentmiklos. Siebert was made managing director of the Austrian firm and managing partner of the one in Hungary.[128] James McFarlane, a member of staff, was sent out from Anniesland to set up the factories and to manage them with the assistance of an experienced rangefinder adjuster, John Dunn. Before production could begin, however, Britain and Austria-Hungary went to war. McFarlane and Dunn were interned for the duration, and the two factories were lost when the Austro-Hungarian Empire was dismantled at the end of the war.[129]

Barr and Stroud were aware that, if they did not set up plants in France and Austria-Hungary, they were unlikely to continue to win orders in either country in the future. However, the partners were concerned at the cost of setting up subsidiaries, and also of the risks involved. Zeiss and Goerz were highly active in establishing new factories in Europe, but their optical businesses were far more broadly based than Barr & Stroud: if the demand for German rangefinders did not materialise, or fell suddenly, they could concentrate on manufacturing microscopes, binoculars, telescopes and other instruments instead, whereas Barr & Stroud did not have other well-established products to fall back on. For this reason the firm preferred to enter into

new areas of activity in tandem with existing companies.

Bausch & Lomb reached an agreement with Zeiss in 1908, allowing the American firm to manufacture the German rangefinders under licence in the USA, and Barr & Stroud had to act swiftly to safeguard this valuable non-European market.[130] Keuffel & Esser of Hoboken, New Jersey, were granted a licence to manufacture range and order indicators in 1909, and in 1910 they were also given permission to begin manufacturing Barr & Stroud rangefinder stands, as the two firms sought to recover business lost to the Zeiss-Bausch & Lomb alliance.[131] At the same time, Barr & Stroud were searching for a partner to help them establish their business in Russia. Oliver Porter was told in St Petersburg in 1910 that the firm would receive no orders to supply the large Russian navy and the Czar's huge army until they could manufacture instruments in Russia, as Goerz and Zeiss had offered to do.[132] The state-owned Obhoukhoff Steel Works in St Petersburg had the contract from Barr & Stroud to clean and adjust instruments returned by the Russian armed forces, but the directors declined an invitation to enter into a partnership with the Scottish firm and begin manufacturing rangefinders in their well-equipped optical department.[133] However, the head of the Obhoukhoff optical department, Professor A . Gerschun, struck up a friendship with Oliver Porter, Harold Jackson and J. Martin Strang during their visits to St Petersburg. When he decided to set up a new firm, the Russian Society for Optical and Mechanical Industry, Barr & Stroud offered to take up £1,500 of shares, and to furnish the Russian company with all the information and

Naval rangefinders submitted for trials at Fort Munro, USA,
c.1912.

expertise required to manufacture their rangefinders under licence.[134]   Zeiss had already won substantial orders from the Russian army and navy, partly because Barr & Stroud's agent, Pierre Balinsky, had neglected the firm's affairs, but after the first trials of field rangefinders in 1913 it seemed likely that the Scottish firm and its new Russian partner would be receiving large orders in the near future.[135] Unfortunately, the outbreak of war in 1914 brought the trials to an end, and Barr & Stroud had to write off their investment in Gerschun's firm after the Bolsheviks siezed St Petersburg at the beginning of the Russian Revolution in 1917.[136]

Harold Jackson believed that 'Zeiss is much more serious for us than Goerz in the marine': he had been told by Zeiss in August 1912 that Goerz had 'never made a successful large rangefinder' and the latter firm's instruments continued to perform poorly in pre-war naval trials. [137] Zeiss had some success, winning large orders for their 3-metre stereoscopic rangefinders from the Imperial German Navy in 1912, and supplying some instruments to other nations, but Barr & Stroud continued to come out on top in most trials and only Germany declined to adopt the Scottish naval rangefinder as standard equipment.[138] A new naval instrument invented by Arthur Hungerford Pollen threatened briefly to provide Barr & Stroud with serious competition for Admiralty orders, but the Pollen-Cooke rangefinder was rejected after trials, apparently on the grounds that it consisted of a large number of optical parts which made it not only expensive, but also prone to derangement.[139] In the USA, Bausch & Lomb's naval rangefinders, embodying Zeiss patents, were ordered in substantial quantities by the US Navy Department. The Barr & Stroud naval rangefinders were considered by the Americans to be 'mechanically simpler' and easier to use than the Bausch & Lomb, but the latter was found to be better for use in poor light, largely because it featured dual magnification and could be used at the lower magnifying power when visibility was poor.[140] Fifty-seven of the Scottish 9-foot FQ instruments were in service with the US Navy by the end of 1910, and although the authorities preferred to order Bausch & Lomb's domestically manufactured instruments thereafter, Keuffel & Esser were asked to make and supply FQ2s to the American fleet after the USA entered the First World War in 1917.[141]

Barr & Stroud's business grew steadily after their range and order systems and rangefinders proved their worth during the Russo-Japanese War and as the firm brought improved instruments on to the market. Between January 1907 and December 1912 they received orders for 3,872 rangefinders, and substantial numbers of improved range, order and deflection instruments, and the total income

A combined transmitter, on the right, and a single order receiver beneath a range and deflection receiver. The Royal Navy preferred indicators with window panels to the dial instruments originally favoured by the Japanese.

from sales during these seven years amounted to the considerable sum of £617,836.[142] As orders continued to pour in, it was decided to transform the firm into a private limited company. The Liberal government introduced a new, higher scale of death duties in 1911, and the estate of a partner who died would be saddled with crippling duties if the partnership remained in its current form. The partners were also eager to ensure that the talented young members of staff stayed with the firm to carry on after the retirement of the founders. Loyalty could be rewarded with a place on the board of the limited company, and talented men were more likely to stay with Barr & Stroud if they had a stake in the business. The new firm, Barr & Stroud Ltd ('Patents' was dropped from the title because it had created some

*Barr & Stroud's fitting shop, looking north-east, in 1913.
Hundreds of field rangefinders passed through the shop each
month during the period 1910-1914 as the armies of Europe
increased their preparations for war.*

- VITA di BORDO -
Misurazione delle distanze
9226

A Barr & Stroud rangefinder with a metallic cover, on board Italian warship at Spezia.

confusion as to the nature of the firm's business), was incorporated on 26 December 1912, with a paid-up capital, by January 1914, of 100,000 ordinary shares and 100,000 6 per cent cumulative preference shares, each of £1.[143] Dr Barr and Dr Stroud were the major shareholders, and Harold Jackson took up nearly 20 per cent of the equity in the new company. James French, who had taken charge of the design department and set up a new optical department for the grinding and polishing of lenses and the manufacture of prisms, and Neil Maclean, an excellent manager whose great organisational talents allowed the firm to increase its labour force and boost output to meet every new demand for its products, were invited to become junior directors, each taking over 4 per cent of the preference and ordinary share capital. The new firm paid the old partnership £147,114 for the Anniesland premises, the business, and its assets, which included the patents. Barr & Stroud Ltd's first year in business was highly successful: the firm received orders for 1,734 rangefinders, achieved sales to the record value of £188,007 and made a record after-tax profit of £57,894.[144]

In 1909, Dr Stroud retired from the chair of Professor at Yorkshire College (which had become a part of Leeds University in 1904) and moved with his family to the suburbs of

Glasgow.[145] Dr Barr retired as Regius Professor of Civil and Mechanical Engineering at Glasgow University six years later.[146] The two friends, now in their fifties, were able to devote more of their time and energies to the firm's affairs after leaving academia.[147] Their long years of experience in the business and their inventive skills made them indispensable to the firm, and their contribution became even more important after Britain went to war in August 1914 and Barr & Stroud were called upon to boost output and to supply a wide range of new and improved instruments for the struggle against Germany and her allies. Harold Jackson voiced the feelings of everyone at the Anniesland factory when he wrote on 12 August that 'the whole of our reputation is now on trial. We face the consequences with hope.'[148]

ANNIESLAND AT WAR: 1914-1919

Barr & Stroud were forbidden by the terms of the Foreign Enlistment Act of 1870 to deliver seventy-five short-based infantry rangefinders and seventy-five artillery instruments of 2-metre base which were on order to Austria-Hungary, after the Dual Monarchy declared war on Serbia on 28 July 1914.[1] No sooner had Harold Jackson written to the agent in Austria, G. R. Siebert, to express his hopes that the fires of conflict in the Balkans could be damped down quickly, than the conflagration began to spread. Germany declared war on Russia on 1 August, and on France two days later, when the Kaiser's troops were already marching into Belgium. Britain, having demanded earlier that Germany respect Belgian neutrality, declared war on the invaders on 4 August. Britain and France then declared war on Austria-Hungary, which promptly declared war on Russia, and a relatively minor confrontation in south-eastern Europe developed into the greatest global conflict in history.

The speed of events in Europe was reflected by a period of hectic activity at Anniesland. Barr & Stroud were prohibited by Royal Proclamation to export instruments of war, although France was exempted from the ban on rangefinder exports in return for a guarantee that supplies of optical glass would continue to be sent to Britain by the French firm, Parra-Mantois.[2] The Admiralty and War Office requisitioned all rangefinders in stock at Anniesland, as well as those manufactured for foreign governments other than the French, and the French and British authorities placed orders for a total of 3,283 new instruments before the end of 1914.[3] Barr & Stroud had to introduce nightshifts and to plan further extensions to their works, in order to be able to complete massive numbers of rangefinders within what seemed to be impossible deadlines.[4]

The difficulties of expanding production facilities at short notice were exacerbated by the unique problems involved in running a business during wartime. Within a week of Britain's declaration of war, 140 of Barr & Stroud's 1,012 employees were ordered to join their territorial regiments.[5] Although Harold Jackson was optimistic that most of the men could be replaced within a short time — he shared a common belief that the war would not last for long - he had to ask the War Office to help secure the release of eight men called up from the firm's new optical shop, as their skills were vital to Barr & Stroud's efforts to boost the output of rangefinders and prisms.[6] Three of the men returned to the works, and the Admiralty arranged for other skilled men to be exempted from service with their territorial regiments, but Barr & Stroud continued to experience difficulty in securing the services of essential workers. Conscription was introduced in January 1916 as the war dragged on and the British Army suffered heavy casualties on the Western Front. Skilled men were exempted from compulsory military service because, in September 1915, the Anniesland works had become a controlled factory under the recently formed Ministry of Munitions. Nevertheless, many semi-skilled and unskilled workers were called up.[7] The firm was still experiencing grave difficulty at this time in attracting craftsmen to replace those who had volunteered to go to war in 1914, as every optical and instrument-making firm in the country was being deluged with orders for

essential military equipment and searching frantically for additional skilled labour. Barr & Stroud were able to replace the men called up with men and boys too old, young or unfit for the armed forces, but the shortage of skilled and experienced men to set up jobs and to train the newcomers was another serious hindrance to efforts to boost output.[8]

The British government's decision in 1916 to promote dilution schemes in industry had important consequences for Barr & Stroud. The dilution of labour, by which employers introduced unskilled workers to carry out many of the tasks previously reserved for men who had learned their trades during long periods of apprenticeship, was intended to release more men for service in the armed forces. It created serious unrest among the membership of the craft unions due to fears that industrialists would use the schemes to undermine the status of skilled men. The opposition to dilution was led in the West of Scotland by the shop stewards, who formed the Clyde Workers Committee to co-ordinate their campaign when the official union leadership failed to take a hard line. A prominent figure in the CWC was John Muir, the shop stewards' convener at Barr & Stroud's works, and there might well have been serious opposition to dilution at Anniesland, had the introduction of new workers not been handled with great tact.[9]   Harold Jackson and Neil Maclean had maintained cordial relations with

representatives of the Amalgamated Society of Engineers, the Society of Instrument Makers, the Scottish Brassmoulders Union and the other trade unions in the factory before the war, and the management's policy of paying a little over the local rates for craftsmen's wages, and of preserving a comfortable working environment on the shop floor, did much to ensure that Barr & Stroud remained largely unaffected by strikes and other manifestations of labour unrest which were so common in other Clydeside industries just before the war. Nevertheless, the challenge presented by dilution to the traditional practices of the craft unions was a serious one, and Jackson knew that he had to tread warily to avoid a confrontation at Anniesland.   His personal belief was that:

A skilled man gets and deserves a high rate because of his particular skill.   His training

Opposite: Large rangefinder assembly department, looking east, 1914. A 9-foot FQ on a naval mounting is in the foreground. FT instruments of 15-foot base, which were delivered to the Royal Navy with turret mountings, are on the benches behind. Note the clock face on the wall on the left: Barr & Stroud installed their own Becker Clock system in the factory in 1904.

Women edging optical parts.

Women at work in the engraving department, with a lone and cheerful-looking male colleague. The women in the foreground are dividing rangefinder scales on machines designed by Dr Barr. In the background, others are working on the engraving machines.

enables him to do a large variety of work.... The job on which he is engaged may be of a very simple character [but] the difference in rate [from that paid to unskilled men] is not founded upon this simple job, but upon the capability of the skilled man for doing any other job which he may be asked to undertake.[10]

The firm underlined its commitment to the retention of a highly skilled workforce by promising that any man who left Barr & Stroud to fight in the war would be re-employed on his return.[11]   Any suspicions which might have remained regarding the firm's motives for employing dilutees were quickly dispelled by the management's readiness to compromise with workers' demands for safeguards.

In January 1916 the Ministry of Munitions Dilution Commissioners arrived on Clydeside to encourage a greater deployment of unskilled labour, and a dilution scheme was applied to Barr & Stroud on 14 March.[12] The Commissioners urged employers to set up joint committees with representatives of their employees, to supervise the application of the scheme, and to deal with grievances concerning breaches of union practices, and Barr & Stroud were one of the first firms to do so. John Muir was a Syndicalist, committed to worker control of industry, and the prospect of the trade unions acquiring a greater say in the administration and organisation of the factory won his support. He ensured that the trade unions gave their support to the creation of the new Industrial Committee at Anniesland on 28 March 1916.[13] Nine representatives, all shop stewards, were elected by the employees from the various departments of the factory. Employees could take complaints on 'matters relating to dilution, [and] other matters connected with the workers' interests' to their representative, to raise at the weekly Committee meeting, and the shop stewards' convener was permitted to visit any department to investigate a grievance which had been expressed there. Harold Jackson, Neil Maclean and Sinclair Reid, the head foreman, represented the management on the Committee, and any matters which could not be dealt with at the weekly meeting were referred to the board. Most of the problems taken to the Committee were settled quickly, and a spirit of compromise prevailed at a time when everyone in the factory appreciated that any confrontation leading to a disruption of supplies of instruments to the

armed forces could only harm the war effort.[14]

Much of the Industrial Committee's time was taken up by problems arising from the introduction of female labour on the shop floor. Twenty women started with the firm in February 1916, and in May 1917 the number reached a peak of 312.[15] The women were employed on jobs as diverse as machine fitting and inspection, optical adjusting and inspection, and as clerks in the stores, and most proved to be hard-working and capable of learning new skills. However, traditional male chauvinism, and an awareness that many industrialists employed female labour as a means of depressing wage rates, made the issue of the introduction of women a sensitive one, to which the unions attempted to attach a variety of restrictions. Barr & Stroud's promise not to introduce women to the machine shop, and to pay them a wage equivalent to that of newly recruited male workers, succeeded in allaying union fears.[16]

The costs of manufacturing rose inexorably in the chaotic economic conditions created by a world war. In just four months, to December 1914, Barr & Stroud's wage bill rose by about 10 per cent, and general costs, which included freight charges and taxes, rose by 5 per cent.[17] Costs continued to rise thereafter, tradesmen's wages rising from 1 shilling (5p) an hour in 1914 to 1s 11d (nearly 10p) in 1918, and although the sheer volume of orders they received allowed Barr & Stroud to make some economies of scale, they were forced to raise their prices by small amounts at regular intervals, to keep pace with inflation.[18] The firm was particularly concerned by the rise in the price of optical glass, which cost almost 50 per cent more in December 1914 than it had done in August, and continued to soar thereafter.[19]   As supplies from European glass manufacturers were disrupted and glass imports from the market leaders in Germany were cut off, and as the relatively small British glass industry was deluged with orders for glass for trench periscopes, telescopes, binoculars and other equipment, supplies became not only expensive but also difficult to secure.   Barr & Stroud's main suppliers, Chance Brothers & Co of Birmingham, were unable to maintain prompt deliveries of the firm's regular orders for thousands of pentagonal prism blocks, and so it was decided that Barr & Stroud, like their German rivals Zeiss, should have their own glassworks.[20] Dr Barr began work on a design for a furnace for the fine annealing of glass, to reduce the firm's dependence on other firms in

this line of work, and several new electrical annealing chambers were in use at Anniesland by the end of 1915.[21] Experimental plant for the manufacture of optical glass was also designed by Dr Barr, with James French's assistance, at the end of the year.[22] The firm received no outside technical or financial assistance in developing their glass-making plant, and could not obtain priority in the acquisition of vital materials, because the Ministry of Munitions did not classify Barr & Stroud as glassmakers. Nevertheless, there were seventeen gas-heated furnaces producing high-quality optical glass at the Anniesland factory by the end of the war.[23]

The   British   government   imposed unprecedented controls on industry during the war, and Barr & Stroud's office was deluged with official   correspondence   and   routine   paper-

An FT6 of 12-foot base, c. 1911. The success of the FT6 convinced Barr & Stroud of the suitability of this design for rangefinders of 15-foot base.

A practical guide to rangefinding, as presented to the readers of The Graphic, 8 June 1918. Most Barr & Stroud rangefinders were provided with a second-range scale window from about 1910, to allow one observer to concentrate solely on bringing the images of the target into coincidence.

work arising from close contacts with the Ministry of Munitions and the government departments responsible for placing orders for the services. The administration of the firm's ordinary day-to-day business became more complex too, as the factory, workforce and output grew rapidly. Harold Jackson showed that he had lost none of his talents as an administrator, reorganising the firm's financial, clerical and commercial methods to meet the changing circumstances of the war years, while his skill and tact in conducting negotiations with government officials ensured that Barr & Stroud's relations with the government Ministries remained harmonious. With Neil Maclean organising the smooth introduction of new men, machinery and working practices in the factory, and both Maclean and Jackson taking responsibility for negotiating with the trade unions and dealing with their grievances, the other directors were free to concentrate on the research and development of new and improved instruments.

Barr & Stroud's first priority was to ensure that the Royal Navy and British Army were fully equipped with the latest of the firm's rangefinders. The firm had been encouraged to persevere with the development of a 15-foot base rangefinder, to give accurate readings at ranges at sea of up to 20,000 yards, by Captain John R. Jellicoe, Director of Naval Ordnance 1905-07.[24] Trial models of the 15-foot FR rangefinder were ordered by several navies between 1907 and 1913, before the FT24 was introduced as Barr & Stroud's standard 15-foot instrument in 1913.[25] The FT24 was accurate to within 170 yards, less than 1 per cent, at 20,000 yards, nearly three times the accuracy which could be attained using the 9-foot FQ2 at that range.[26] However, many prominent British naval officers did not believe that naval engagements would take place at ranges much greater than 10,000 yards, and the Royal Navy continued with its pre-war plans to fit the FQ2 in the gun turrets of all existing British capital ships.[27] Only twenty-eight FT24 rangefinders of 15-foot base were ordered before the war, along with about a dozen 12-foot FT and FQ instruments.[28]   The Battles of Coronel, the Falkland Islands, and the Dogger Bank in 1914 and 1915 revealed that firing at ranges of up to 20,000 yards was indeed feasible, and that the FQ2 was not a sufficiently accurate instrument at such great distances.   Nevertheless, the first 15-foot FT24 rangefinders were fitted in the four turrets and the control tower of the newly completed *Queen Elizabeth* class battleships only in 1915, and although the Royal Navy ordered fifty-nine more 15-foot rangefinders between October 1914 and May 1915 for new warships under construction, capital ships of pre-war vintage retained their complement of up to seven 9-foot FQ2 instruments.[29]

The British Army received a total of over 16,000 FT17 and FT27 field rangefinders from Barr & Stroud between 1913 and 1918, and their French allies were equipped with over 3,300 of these and earlier models of the FT.[30] Most of the field rangefinders were carried to the Western Front, but they seem to have played a less important role in the fighting there than army officers had expected.   Once the two opposing forces settled down along virtually static lines of defence, the artillery was used to bombard targets from well behind the front lines.   Most targets were identified by map grid references, and the gunners often relied on aircraft pilots to act as spotters.   As the gunners rarely, if ever, saw their targets, they had no need for their rangefinders, and the instruments were usually locked away in the battery's store.[31] At the front, the machine-gunners, riflemen and mortar teams generally had plenty of time to discover the distances separating their trenches from those of the enemy.   However, the rangefinders proved useful in calculating new ranges on the rare occasions when a

breakthrough was made and new forward positions were established.   The instruments also proved to be useful in the hands of the snipers and scouts who patrolled no-man's land.[32]   The Barr & Stroud rangefinders would have been of far greater importance to the army in a war of movement, and the firm regretted that few were sent for use against the Turks in Palestine and Mesopotamia.[33]

The rapid development of the aeroplane as a fighting machine during the First World War led to the introduction of a new type of rangefinder by Barr & Stroud.   The firm had been asked in 1911 to supply the French with a high-angle mounting for rangefinders which were to be supplied to anti-aircraft batteries, and sent the first MT mountings across the English Channel in 1913.[34]   The original MT mountings allowed a standard FT field rangefinder to be swung freely both in altitude and azimuth, to find a high-flying target and to follow it as it crossed the sky, but it measured only the true range of the enemy aircraft. British Army units took some of these early high-angle rangefinders with them to France in 1914, and the Royal Navy acquired others for trials, but the instruments were not considered entirely suitable for anti-aircraft work.   The gunners required information on the height of a target to assist them with the setting of their gun-sights, and Barr & Stroud were asked to design a new instrument to meet their needs.[35]

The first heightfinders manufactured by Barr & Stroud were FT rangefinders of up to 2-metre base, on mountings which allowed them to swing in a vertical plane.   An eye-piece was situated in the line of trunnion, so that the observer could view the target at any altitude, without having to strain his neck muscles in the

A 13-pounder, 9-hundredweight anti-aircraft gun unit, 1916. In the foreground, an observer uses a Barr & Stroud rangefinder on a high-angle mounting to determine the range of an enemy aircraft.

process. The observer operated a hand-wheel which controlled the elevation of the instrument, and his prime function was to keep the images of the target in coincidence at the eye-piece, and to take readings of the range. A second observer viewed the target through a finder, keeping it in the field of view as it crossed the sky by operating the azimuth-training hand-wheel. Because the heightfinder swung in a vertical plane, its angular position indicated the height of the target, depending on the range. A pointer fixed to the instrument travelled over a scale, which gave different readings of the height according to the range when the instrument was at different angles of elevation. The third observer, who was informed of each change in the range, was responsible for calculating the height of the target from the scale.[36]

The early heightfinders were somewhat cumbersome, and while they might provide good readings of the height and range of early aeroplanes and airships, it proved difficult to 'track' and measure the range and altitude of the faster-moving aircraft which began to appear over the battlefields in 1915. Barr and Stroud, however, were able to come up with a new design for the instrument, and the firm

The anti-aircraft gun and crew on board the light cruiser HMS Undaunted, *with two sailors operating an early Barr & Stroud FT28 heightfinder on the canopy above the covered 9-foot FQ2.* HMS Undaunted *was the first warship to shoot down a German Zepplin airship.*

began to manufacture the first UB2 heightfinders in 1917. The UBs were also manned by three observers, but were simpler to operate and more manoeuvrable. A complicated system of differential gearing in the instrument solved the problem :

$$r \text{ (range) } \sin a \text{ (angle of elevation)} = h \text{ (height)}$$

and the third observer could find the height, the range and the elevation of the target simply by reading the appropriate scale on the instrument.[37] The War Office ordered 400 UB2 heightfinders in November 1917, and as the aircraft became an ever-deadlier threat to ground and naval forces, Barr & Stroud could rest assured that their invention would be in great demand for many years to come.[38] Dr Stroud, who was proud of his achievement in devising such an effective instrument as the UB, regretted nevertheless that 'if we had only devised this at the outbreak of the war, things would have been very different at the front.'[39]

The development of a rangefinder to measure ranges and heights of airborne targets was accompanied by the invention of another new instrument, to measure ranges from beneath the sea. Dr Barr and Dr Stroud had been invited by the Holland Torpedo Boat Co to design a rangefinder for submarine periscopes as early as 1903, only one year after the Royal Navy's first Holland submarine went into service.[40] They received other enquiries before the war, and decided that the most suitable arrangement was to incorporate a rangefinder of vertical base in the upper part of the periscope tube itself.[41] However, in the absence of encouragement from the Admiralty, or of firm commitments from foreign powers which

*An FT28 rangefinder of 1-metre base, on an MT4 high-angle
naval mounting which was fitted with a height indicator.*

might make the development of such an
instrument viable commercially, Barr & Stroud
did not take their ideas to the design stage. The
Royal Navy relied on Howard Grubb of Dublin
for submarine periscopes until about 1910,
when Barr & Stroud's old friends, Kelvin,
Bottomley & Baird (formerly James White &
Co), were awarded some Admiralty contracts.[42]

The experience gained by British
submariners during the early months of the war
pointed to the need for a method of
ascertaining distances while submerged, with
sufficient accuracy to ensure that precious
torpedoes were not wasted on targets outwith
their effective ranges. As Britain's leading
manufacturers of rangefinders, Barr & Stroud,
had their own lens computation department
and were already producing small periscopes
for the gun turrets on British warships.[43] They
therefore seemed the most suitable firm to
manufacture submarine periscope
rangefinders. Commodore S.S. Hall of the
Submarine Service met James French in
December 1915 to discuss the Admiralty's
requirements, and Barr & Stroud produced
preliminary designs for him to study early the
following year. A mock-up of the periscope
rangefinder was set up in July 1916 and in
September, after Hall submitted his report on
Barr & Stroud's work to the Admiralty, the firm
received an order for six instruments.[44] Barr &
Stroud designated their periscope rangefinder
the FY1, and the first one was despatched from
the factory, to be fitted in the new submarine
M3, within a year of the order being placed.[45]
The firm received orders for seven more
periscope rangefinders in September 1918.[46]

The FY1 consisted of a periscope 30 feet in
length, incorporating a rangefinder of 3-foot

A UB2 heightfinder with four operators, c. 1920.

base. The need for the top window to act as both the periscope window and as the window for one of the end reflectors for the rangefinder made it necessary that it could admit a beam of light of wide angle, but it was also essential to make the diameter of the top of the periscope-rangefinder tube as narrow as was possible, and that there should be no shift of image caused by the location of optical parts there. Dr Stroud dealt with these problems by inserting a telescope of unit magnification in the upper tube, and the telescope was designed so that it could be tilted in any direction without affecting the beam of light it transmitted.[47] Submarine officers who tested the FY1 were impressed by the quality of the image received at the eye-piece, and their preference for the

periscope itself, over others in service with the Royal Navy, persuaded the Admiralty to place orders with Barr & Stroud for new periscopes which did not require a built-in rangefinder. In May 1917 the Admiralty ordered twenty periscopes of single magnification and twenty instruments of dual magnification from Anniesland.[48] The order for these 30-foot long CH1 and CH2 periscopes came too late to allow Barr & Stroud to complete them before the end of the war, and only six CH1 periscopes and eleven CH2 periscopes were finally delivered, between 1918 and 1921, because the orders for the others were cancelled once hostilities ceased.[49] Nevertheless, Barr & Stroud's ingenuity and skill in the design and manufacture of the periscopes did not go unnoticed, with important consequences for the firm after the war.

In January 1916, the Admiralty placed an order with Barr & Stroud for forty depth and roll recorders.[50] These instruments were designed to fit into a chamber in a torpedo, and to measure and record the depth and roll of the projectile during its running trials, in order that the Royal Navy could be reasonably confident that well-aimed torpedoes would strike their targets when fired in action. Drawings and specifications for the recorders were sent to Anniesland, where Barr & Stroud discovered serious defects in the design. The Admiralty, which had received complaints from officers conducting running trials to the effect that the recorders already in service were neither accurate nor reliable enough to serve their purpose, readily accepted Barr & Stroud's suggestion that they devise an improved instrument. Dr Barr set to work in March, and his design was approved by the Admiralty in

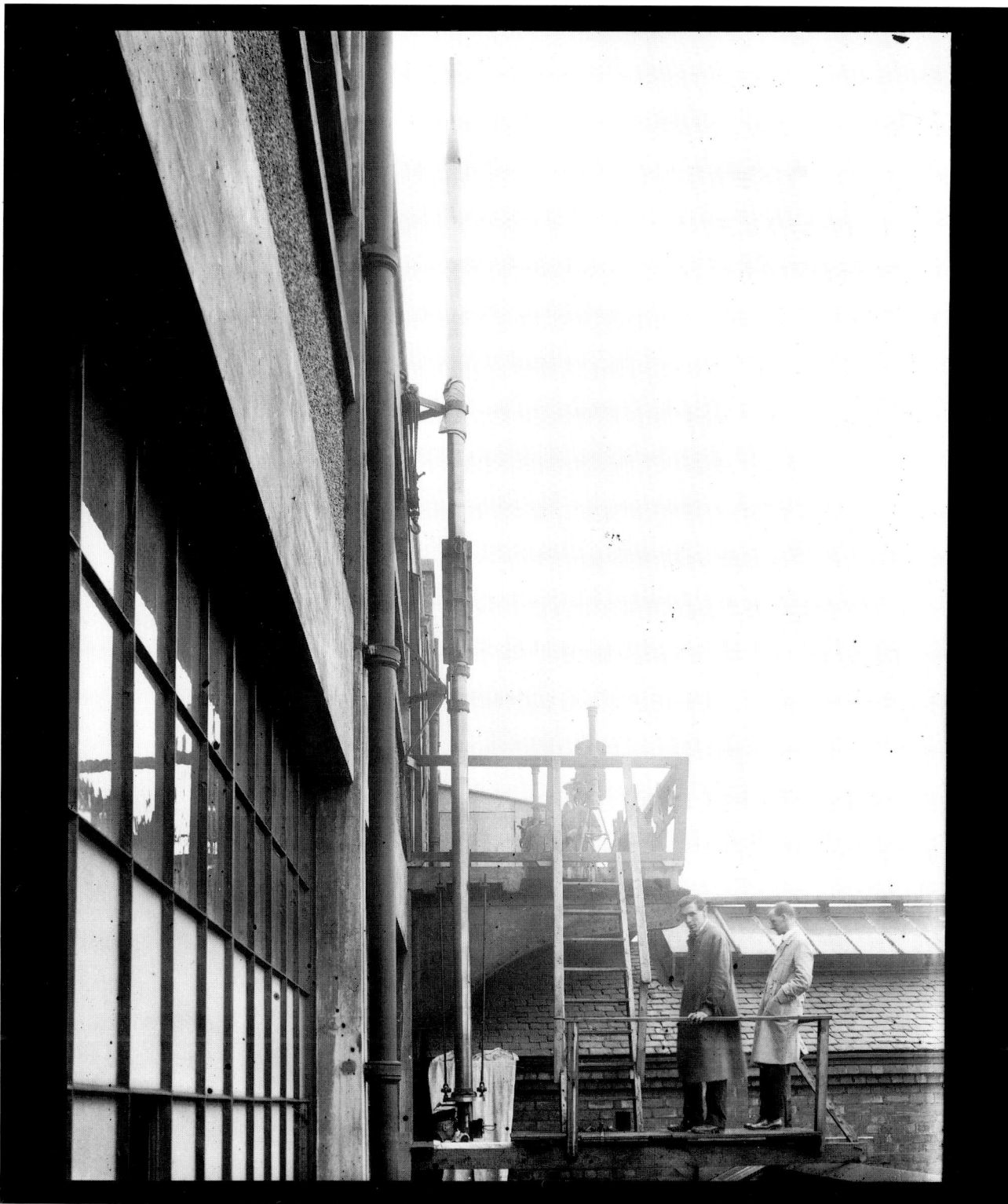

A faded but historically important photograph of the FY1 periscope rangefinder being tested in Anniesland, probably in 1916.

August. The first of a sample batch of eight new Barr & Stroud recorders was delivered in April 1917, and fifty more were ordered in June.[51] The depth and roll recorder was another of Barr & Stroud's great successes of the war years, and, like the submarine periscope, it was a product which attracted customers from all over the world after 1918.

Several of the inventions developed by Barr & Stroud between 1914 and 1918 were intended to be incorporated in naval fire-control systems. Fire-control became an increasingly important and complex subject during the early years of the twentieth century, as effective gun ranges and the speeds at which warships could steam, increased at rates far beyond those predicted by most Victorian naval experts. At short ranges, even of up to 6,000 yards, the distance of a target could be overestimated by more than 200 yards and yet hits could still be scored. This was because projectiles fired at short range from large calibre guns flew on a relatively flat trajectory, and might still strike the superstructure of a target ship even if the enemy vessel was closer than had been estimated. At close range, too, differences in the speeds of the firing ship and the target did not affect the relative positions of the vessels, between the time a shot was fired and when it began to fall towards the sea, so greatly as at long range. It was easier to spot the fall of shot at short range, and correct the allowances made by the gunners for deflection and the rate of change of range. At ranges of between 10,000 yards and 20,000 yards, however, the guns had to be fired at a far higher elevation, while the effects of 'aerodynamic drag' were greater and caused the projectile to plunge from the sky at far steeper angles. Most hits at long ranges were scored by shells falling on the horizontal armour of the target, rather than hitting the enemy ship side-on. As a 12-inch shell fired at only 12,000 yards took 22 seconds to reach its target, it was essential that the gunners be supplied with accurate predictions of the future position of an enemy vessel, so that they could 'lob' their shells into the area the target would enter as a shell completed its flight.[52]

Before the war, the Royal Navy adopted various fire-control inventions. The most important was the director firing system developed by Captain Percy Scott RN, to enable an officer at the director sight in the foretop of a ship to lay, train and fire all the heavy guns simultaneously. Directors were fitted in most of the Royal Navy's capital ships before or in the first months of the First World War, and greatly increased the effectiveness of salvoes fired from the main armament.[53] Other inventions adopted by the Royal Navy proved more controversial. The Dumaresq trigonometric slide calculator could translate estimates of the course, speed and course bearing of the target and host ships, and the instantaneous bearing of the target, into indications of the rate at which the range was changing, and provide corrected information for gun control.[54] The Vickers Clock, which was fed with the initial range and the change of range rate, ran automatically to give predictions of future ranges, and was intended to supply information on the target's future position when visual contact was lost.[55] The Dreyer Fire-Control Table took information from the rangefinder and the other fire-control stations on rates of change of range and bearings and produced a plot of the course and the predicted future positions of the target, to feed additional data to

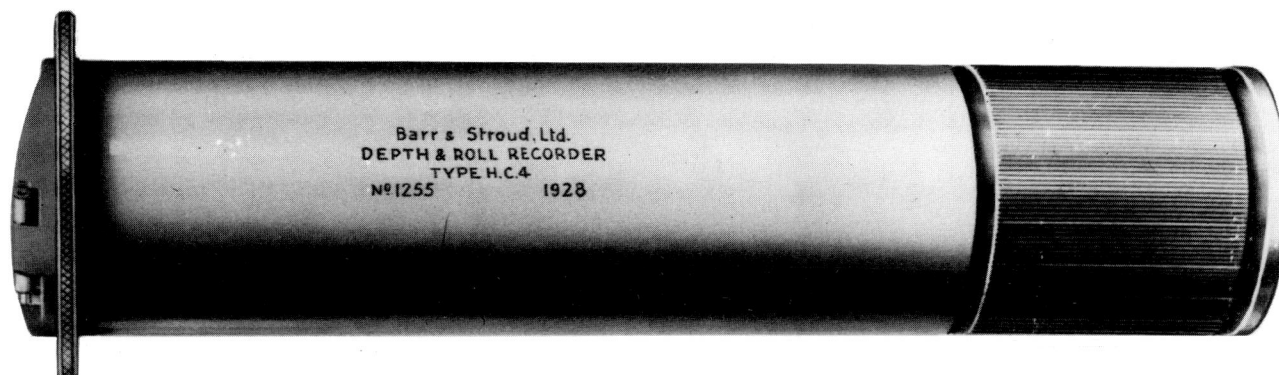

A later model of the depth and roll recorder, with the casing removed to reveal the internal arrangements.

the Vickers Clock.[56] These instruments were criticised by some naval officers, and by the controversial inventor Arthur Pollen, because they did not comprise a fully integrated system of fire-control and because they relied on estimated data on such subjects as target speeds and bearings, and so could not provide precise predictions of the target's changing position relative to the host ship. Pollen, a virulent critic of the Dreyer Table in particular, devised an integrated fire-control system himself, and conducted a highly publicised but ultimately unsuccessful campaign to have it adopted by the Royal Navy.[57] Barr & Stroud sought less attention for their own fire-control system, although Dr Stroud and his friend, the retired Dutch Admiral Mouton, were on the verge of completing work on a new fire-control table when the war began.[58] Without the table, the nerve centre of fire-control, Barr & Stroud were unable to submit their system for trials. Nevertheless, many of the instruments developed to be incorporated in it were incorporated in other systems on Royal Navy ships.

After 1915, all of the firm's naval rangefinders of 9-foot base or longer were fitted with the uniform scale gear. The gear consisted of a complicated arrangement of spiral cones, which translated the reciprocal range scale of the rangefinder into a scale of uniform ranges which could be transmitted to the plotting station electrically by pressing a button on the rangefinder when the images of the target were brought into coincidence.[59] Barr & Stroud also developed ROCORD, the Rate of Change of Range and Deflection indicator, which was fed with data on the known line of sight between firing ship and target, the known speed of the firing ship, and the estimated speed and course of the target, and ran automatically to indicate future positions of the enemy vessel.[60] Like the Vickers Clock, ROCORD was designed to meet the need of the gunlayers for information on ranges and deflection during periods when the rangetakers and spotters could not make visual contact with the target through mist, smoke or spray. It shared the weaknesses of the Vickers Clock, in that it relied on estimated data, and it was supplied only in small numbers to the Royal Navy during the war.

Barr & Stroud received orders for several types of the Royal Navy's standard gun-sights during the war and, in response to a special request from the Admiralty in 1915, James French designed the firm's own GB dial sight, which indicated the bearing of the target ship.[61] In August 1916 the firm was informed that the Royal Navy required more accurate means to

An SF2 inclinometer, complete with automatic slide-rule and what appear to be three bicycle saddle seats for the team of operators.

detect changes of course by a target, and Barr & Stroud were asked to design 'a simple optical instrument working on the coincidence principle' to meet the need.   The SF Inclinometer was used to bring the images of the target's bow in one field of view into coincidence with the image of the stern in the other field.   A special slide-rule was set with the reading from the inclinometer, as well as the range and the length of the target, to show the target's inclination to the line of sight.   The data was then fed to the fire-control station.[62] The SF Inclinometer was only put into production near the end of the war, but it attracted orders from all over the world, and with ROCORD, the uniform scale gear, and the dial sight, it became a feature of the integrated fire-control system developed at Anniesland during the 1920s.

Of all Barr & Stroud's wartime products, naval rangefinders were probably the most famous and the most vital to the nation's war effort, and they were certainly the most controversial.   They were used in action on several occasions during the first twenty-one months of the war, although not in conditions best suited to gauging their worth. Then, on 31 May 1916, came the showdown in the North Sea between the British Grand Fleet and the German High Seas Fleet, a confrontation which had been anticipated eagerly by press and public in both countries. After years of trials in peacetime, the Barr & Stroud 9-foot FQ2 rangefinders were finally tested in deadly competition with the Zeiss 3-metre stereoscopic instruments, in a full-scale fleet action which neither side could afford to lose.

The Battle of Jutland resulted from Admiral Scheer's instructions to Konteradmiral Hipper, to take the five battle-cruisers of his 1st Scouting Group out to raid British shipping off Norway and entice a British force to sea.[63] Hipper was to engage the enemy, and deliver them into the hands of Scheer, lurking to the south with the sixteen dreadnought battleships and six pre-dreadnoughts of the German High Seas Fleet. Hipper encountered Vice-Admiral Sir David Beatty's 1st and 2nd Battle Cruiser Squadrons, supported by the four battleships of the 5th Battle Squadron, in mid-afternoon on 31 May, and the battle began in earnest when Beatty's six battle-cruisers opened fire on the 1st SG from just over 15,000 yards. The engagement continued at ranges of 14,000 to around 20,000 yards, as Hipper chose a southerly course which would deliver the British squadrons to Scheer. In just twenty-two minutes the Germans sank the *Indefatigable*, which blew up after a shell penetrated her horizontal armour and cordite flash ignited a magazine, and succeeded in scoring a total of twenty-five hits on the British battle-cruisers, receiving only six in return.

The accuracy of German gunnery was markedly superior to the British during this opening stage of the battle, but British gunlayers and spotters were labouring under a number of disadvantages. The 1st and 2nd BCS had had little practice firing at ranges of over 10,000 yards, and during the opening minutes of the action the British guns were fired while the ships were under helm, a situation in which their fire-control instruments were of little use in keeping the range.   The poor weather conditions favoured the Germans: their ships were difficult to spot against a dull grey sky and a misty horizon in the east, and funnel smoke from British destroyers blew across the engaged sides of the British battle-cruisers to make rangefinding and spotting even more difficult, while the British ships stood out quite clearly against a bright western sky. The British 'bracketing' system of firing single salvoes of ranging shots proved far less effective than the German 'ladder' system, which involved firing three consecutive salvoes, including one over and one under the range given by the rangefinder, and Hipper's gunners were able to 'straddle' their targets sooner than their British counterparts. Luckily for Beatty, the four battleships of Rear-Admiral Evan-Thomas's 5th BS, which had fallen behind the battle-cruisers before the engagement began, came into range of the two ships at the end of Hipper's battle line just after the *Indefatigable* went down, and opened fire on the *Moltke* and *Von der Tann* with great accuracy.

The *Queen Elizabeth* class battleships of the 5th BS, the *Barham, Valiant, Malaya* and *Warspite,* were four of only seven battleships at Jutland which were equipped with Barr & Stroud's 15-foot rangefinder, the FT24 (the others were the battleships *Royal Oak* and *Revenge,* each with five FT24 rangefinders, and the *Orion,* equipped with only one of these instruments).[64] Fire-control officers reported later that the longer instruments provided accurate ranges as the battleships opened fire at up to 19,000 yards, and the Germans later expressed great admiration for the speed with which the battleships' gunners were able to 'straddle' their targets.[65] The ships of the 1st and 2nd BCS continued to take more punishment than they could inflict on the German battle-cruisers. The *Queen Mary* was lost in an explosion, when cordite flash penetrated a magazine just as it had done in the *Indefatigable* eighteen minutes earlier, and Beatty was moved to make his famous remark that 'there seems to be

something wrong with our bloody ships today.' Nevertheless, Hipper was outnumbered and unable to escape for long the heavy fire of the British battleships, and he must have been relieved to see Admiral Scheer's High Seas Fleet appear from the south-east. Beatty was surprised to meet the enemy battleships, but acted quickly to extricate himself from the trap and turn the tables on his foes. He ordered his ships to turn back to the north and they raced back from whence they came, with the Germans in hot pursuit and, unwittingly, heading into the jaws of the twenty-four battleships and three battle-cruisers of the Grand Fleet, which Admiral Sir John Jellicoe had taken to sea in the hope of springing his own trap on the Germans.

During the 'run to the south', British capital ships were hit by over forty heavy shells, while the Germans sustained only seventeen hits in return. However, from the time the battleships of the 5th BS began their turns to the north until the 1st SG and the leading ships of Scheer's battle line sailed into range of the rest of the British Grand Fleet an hour and twenty minutes later, the British generally enjoyed better conditions of visibility. During the 'run to the north' the Germans scored a further eighteen hits on British capital ships, but at least five of these were made on Evan-Thomas's battleships as they turned in succession at the end of the run to the south and presented a relatively easy target. The 5th BS went on to take all the gunnery honours on the British side after completing the turn and racing northwards: of nineteen hits scored on the German capital ships during this phase of the battle, all but one were made by the battleships' 15-inch guns.

Jellicoe's battleships had been steaming in six parallel columns of four when the Admiral heard that the Germans would soon come into view, and he ordered the ships to deploy to port and form a line ahead to 'cross the T' of Scheer's and Hipper's battle lines. This would provide the British with the opportunity of pouring the combined broadsides of twenty-four battleships into the leading German battleships and battle-cruisers, which would be able to return fire only from their forward guns. Scheer's spotters could not see clearly through the haze to the north-east, where British battleships began to fire accurately on the German line as it emerged from the smoke and mists. Realising that conditions of visibility favoured the British and that he had in any case entered a trap, Scheer ordered the first of his famous battle turns, every German ship turning simultaneously through 180 degrees and escaping back into the mists.

Before executing the battle turn, the battleships of the 1st SG came under heavy and accurate fire from the three battle-cruisers of Vice-Admiral Hood's 3rd BCS, from around 10,000 yards. Significantly, the 3rd BCS had only just completed long-range gunnery practice at Scapa Flow, and it inflicted serious damage to Hipper's flagship, the *Lutzow*. However, the Germans fought back furiously. When the mists and smoke cleared for a few minutes to allow the German spotters to see their enemy clearly, several salvoes were fired off at Hood's flagship and hits were scored. The weakness in magazine protection, which had resulted in the loss of two battle-cruisers earlier in the day, was responsible for another explosion which destroyed the *Invincible*.

Scheer ordered his ships to execute a second battle turn a short time after the first, probably hoping to cross unnoticed behind the British battle line and, by positioning himself to the north of the Grand Fleet, to obtain the slightly better conditions of visibility which Jellicoe had enjoyed earlier. However, he came under fire from the rearmost British battleships from as little as 10,000 yards, and shortly afterwards from the rest of the British line, which had veered southwards. He then ordered his third battle turn, and despite some brief, isolated engagements before nightfall, succeeded in escaping from the British trap. The battered *Lutzow* was scuttled during the night, and a German pre-dreadnought battleship was torpedoed, but the remaining capital ships of the High Seas Fleet returned to home ports the next day.[66]

The Royal Navy lost three battle-cruisers at Jutland, as well as three armoured cruisers and eight smaller warships. The German High Seas Fleet lost only one battle-cruiser, an obsolete battleship, four light cruisers and five smaller vessels, and inflicted far greater casualties than it sustained, but the relative strength of the two fleets were little affected by the results of the fight. It is generally agreed that the battle, in which nearly 250 warships fought in a series of sporadic and confused actions whenever the mists and the smoke from funnels and guns cleared away to reveal the enemy, was strategically indecisive. It proved more conclusive as a test of the relative merits of the British coincidence and the German stereoscopic rangefinders.

Because the gunnery of Hipper's battle-cruisers was so effective during the run to the south, some historians have suggested that the German rangefinders must have been superior to the British instruments.[67] However, the German battle-cruisers also overestimated the

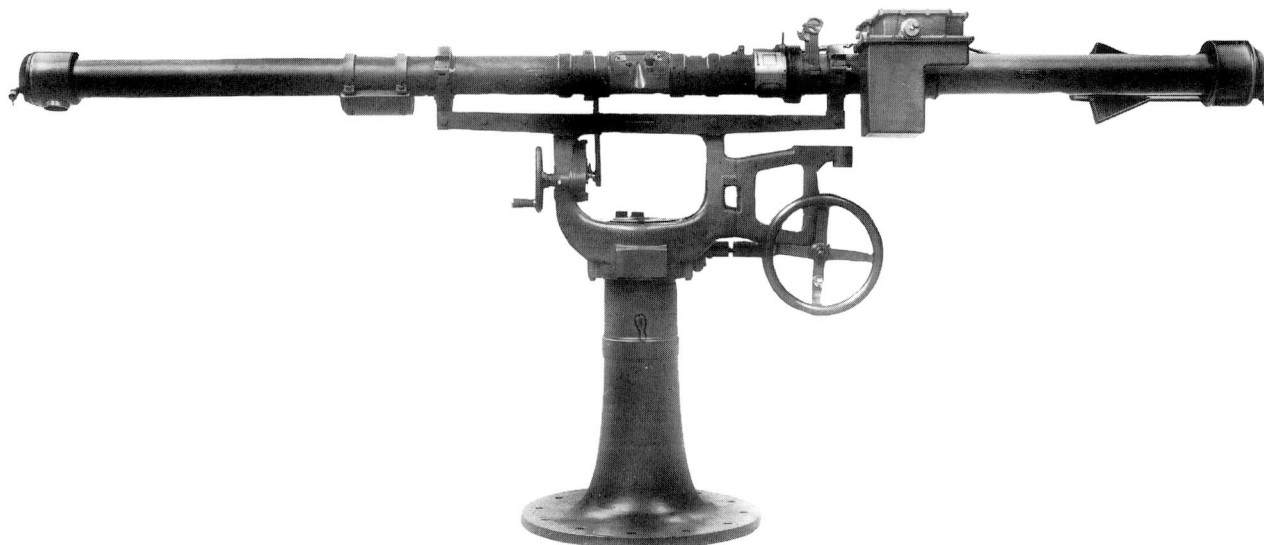

An FQ2 of 9-foot base, complete with uniform scale gear and training wheels. While most British capital ships at Jutland had rangefinders mounted in the gun turret hoods rangefinders on mountings such as these were located in fighting tops and other fire-control stations.

initial ranges at the start of the battle, even though, with the advantage of a clearer view of their opponents, they did not make such great errors as the British. Hipper noted after the battle that 'the fire of the [1st and 2nd BCS] resulted in no serious damage to our battle-cruisers …. In contrast to this, the fire of the [5th BS] and later of the enemy's main fleet created an excellent impression.'[68] It was to be expected that the battleships of the 5th BS would find ranges more quickly than the battle-cruisers, as their FT24 rangefinders were designed to measure ranges of up to 20,000 yards. However, many other British ships found ranges quickly during the later stages of the battle, when conditions of visibility restricted most of them to firing at ranges within those at

which the FQ2 was designed to operate. Admiral Jellicoe's flagship, the *Iron Duke*, scored hits on the battleship *Konig* with her second, third and fourth salvoes fired at about 12,500 yards, the *Thunderer* straddled a battleship with her first salvo at a similar range, the *Inflexible* of the 3rd BCS scored a hit on the *Lutzow* with her opening salvo from around 10,000 yards, and eight of about fifty shells fired in just eight minutes by the battle-cruiser *Invincible* at the *Lutzow* from under 10,000 yards, are believed to have struck their target.[69] German gunnery deteriorated markedly after weather conditions began to favour the British, and after two hours they scored no hits from over 10,500 yards on ships other than those disabled and presenting relatively easy targets.[70] They scored only three hits during the final two and a half hours of the daylight battle, sustaining forty-five in return. The decline in the accuracy of German fire can be attributed partly to the failings of the stereoscopic rangefinder in battle conditions.

Reports of the Battle at Jutland did little to change Barr & Stroud's opinions, formed before the war, about the relative merits of coincidence and stereoscopic rangefinders. Zeiss naval rangefinders were better than Barr & Stroud's for ranging on indistinct targets, such as a pall of smoke, which did not provide partial images with sufficiently distinct outlines to be brought into coincidence. A binocular instrument could often be used in darker conditions than a coincidence one, because there is a physiological advantage in using both eyes, rather than one, when attempting to see in poor light. The Zeiss rangefinders are almost certain to have featured dual magnification, allowing operators to use the lower magnifying power in poor light. The Barr & Stroud rangefinders seem also to have been more adversely affected by vibration, which sometimes made it difficult to achieve coincidence owing to the blurring of the partial images at the eye-piece.[71] However, Barr & Stroud's claims for the superiority of their instruments over stereoscopic rangefinders, of the same length and magnification, were confirmed by the results of post-war trials conducted by the Royal Navy.

A report entitled *Progress in Gunnery Material 1922 and 1923* summarised the disadvantages of stereoscopic rangefinders clearly:

> The operation of aligning two lines in coincidence may be described as a physiological process: the accuracy of such alignment depending upon the quality of a man's vision (i.e., his ability to see straight).
>
> Stereoscopic rangefinding, on the other hand, is a psychological action, as yet imperfectly understood. The interpretation of sensation of depth is contingent upon the mental as well as the physical condition of the operator. Very hot weather, indifferent health, excitement and other factors may seriously affect the capacity of the operator to range stereoscopically.[72]

The difficulties involved in stereoscopic rangefinding could be formidable. Even after a suitable operator with good vision in both eyes had been found, he had to be given extensive training to be able to judge accurately when the 'wandermark' in his field of view lay at the same

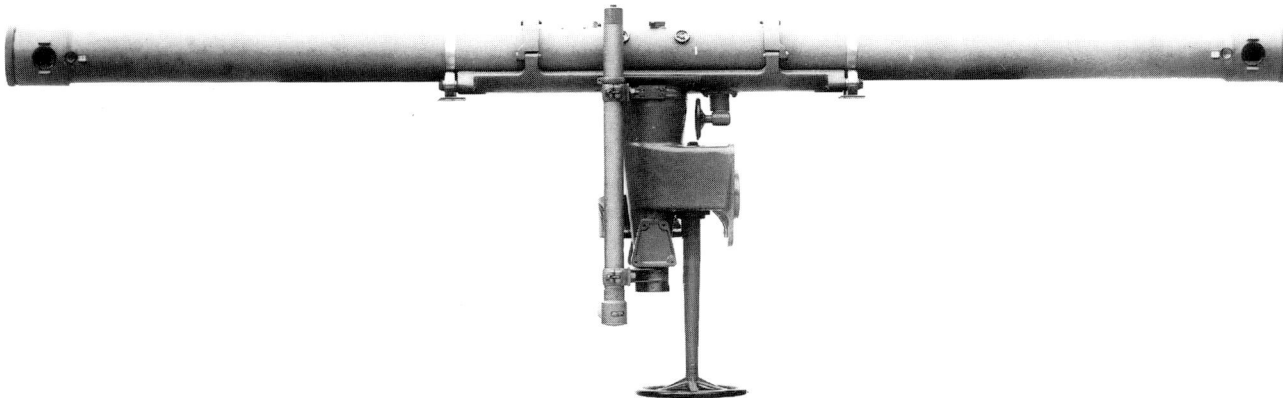

An FT13 of 15-foot base, with a turret mounting.

Three FT25 rangefinders on a triplex mounting. The French were first to order triplex mountings for the battleship Courbet. *The Italians ordered six more in 1916.*

distance as the target. It was found that a fully trained man could still make serious errors if, for example, he suffered from ill-health or was under some psychological pressure, and it was rumoured that German operators were ordered to abstain from such distractions as alcohol and sex while their ships awaited orders to put to sea.[73] Of even greater importance was the strain imposed on a sailor's nervous system by the shock of coming under fire. Tension and fear were discovered to have a serious detrimental effect on the ability of many men to take ranges stereoscopically. The despatches of Royal Navy officers who fought at Jutland contain numerous references to the accuracy of German gunnery deteriorating once their ships came under fire. The 1923 report claimed that all the rangetakers on board two German warships at Jutland became incapable of taking ranges stereoscopically after their vessels were struck by enemy shells.

James French became a member of the Inter-Allied Commission of Control after the war, and in this capacity he interviewed German naval officers responsible for rangefinder maintenance. He was told by one expert, Commander Rencken, that the Zeiss gun turret rangefinders were prone to derangement, caused by changes in temperature and by the vibration caused by the firing of guns, and that at Jutland they had to be adjusted before each reading or set of readings could be taken. Rencken believed that the majority of German officers preferred coincidence to stereoscopic rangefinders, supporting Barr & Stroud's case that their instruments were superior in terms of ease of use, mechanical reliability and general all-round performance. He claimed that German officers had reported their preference for the Barr & Stroud 9-foot FQ2 rather than Zeiss's 3-metre instrument, after secret trials in 1912.[74]   Their findings seem to have been confirmed by a German report compiled after the Battle of Jutland, in which it was noted that 'the British rangefinders are superior to the German.'[75]

The successes of the 5th BS's gunners at Jutland convinced Barr & Stroud, and the Admiralty, of the importance of stepping up production of longer-based rangefinders. Seventy-five 15-foot-base rangefinders were ordered after the Battle of Jutland, fifteen of them to be supplied on triplex mountings for the Italian Navy, and 174 of 12-foot base were ordered, primarily for the Royal Navy's cruisers but also to replace the 9-foot FQ2 in the fighting tops of capital ships.[76]   The Admiralty also ordered thirty-four 18-foot FT25 rangefinders for the Russian Navy, but preferred to purchase instruments of a new type when it began to re-equip British warships.   The FX2 contained larger optical parts than the old FQ and FT instruments, giving it a greater light-gathering capacity, and the Admiralty ordered nineteen of 25-foot base and forty-eight of 30-foot base in 1917.[77]   Although orders for over 170 of the long-base rangefinders were cancelled at the end of the war, the Royal Navy was by then equipped with 148 15-foot base FT instruments, and had begun to fit a minimum of two FX2 instruments of 25-foot or 30-foot base on Britain's most recently completed battleships and battle-cruisers.[78]

After the Battle of Jutland, the Royal Navy's requests for longer rangefinders with higher light-gathering capacities were accompanied by suggestions that Barr & Stroud improve their instruments' resistance to the effects of vibration.   At Jutland, and particularly during the battle-cruiser action, British warships steamed at far greater speeds than had been attempted in pre-war gunnery practices, and this created severe vibration which affected the rangefinder, blurring the partial images to such an extent that it was difficult to bring them into coincidence.[79]   The Barr & Stroud FQ2 was a relatively light instrument, weighing just 1,050 pounds compared to the 2,144 pounds Zeiss 3-metre instrument, and the circular coir mats provided with the firm's mountings since 1908 were not intended to absorb such high levels of vibration as those experienced in fast-moving ships during the First World War.[80]   The Admiralty approached Barr & Stroud in 1916 to ask for an improved anti-vibration mounting, and Charles Macgill, chief engineer in charge of the firm's Drawing Office, designed a new model embodying strong vertical springs and dampers to meet the specifications he received.[81]   The new MS type mounting proved successful in protecting the rangefinder from the effects of vertical vibration when it was tested at sea in 1918, but the Admiralty returned to Barr & Stroud later to request that the firm develop a means of reducing vibration along the longitudinal axis of the instrument. Macgill's new mounting design, using sponge-rubber damping cylinders and later springs and dashpots to support the rangefinder tube, proved highly effective and was especially important in improving the performance of rangefinders mounted on torpedo-boats and destroyers.[82]

The design and production of improved instruments at Anniesland near the end of the war was achieved at a time when friction had begun to develop between the management

An FX3 rangefinder, with a turret mounting.

and the employees of Barr & Stroud. For most of the war, the firm's record in industrial relations was excellent. During the opening months of the conflict, there was great concern about 'lost time' in Clydeside munitions industries, but Barr & Stroud were able to report that their men 'lost' only 3 per cent of working hours, for all reasons including illness.[83] Very little time was lost due to strikes. In February 1915 fifty brassmoulders answered the call of their union to walk out in support of a largely unofficial strike by Clydeside engineering workers calling for wage increases of 2d an hour. The firm promptly dismissed the men 'in order to make a clear issue', and obtained castings elsewhere until the strike ended and the men were re-engaged.[84]   In February 1916, Barr & Stroud's employees joined those of other Glasgow firms in downing tools in protest at the arrest of their shop steward's convener, John Muir, along with William Gallacher and Walter Bell, who were arrested and charged with sedition for their roles in the publication of an article entitled 'Should the Workers Arm?', which appeared in the socialist newspaper *The Worker*. The men returned to the factory the next day, after Muir and the others were released on bail.[85]   At Muir's trial in April, Harold Jackson testified that 'as convener of shop stewards [Muir] exercised his influence for the good, and his employers had every confidence in him. . .He had also done his best to carry out the scheme

for the dilution of labour.' His evidence of Muir's reliability, and the faith placed in him by the firm, was corroborated by Neil Maclean at the trial.[86] Their views may have surprised those who considered the accused to be a dangerous radical, but Jackson and Maclean had great respect for their shop stewards' convener and had worked closely with him in organising the introduction of the dilution scheme at Anniesland. The two directors could not prevent Muir being found guilty and receiving a sentence of twelve months in gaol, but Jackson promised that the convener would be reinstated by the firm on his release, a gesture welcomed by the workers' representatives on the Industrial Committee.[87]

Industrial relations at Anniesland became more strained near the end of the war. The withdrawal by the government of the Trade Cards scheme in 1917 resulted in the conscription of many of Barr & Stroud's skilled workers, when the firm was already struggling to meet the demands of the War Office and Admiralty for new instruments. In July 1917, Harold Jackson complained to the Investigation Officer at the Ministry of Munitions that, while the output and quality of lenses from the factory remained satisfactory, it 'was obtained with difficulty and much spoiled work'. He noted that 'we have not a single trained lens worker in our Establishment', and requested that experienced men be diverted to the firm immediately, to supervise and train the grocer, fishmonger, plumber's help, tailor and others who were now working in the optical department.[88] Jackson's request for assistance in recruiting skilled men met with no response. The calling-up of skilled workers continued, forcing the firm to entrust still more jobs to unskilled men, and the morale of Barr & Stroud's war-weary employees began to suffer.[89] The shop stewards called the workforce out on strike at the end of 1917, as Barr & Stroud were caught between the Ministry of Munitions' insistence that wages be pegged at government-approved levels and the unions' demand that unskilled and semi-skilled men be awarded pay rises in recognition of their growing responsibilities in the factory. Although the firm was able to obtain permission from the Ministry of Munitions to grant one of the workers' demands, for wage rises of 12.5 per cent for the unskilled and semi-skilled men, the directors were not prepared to meet a demand for the abolition of the premium system of bonus payments.[90] Dr Barr lamented the strike, which he ascribed to war-weariness and 'a terrible manifestation of the unrest in the labour world at this time'.[91]

The other directors took a hard line over a matter they regarded as likely to set a precedent. The shop stewards referred the matter of the premium system to the County Sheriff for arbitration, but he dismissed their case and the firm immediately dissolved the Industrial Committee. Harold Jackson explained later that 'the action of the Shop Stewards' [sic] Committee... was considered a breach of discipline, and if they had been successful in their endeavours, the management of the business would no longer have remained in the hands of the Directors.' The Industrial Committee, which had contributed so much to the smooth running of the factory for nearly two years, was not resurrected, and Barr & Stroud reverted to the pre-war practice of dealing with the trade union officials by direct correspondence.[92]

The workloads thrust upon the directors of Barr & Stroud during the war were great, and the staff of seventeen (seven of whom joined the firm only for the duration of the war) took greater responsibilities than ever before in the running of their departments.[93] In 1917, the directors decided that two of the members of the staff should be rewarded for their loyalty and hard work with places on the board. J. Martin Strang, who had begun working for the firm during his holidays, after beginning his BSc course in Mechanical Engineering at Glasgow University in 1905, and had joined the technical staff soon after his graduation in 1908, was one of the new directors. Strang's knowledge of methods of manufacturing lenses and his formulae for the computations of lenses, both of which were acquired when he was sent to supervise the cleaning of rangefinder parts at the Obhoukhoff optical works in St Petersburg in 1912, proved invaluable during the war. A new computing department was set up under his direction, and the success of the firm's periscope, among other instruments, was a testament to his achievement.[94]

The other new director of Barr & Stroud was Francis Morrison. Morrison enrolled in Dr Barr's classes in 1908, to complete a BSc course in Electrical Engineering which he had begun at Aberdeen University. He had already gained eight years' practical experience in electrical and mechanical engineering before he arrived in Glasgow, and had a brilliant academic

An FQ2 on an MS2 anti-vibration mounting, c. 1920.

record. Dr Barr recruited this latest in a long line of his students after his graduation in 1910, to work in the scientific department. The new man worked with Dr Stroud on the improved step-by-step receivers which the firm was developing for the Admiralty, and then on a number of important projects.[95] His knowledge of the firm's products was so impressive that, when the directors decided to open a London office in 1919, Morrison was asked to take charge. The firm felt that an office in London was essential, because high-ranking British army and navy officers, foreign military attachés and representatives of companies with which Barr & Stroud hoped to

do business, usually lived and worked in or near the capital. Morrison and his small staff were able to offer information on Barr & Stroud's products and give demonstrations at short notice, and to liaise more effectively with clients' representatives, while technicians based at the office could be sent off quickly to British ports or army bases in the south when military or naval instruments needed repairs or adjustments.

Harold Jackson announced to the board in February 1916 that he intended to resign as an active director once the war was over. However, his immense contribution to the smooth running of the firm and its complex business and administrative affairs between 1914 and 1918 made his fellow directors loathe to accept his resignation. By putting Francis Morrison in charge of commercial affairs at the London office, and giving James French and J. Martin Strang greater authority to liaise and negotiate with customers on technical matters relating to the firm's instruments, the board was able to reassure Jackson that he could be relieved of many of his duties. He became Managing Director of Barr & Stroud in 1919, a position he had held in all but name since 1903.[96]

Dr Stroud and Dr Barr were called upon to devise and design many new instruments for the firm during the war, but they did not restrict their involvement in the war effort to the work of their firm. Both men were invited to join the government's Board of Invention and Research during the war, but declined politely on the grounds that they might be put in the awkward position of considering the merits of inventions which would be produced in competition with those of their own firm.[97] Nevertheless, they were quite willing to offer expert advice on general problems which arose during the war, and visited London in consultative capacities to advise government experts on means of improving anti-aircraft and anti-submarine defences.[98] Their contribution to the war effort, both through their work for Barr & Stroud and their activities as consultants, was highly appreciated in Whitehall. Both men were offered knighthoods in 1918, but Dr Stroud felt that he had merely 'done his bit' for his country, and that others had made greater sacrifices and contributed more than he, without obtaining recognition. When he declined the honour, Dr Barr decided to do likewise.[99]

Hundreds of thousands of young Britons lost their lives during the First World War, and thirty-five of Barr & Stroud's employees were numbered in the ranks of the fallen. Many more of the men and women working at Anniesland lost friends and members of their families, and Dr Barr and Dr Stroud themselves suffered bereavements. Lieutenant Jack Barr of the Argyll and Sutherland Highlanders, Dr Barr's second son, was killed at the Second Battle of Ypres in 1915, and Bertie, Dr Stroud's youngest son and a pilot in the RAF, was shot down over Bailleul, near the Franco-Belgian border, in 1918.[100] After the Armistice had been signed, the firm honoured the promise to re-employ old hands returning to Glasgow after their units were demobilised. Joining those who returned to Anniesland were Dr Barr's sons — Douglas, who served as a captain in the Royal Engineers and then as an equipment officer with the RAF, and Gordon, who had just reached the age of eligibility for military service when the war ended, and Dr Stroud's eldest son Reggie, who returned from his regiment to complete the final year of his engineering course at Glasgow University before starting work at Anniesland.[101] They found that there was already serious concern about Barr & Stroud's future in the aftermath of the war.

Barr & Stroud's sales had risen dramatically during the war, as orders soared to record levels and the firm increased its production capacity to cope with higher demand for their instruments. The value of sales climbed from £234,423 in 1914 to £468,611 in 1915, £559,674 in 1916 and £614,660 in 1917, before dropping back to £473,780 in 1918.[102] Large orders enabled the firm to manufacture in bulk and to make economies of scale, but higher labour and

Opposite: *Aerial view of Barr & Stroud's factory, 1923. The North-West Works, the eight-bay building standing beyond the West Works on land which is now crossed by Bearsden Road, was built by the Ministry of Munitions early in 1918. It was intended to provide Barr & Stroud with more spacious premises for the manufacture of long-base rangefinders and other confidential Admiralty work, and was used for these purposes by the firm after the end of the war. However, the Ministry erected the building without the permission of Glasgow's Dean of Guild Court, over-ruling the objections of the city's planning authorities on the grounds that the navy's requirements were pressing. The North-West Works was finally demolished early in 1924, shortly before the construction of Bearsden Road.*

Members of staff from the Scientific Department at Anniesland, 1915. The department was set up by Dr Barr during the early years of the firm's history, to assist him in the development of new instruments and to manufacture the first models.

materials costs and inflation, which halved the purchasing power of the pound between 1914 and 1918, held profits down in real terms. The government introduced an Excess Profits Duty in 1917, which reclaimed 40 per cent of profits in excess of those made by a government contractor in the two years prior to the war, and Barr & Stroud had to repay £217,140 to the government in 1917.[103] While the firm made good profits during the war, after these considerations were taken into account, it was not possible to build up sufficient balances to cushion it from the effects of the economic slump which followed. The Admiralty and War Office had included cancellation clauses in contracts placed with Barr & Stroud during the war, and many instruments on order from the firm were cancelled after the Armistice in 1918.[104] The firm's after-tax trading profit for 1918 was only £13,109, the lowest recorded, in real terms, since 1903, and although the government granted a rebate on Excess Profits Duty of £38,000 that year, Barr & Stroud's immediate future looked bleak.[105] Orders for only nineteen rangefinders and a handful of other military and naval instruments were received during 1919, as the great powers demobilised millions of troops and mothballed their massive naval construction projects.[106] While the 'war to end wars' dragged on in some parts of the world, most notably in Russia and on the Greco-Turkish border, the world demand for munitions had been largely sated during the previous four years, and second-hand equipment was freely available to those few nations which had not yet acquired sufficient quantities to meet immediate needs. Barr & Stroud were forced to reduce their workforce to just 1,200 men in 1919, by laying off most of the workers recruited during the war.[107] The firm had then to adjust to the harsh realities of the post-war world, when the consequences of a severe economic depression which afflicted the whole of Europe created massive problems for British industry, and threatened the continued existence of Barr & Stroud.

Dr Archibald Barr in court dress, de rigeur for Royal garden parties at Holyrood, c. 1911. Dr Barr enjoyed mixing with members of high society, and the social prestige of being a successful academic and industrialist. However, he agreed with Dr Stroud that it was inappropriate to accept the knighthoods offered to them in 1918.

DEPARTURES: 1919-1939

By the beginning of 1919, Barr & Stroud's directors were resigned to the fact that there was no prospect of a revival in orders for rangefinders and other military and naval instruments in the foreseeable future. They had then to face the problem of finding suitable work for their highly skilled workforce and the technologically advanced manufacturing facilities of the Anniesland factory, but had to meet this challenge in extraordinarily difficult circumstances. Four years of war had sapped the economic strength of Europe's leading industrial powers. Economic recovery was hampered by the disruption caused by revolution in Russia and Germany, by the partition of the Austro-Hungarian Empire, by rampant inflation, and by the erection of a maze of tariff barriers across the continent. The British government's commitment to a policy of drastic deflation precipitated a severe contraction in demand for goods and services at home, just as British manufacturing industries were discovering that pre-war export markets had collapsed or had been lost to foreign competitors, and a severe depression set in. Barr & Stroud's directors had hoped to keep their business afloat by undertaking subcontracting work for other companies and by developing and marketing a new range of products for domestic markets. With the onset of the depression, finding contract work and selling consumer goods in Britain proved to be a frustrating business.

The first tentative attempts at diversification were made in 1919 with the manufacture of cinematograph machines, binoculars, and 'Impactor' golf machines at the factory. The cinematographs, or film projectors, were manufactured for the Alliance Cinematograph Co, which placed an order for 500 in April. Barr & Stroud supplied the company with reliable and moderately priced machines, but Alliance were unable to sell them once the recession set in, and by September 1920 owed Barr & Stroud the considerable sum of £11,000. Many of the machines were returned to Anniesland in lieu of cash, and Barr & Stroud sold a few each year during the following decade, but the directors were forced to write off a debt of £5,032 for machines which Alliance had managed to sell but for which they were unable to pay the manufacturers.[1]

Dr Barr and Dr Stroud had perfected their

Alliance cinematographs, all lined up with nowhere to go during the post-war recession.

own design for prismatic binoculars during the early 1890s, and Dr Barr was actually at work drawing up the patent papers when the professors discovered that Zeiss had patented a very similar design and had just begun to manufacture a range of excellent instruments.[2] Barr & Stroud subsequently abandoned their plans to make prismatic binoculars, leaving British firms such as Ross Ltd of London to compete with Zeiss, Goerz and the other German companies while they concentrated on the development of their rangefinders. However, the British generally failed to match the optical qualities of German binoculars, and in 1919, when the German companies were struggling to survive in a country racked by economic and social problems, Barr & Stroud decided the time was right to make their own bid to win a share of the market for prismatic as well as simple Galilean binoculars.

Barr & Stroud were soon regretting their lack of experience in marketing civilian products and the fact that they had no established contacts with British retailers. Galilean binoculars did not require a high standard of optical or mechanical work, and Barr & Stroud were unable to woo retailers away from field glasses with a poor finish, but which were less expensive than those made at Anniesland.[3] Thousands of binoculars were returning to Britain in the hands of ex-servicemen who had 'acquired' them from stores or 'liberated' them from the enemy during the war, just when the government began to sell army-surplus instruments at very low prices through special disposal centres.[4] Barr & Stroud quickly abandoned their unprofitable Galilean glasses venture, but persevered with prismatic instruments in the hope that they would find

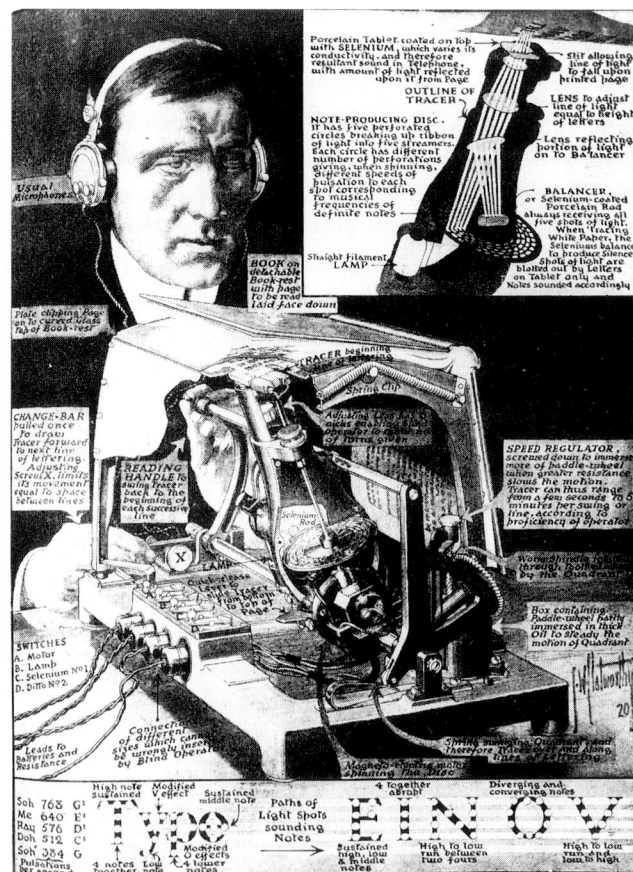

The Graphic's *view of the optophone, 12 June 1920.*

favour with discerning racegoers, yachtsmen and Royal Navy officers willing to pay a reasonable price for a superior instrument. The firm had completed an order for 120,000 prisms for service binoculars during the war, and had the skilled workers and production facilities required to manufacture instruments with superb optical qualities. However, their brass prismatic binoculars were too heavy for popular tastes, and when Zeiss became active in Britain once more during the early 1920s, the high reputation of German optical instruments and Zeiss's greater experience in marketing enabled them to re-establish their position as the leading manufacturer of binoculars for the British public.[5] Barr & Stroud had to develop new, lighter instruments, and Francis Morrison had to improve the firm's sales organisation in London, before the firm's binoculars could become viable.

The production of the cinematographs and binoculars may not have been a great success commercially, but the manufacture of these products did serve to keep instrument-makers and optical workers gainfully employed during the early years of the recession.   The 'Impactors' served the same purpose, and many of the apprentices were kept busy manufacturing them.   The 'Impactor' consisted of a golf ball, attached by a cord to a machine which measured the force with which the ball was struck by a golf club, and the direction of the flight of the ball. The golfing enthusiast could use it to see how far he was striking the ball, and the extent to which he was slicing or hooking his shots. As the kit came complete with maps of famous golf courses, showing lengths of holes and the positions of bunkers and other hazards, the retailers, British Impactors Ltd, were able to exhort golfers to purchase it and 'play a golf match without a golf course'.   Barr & Stroud made 500 of the machines for British Impactors in 1919, but golfers refused to share the retailers' enthusiasm for 'the most wonderful invention of the century'.   British Impactors went into liquidation early in 1921, owing Barr & Stroud £1,225.[6]

While the firm persevered with the manufacture of these new lines, Dr Barr was hard at work on a project of his own. Before the war, Dr Fournier d'Albe had invented the 'optophone', a machine which translated letters printed on a page into sound to enable blind people to 'read' books by ear.[7]   The inventor came to Barr & Stroud shortly before the end of the war, to ask if the firm could manufacture a better model for him, and Dr Barr was so impressed with the idea that he set about improving on the original design.[8] The new instrument featured two of Dr Barr's inventions: a balancer selenium bridge which cancelled the effect of white paper and allowed only the 'black noise' from the print on a page to reach the earphone, and a speed regulator, which Sir Charles Parson described as a greater innovation than even his famous turbine engine.[9] Relatively few books were available in Braille, while people with physical disabilities or a poor sense of touch were unable to learn it, and so Dr Barr believed that the improved optophone would be a boon for the blind. Margaret Jameson, a blind lady who had learned to use d'Albe's original machine and who could 'read' up to forty words per minute using the improved model, visited exhibitions all over Britain and France to demonstrate the optophone.[10]   However, Dr Barr's hopes that the instrument would become widely used, especially to help in rehabilitating blinded ex-servicemen, were soon dashed. The price of £80 per instrument proved to be too great for the Blind Asylums, while London County Council decided in 1922 that it could not afford the expense of training and employing teachers to instruct the blind in using the optophone.[11] Although some individuals in Britain and a number of US institutions purchased optophones, the firm lost several thousand pounds on development costs, and only about eighty were made by Barr & Stroud.[12]

The most famous of the new products to be manufactured at Anniesland after the First World War was the single-sleeve valve motor-cycle engine. Most two- and four-stroke motor-cycle engines of the day featured poppet valves, and while these engines were often very powerful, they were usually extremely noisy. The poppet-valve engine was also difficult to maintain, and its owners found the grinding of valve settings and the adjustment of tappet clearances to be tricky tasks.[13] The double-sleeve valve engine had been developed in the USA during the early 1900s, and had proved to be highly popular and successful when adapted for British cars such as the Argyll. The engine offered many advantages over the old poppet-valve types, and in 1919 Barr & Stroud were offered a licence to build single-sleeve valve engines for motor-cycles, under the patents of two local engineers, Messrs Burt and McCollom.[14] They decided to proceed with the new venture in December 1920. Dr Barr's son, Douglas, was put in charge of the project, and the old Fire-Control Shop at Anniesland became the home of Barr & Stroud's new engine department.[15]

The single-sleeve valve engine contained a piston working inside a reciprocating sleeve, which was mounted eccentrically so that it was given a slight rotating motion as it reciprocated. Five ports were cut in the sleeve, and six in the

A Beardmore Precision motor-cycle with a Barr & Stroud single-sleeve valve engine, c. 1922.

cylinder, and the ports were so arranged that the exhaust ports on the cylinder and the sleeve coincided on the exhaust stroke, and the inlet ports coincided on the inlet stroke. Although the engine had more frictional surfaces than the ordinary poppet-valve type, a splash system provided effective lubrication. The new engine had no valves, tappets or cams, and so it emitted virtually no mechanical noise when it was running. The absence of striking gear and the provision of an effective system of lubrication reduced friction to an absolute minimum, giving the engine a longer life than most others.[16] The engine was also compact and easy to dismantle and reassemble, while the lack of mechanical noise, its fuel efficiency, the ease with which it could be maintained and the fact that it could develop speeds of up to 60 mph, attracted admiring comment from motor-cycle enthusiasts.

Barr & Stroud launched a major advertising campaign in the trade press, pointing out the advantages of their engine under the slogan 'It's the ENGINE that Counts'. The experts were enthusiastic, describing it as 'a new departure in air-cooled engines', 'really phenomenal', 'wonderfully successful', 'the last word in internal combustion engine design' and 'the most revolutionary power unit of recent years'.[17] By August 1924, Barr & Stroud could boast that motor-cycles fitted with their engine had won a total of seven cups, one special award, four first-class awards, twelve gold medals, two gold centre medals and two awards for best performances at race trials held throughout Britain.[18] Despite critical acclaim and success in competitions, however, the Barr & Stroud engine did not achieve the volume of sales the firm had hoped for. The engine

required a high degree of workmanship, and so it was impossible to compete with the low prices of poppet-valve engine manufacturers in what was a highly competitive market, and at a time when army-surplus bikes, like cheap binoculars, were being sold in Britain in large quantities.[19] Barr & Stroud's losses on the venture began to mount, and the firm was forced to look for a new market for their engines.

During the early 1920s, the Board of Trade gave serious consideration to making emergency wireless sets compulsory items of equipment on ships' lifeboats, and Barr & Stroud collaborated with the Marconi Wireless Telegraph Co, for a time, on a scheme to adapt the single-sleeve valve engine as a power unit for wirelesses. This imaginative venture came to nought, however, when the Board of Trade decided not to impose greater financial obligations on hard-pressed shipowners while the depression in the shipping industry continued, and the proposed emergency wireless legislation was dropped.[20] Barr & Stroud then joined with the Austin Motor Co in 1925 to set up the Austin Lighting Co. The company, with Francis Morrison as one of the directors and Sir Herbert Austin as chairman, was set up to sell lighting sets to farmers and other inhabitants of rural areas, and the units were to be powered by the efficient, quiet, and easily maintained single-sleeve valve engines.[21] Once again, however, Barr & Stroud's hopes were frustrated by events beyond their control, when the government announced that it would endeavour to connect country-dwellers to the new national grid at the earliest opportunity. The Austin Lighting Co realised that people were unlikely to invest in independent power units when they could soon obtain cheap

A Barr & Stroud 1,000 cc V twin motor-cycle engine, c. 1922.

electricity from the grid, and so it was decided in December 1927 to abandon the scheme and go into voluntary liquidation, settling in full all the claims of its creditors.[22] Having sold over 3,000 engines and provided customers with thousands of spare parts, but having made heavy losses on the venture, Barr & Stroud reluctantly ceased full-time production.[23] Douglas Barr was so disappointed by the commercial failure of the highly-praised engine that he left the firm.[24]

The great efforts made by Barr & Stroud during the 1920s to develop a range of civilian products did not prevent work continuing on the improvement of naval and military instruments at Anniesland. Demands for rangefinders remained low after 1919, and in

1920 an order from the Siamese Army for 350 of the new FT32 instruments of 1-metre and 0.8-metre base boosted the total for that year to just 492 rangefinders and heightfinders. Orders for 159 instruments in 1921 and for 161 in 1922 were mostly for short-based rangefinders— in particular the FT32, which became popular as a navigational aid for oil tankers, cable-laying ships and other civil vessels between the wars — but included some for longer, more expensive instruments.[25] Nearly all of the latter were ordered by the Imperial Japanese Navy, which was striving to match the rising power of the USA in the Far East after 1918. Naval rearmament was checked rather than halted by the Washington Naval Treaty of 1922, and Barr & Stroud were encouraged to continue with the development of improved rangefinders by the realisation that the limitations imposed on warship construction in the USA, Britain, Japan, France and Italy by the Treaty would force the great naval powers to concentrate more on improving the fighting efficiency of their ships. As no navy would be able to impose its will on another through weight of numbers alone, improved rangefinding and fire-control became matters of even greater priority to naval officers than they had ever been before.

The results of trials conducted at Fort Cumberland in 1923, of Barr & Stroud, Cooke-Pollen and Zeiss rangefinders, convinced the Royal Navy that 'the FX type of coincidence rangefinder as designed by Messrs Barr & Stroud is better suited for Naval Service than any other type, and the future policy will be to supply the FX ... wherever conditions of space, etc submit.'[26] The 1923 report confirmed the decision, taken in 1917, to equip all British capital ships with a minimum of two FX rangefinders of 25 feet or 30-feet. HMS *Hood*, then under construction, was to be fitted with a 30-foot instrument in each of her turrets and a fifth in her main director hood.[27] By 1923, British capital ships were equipped with between nine and eleven rangefinders, to send information to the gun, torpedo and anti-aircraft fire-control stations, and three 12-foot instruments had replaced the two 9-foot FQ rangefinders which were fitted on British cruisers during the war.[28] The re-equipment of the British fleet between 1918 and 1923 was carried out mostly with rangefinders ordered at the end of the war, but in 1924 the Royal Navy ordered six FX3 instruments of 42-foot base, for the turrets of the battleships HMS *Rodney* and HMS *Nelson*, then being built.[29] The FX3 was accurate to 1.3 yards at 3,000 — that is, within 0.043 per cent, or to an accuracy seventy times greater than the Admiralty had specified in 1893.[30]

HMS *Nelson* and HMS *Rodney* were equipped with another new Barr & Stroud product, the FM duplex rangefinder. The firm had supplied

GLASGOW UNIVERSITY ARCHIVES

The battle-cruiser HMS Hood, *shortly before leaving John Brown's yard in Clydebank in January 1920. The 30-foot FX rangefinders in her forward turrets and director control tower are clearly visible, as are the 9-foot rangefinders in the foretop, where the aloft director with its 15-foot rangefinder was installed later. The torpedo control towers were also equipped with 15-foot rangefinders.*

An FM2 duplex rangefinder.

a few triplex mountings, each holding three 15-foot FT25 rangefinders, to the French and Italian navies during the war.[31] In 1922 the Royal Navy began trials of the FMI, which contained a coincidence and a stereoscopic rangefinder in a single barrel, but the Admiralty finally decided to adopt the FM2 duplex, consisting of two coincidence rangefinders.[32] The advantage of the duplex instrument was that it could send two independent readings to the fire-control station, where ranges were averaged for the plotting table, but occupied little more space than a single instrument on a conventional mounting. The Japanese ordered the first two FM2 instruments, of 8-metre base, in 1924, and the Royal Navy ordered four of 15-foot base two years later. The Japanese acquired eight more of the instruments before 1930 and the Royal Navy a total of seventy-seven before the outbreak of the Second World War.[33] Each FM cost up to £5,000, as compared with £80 or £100 for the short-based FT32, and the price offers an indication of the amount and complexity of the work involved in its manufacture.[34]

After 1918, most of the world's leading naval powers ordered their rangefinders from domestic manufacturers. The US Navy relied mainly on Bausch & Lomb for their instruments, the French on Optique et Précision de Levallois and Société d'Optique et de Mécanique; the Italians, initially, on San Giorgio and Galileo, while Zeiss continued to supply rangefinders for the few small warships Germany was permitted to build.[35] Japan, however, relied almost exclusively on Barr & Stroud for naval rangefinders, continuing links with Anniesland which stretched back to the mid-1890s. Ninety-six of the first 185 visitors to Barr & Stroud's works before 1906 were Japanese officers, sent to learn about the firm's latest rangefinders and fire-control instruments, and Admiral Count Togo, the victor at Tsushima, visited the factory himself in 1911.[36] Pairs of Japanese workmen stayed for long periods at the Anniesland factory before the war, to learn how to adjust and repair rangefinders, and Japanese enthusiasm for

Mr Yamada's predecessor with Barr & Stroud's staff foreman in 1923. Sinclair Reid is seated on the Japanese inspector's left, John McCann, in charge of the machine shop at Ashton Lane and then at Anniesland, is seated on the far right, and Roy Grant, the SD foreman, is standing third from right.

Barr & Stroud's coincidence rangefinders continued after the war.[37]

The Japanese ordered only two 4-foot 6-inch rangefinders in 1919, but ordered eighty of up to 8 metres in length in 1920, fifty-eight in 1921, 122 in 1922 and forty-six in 1923. Instruments for Japan accounted for nearly a third of the rangefinders ordered from Anniesland during these years, when Barr & Stroud received orders for only ninety rangefinders from the Admiralty, and the firm's relationship with Japan grew even closer.[38] A Japanese inspector, Mr Yamada, was given his own office in the factory when further large orders from Japan were placed in 1924.[39] The firm continued to receive many visits from Japanese naval personnel, and Isoroku Yamamoto, who became Commander-in-Chief of the Combined Japanese Fleet which attacked Pearl Habour in 1941, as well as two princes, two counts, a viscount and many admirals were among those to follow in the footsteps of Admiral Count Togo to visit the works.[40] Mr Yamada returned to Japan during the late 1920s, to set up his own optical manufacturing business and, it is said, to put into practice many of the techniques he had learned of from Barr & Stroud.[41] The firm's close links with the Imperial Japanese Navy lasted until the early 1930s, when Britain's relations with Japan deteriorated following Japanese aggression in Manchuria. Barr & Stroud received no orders from Japan for rangefinders after 1936.

One other new rangefinder which appeared during the 1920s is worthy of note. The FZ was designed after a request from the War Office in 1916 for a rangefinder for a coastal defence station, of greater length and accuracy than the 30-foot instruments then being developed at Anniesland. Designs were submitted for approval, and in March 1919 Barr & Stroud received an order for the longest rangefinder in the world, of 100-foot base. Barr & Stroud overcame many problems in producing this monster instrument. They had to provide a means of circulating air within the tube to prevent the deterioration of the images which, it was feared, would result when the light from the end reflectors had to pass through the long columns of air in the tube to the eye-pieces. The rangefinder itself was extremely heavy; but a mounting consisting of a rigid horizontal framework connecting two trucks which ran along a roller path of about 50 feet in diameter, proved capable of supporting it. The FZ was delivered to a coastal defence position at Portsmouth in 1922, and it was found to be accurate to within 17 yards (0.055 per cent) at 31,000 yards. During the 1930s, when the British began to erect huge 18-inch guns to defend Singapore harbour, the FZ was shipped out to join them. However, like the guns it was sent to serve, the FZ was specially sited to defend Singapore from a naval assault from the south. In February 1942 the Japanese Army attacked Singapore by land from the north. The FZ was destroyed by British officers to prevent it being used by the enemy, and the longest rangefinder ever made was probably broken up for scrap during the Japanese occupation.[42]

During the 1920s, Barr & Stroud became the sole suppliers of submarine periscopes to the Royal Navy and established themselves as one of the world's leaders in this field by introducing a number of new features to their instruments. An internal focusing lens was provided to enable the observer to change focus without removing his eye from the eye-piece, as he had to do when changing the external focusing lenses in older instruments. Internal colour

The FZ 100-foot rangefinder, the largest ever built, 1923. The observer standing outside the control room is taking ranges using a standard FT field rangefinder of just 0.8 metres.

glasses replaced the old coloured Dutch caps which had to be fitted over the eye-piece and rotating grips were provided on the training handles so that the observer could change the magnification and alter the elevation of the top prism of the periscope, without having to turn to operate the levers which had previously been used to control these functions. Barr & Stroud supplied their periscopes with new range estimators after 1920. The range estimator consisted of an arrangement of prisms fitted inside the periscope, which enabled the observer to measure the angle subtended by the height of the target, and to discover the approximate range when the height was known or could be estimated with reasonable accuracy. It could also be used to measure the angle in the horizontal plane, between the bow and stern of the ship, and so it provided an indication of the target's bearing if the length of the target vessel was known.[43]

Four CH3 and three CH4 periscopes were sent by Barr & Stroud to the Portland naval base in 1921, and a CH7 followed in 1923.[44] All had the same optical length and diameter as those manufactured during the war by Sir Howard Grubb and they were probably intended as replacements for the latter.[45] In 1924, however, Barr & Stroud were set a new task. Many submarine officers complained of eye-strain after spending long hours on duty with monocular search periscopes, and in 1924 Barr & Stroud were given the go-ahead by the Admiralty to produce a trial model of a binocular instrument, which they believed would relieve the problem. The production of a binocular periscope involved solving many difficult technical problems, particularly in finding ways of keeping the size and weight to a

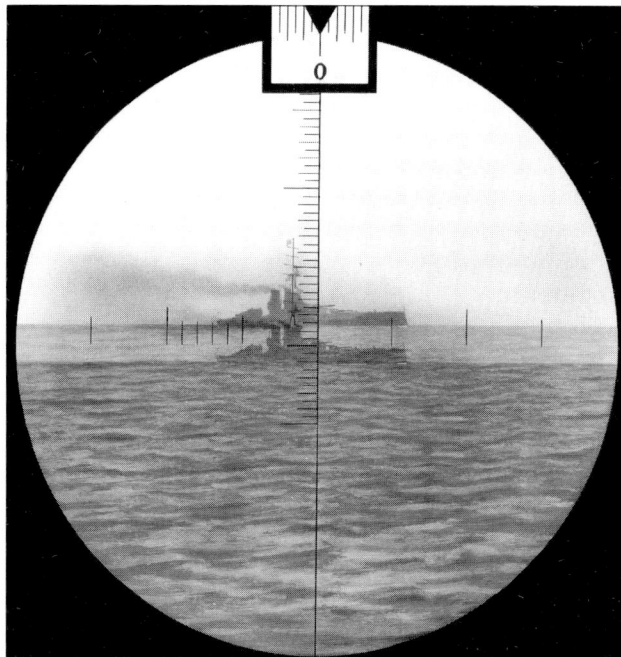

The field of view in a CH periscope, fitted with a range estimator.

minimum. The solution arrived at by Dr Barr, Dr Stroud and J. Martin Strang was to design an instrument in which the beams of light from the top windows could be directed down along the length of the instrument, through lenses common to both beams, and then crossed at a point at the bottom of the tube. Light entering at the left window above the sea emerged at the observer's left eye-piece, and the light from the right window emerged at the right eye-piece, to give a stereoscopic view of the target.[46] The first binocular periscope, designated the CK1, was just 9.5 inches in diameter, 60 per cent greater than a monocular instrument, but half the diameter which would have been required for a double lens system. It was delivered to the Royal Navy in the autumn of 1925, and proved highly popular with officers who used it in trials. Binocular search periscopes became standard in British submarines, although attack periscopes remained monocular.

Barr & Stroud's energetic attempts to diversify their range of products and the development of improved military and naval instruments during the early 1920s were carried out during a period of mounting financial crisis. Sales fell in value from £369,274 in 1919 to £310,822 in 1920, £259,226 in 1921 and £181,591 in 1922, rising slightly to £194,911 in 1923 and then falling again to £139,886 in 1924. Slight profit margins on civilian products, on small rangefinders, and on subcontracting work such as the manufacture of brass steam whistles and mild steel nozzles for the boilermakers, Babcock & Wilcox, were not sufficient to offset losses on products such as motor-cycle engines, and the firm's future hung in the balance. Barr & Stroud's after-tax profit for the six years 1919-1924 amounted to just £41,496, even after taking into account government rebates of Excess Profits Duty in 1919 and 1920 which amounted to a total of £131,614.[47] Unable to achieve profitability, the directors were forced to take drastic measures to reduce costs in 1924. Barr & Stroud's employees were put on short-time, working only two weeks in every three.[48] This arrangement was considered preferable to making more men redundant, but there were fears that it would hamper the education of apprentices. Consequently, the youngsters were allowed to work under supervisors in a special department during their 'free' week, to manufacture tools for themselves from materials provided by the firm free of charge, and time spent in this department was allowed to count towards the youngsters' apprenticeships.[49] The arrangement was successful in keeping apprentices at the factory but the firm could only offer the youngsters a secure future at Anniesland if money was found to keep Barr & Stroud afloat.

The year 1924 marked the lowest ebb in Barr & Stroud's post-war fortunes, but the workforce had to make further sacrifices during the following years to enable the firm to take the first painful steps to recovery. The value of Barr & Stroud's sales increased after 1924, but largely because of orders for relatively expensive instruments such as periscopes and rangefinders. The volume of work for the men in the machine and adjusting shops continued to fall, as demand for binoculars, motor-cycle engines and other products failed to develop, and the directors had to face up to the fact that over-capacity and surplus labour costs were holding back recovery. The two weeks on, one off work-sharing arrangement became one week on and two off. After the discontinuation of the single-sleeve valve engine in 1927, some of the unmarried men had to be laid off for a short period owing to the shortage of work in the machine shop.[50] Barr & Stroud had already quit the North-West Works by 1924 — the erection of the building by the Ministry of Munitions had been carried out without the approval of Glasgow's Dean of Guild Court, and the building was demolished after the war according to the building authority's wishes — and in 1922 there were plans to sell the West Works to Glasgow Corporation, which was intending to open a bus garage in the Anniesland area.[51] Fortunately for Barr & Stroud, in the light of events in the 1930s, the West Works were not sold and the bus garage was built further to the west in Knightswood.

An increase in demand for naval instruments underpinned Barr & Stroud's recovery after 1924. Sales rose in value to £224,929 in 1925 and £356,012 in 1926, slipping back to just under £290,000 in 1927, and rising by a few thousand pounds the following year. Improved profits during these years, boosted by a final settlement of war-time Excess Profit Duty claims and small tax rebates in respect of over-payment during the early 1920s, ensured that concern over the firm's continued existence was eased.[52] Harold Jackson lived to see the first signs of recovery, but the man who had done so much to establish and promote Barr & Stroud's reputation died on 14 January 1928. His fellow directors acknowledged their debt to him in the minutes of a board meeting held three days later, when they noted that 'they believed that the success which had attended the company was very largely due to his whole-hearted devotion to the interests of the company and to the exceedingly wise and tactful way in which he had guided its business affairs'.[53]

During the early 1890s, Harold Jackson's assistance in mounting and adjusting the optical parts of the first naval rangefinders, and his assumption of the clerical duties of the fledgling business, permitted Dr Barr and Dr Stroud to devote more of their limited spare time to devising and designing improvements to their inventions. The young assistant then proved his worth as an efficient office and workshop manager, after Barr & Stroud's Patents moved to the premises in Byres Road and engaged the first workmen and part-time scientific assistants. However, Jackson was more than just a secretary-cum-manager. He worked closely with Dr Barr and Dr Stroud in the early stages of the development of new instruments, and was well versed in the scientific principles they applied and in the manufacturing techniques employed in producing the new inventions. As secretary, he knew more about the nuts and bolts of the business and its financial affairs than either of his employers, and they relied on him for sound advice on pricing policies and the risks involved in investing in new plant and buildings. Dr Barr, the managing partner, also delegated to Jackson a great deal of authority in commercial matters, and while he retained the final say on the direction of the firm's affairs, he rarely disagreed with the secretary's expert advice.

Jackson made frequent trips to the south of England during the 1890s, when Dr Barr was detained at the University, to attend naval trials and to meet with Admiralty officials in London. He also entertained naval officers from around the world, and many of the firm's customers, when they travelled to Glasgow to see Barr & Stroud's workshops and the latest instruments being manufactured there. His great personal charm and lively sense of humour, as well as his expert knowledge of the firm's products, his frankness in discussing business matters and his firmness in upholding what he considered to be Barr & Stroud's best interests, won him many firm friends, as well as a level of respect and trust which was uncommon in the often shady world of the armaments business. He made many more sales trips before 1914, to the USA, France, Germany, Russia, Italy, Austria-Hungary, Belgium and the Netherlands. The stream of letters he sent back to Anniesland contained news of the latest rangefinder trials and prospects for new orders, appraisals of the achievements of the firm's agents and of the opinions of foreign officers, officials and other men on the spot concerning the types of instruments most suited to the needs of their armed forces. His considerable talents as a salesman, his achievements in building up a network of industrious agents, and his appreciation of the state of the market, were important factors in Barr & Stroud's rise to pre-eminence as rangefinder manufacturers.[54]

Jackson's most important role in Barr & Stroud was as a brake on the enthusiasm of the two founders. Dr Barr and Dr Stroud believed, with good reason based on experience, that they and their team of scientists and designers could apply their expertise in optical and mechanical science to the development of a wide variety of instruments, many of them entirely unrelated to Barr & Stroud's traditional areas of enterprise. Jackson, however, always kept a wary eye on costs, and he noted in 1921 that 'I carry the responsibility on my shoulders of having to say "No" at some time, unless there is a reasonable prospect of a return ... for all the expenditure [on the research and development] of new products.'[55] His attitude to the business was expressed clearly in a note sent to Dr Stroud in 1901, after the latter had insisted that 2-foot-base rangefinders were of little practical use, and that the firm should inform the War Office of this fact and offer to develop a new and far more accurate field instrument of longer base instead. The secretary commented simply that 'It is what the War Office has asked for, not what we think.'[56]

Dr Barr's optimism often led him to suggest that the firm acquire new plant and floor space, while Dr Stroud was by nature a pessimist, and generally opposed investment in new machinery and buildings, fearing that the firm would be unable to win orders to justify the risk of capital expenditure.[57] Jackson became the mediator on these occasions, and he would only agree to proposals for expansion when they had sufficient capital reserves and the prospects of valuable orders in the future to justify large outlays. His business caution was vital in enabling the firm to expand without over-extending resources, and to survive during hard times when orders were difficult to come by. Jackson was essentially a happy-go-lucky character, who joked with suppliers and agents in his business correspondence and chatted amiably with the workmen at Anniesland. His prudence in business sprung not from his personality, but from a shrewd understanding of the requirements of the job, although Jackson himself had his own, typically whimsical explanation. After offering a bleak view of the prospects for the success of the optophone in 1921 he joked with a client, C.P. MacCarthy, 'Don't think I am not cheerful. I'm nearly always that by nature, but I've been thirty years in Scotland and have naturally imbibed some caution.'[58]

Shortly before Harold Jackson's death, Dr Barr announced to his fellow directors 'that he and Dr Stroud desired to continue their connection with the company but did not wish to bind themselves to give their whole time to it'.[59] For many years, Dr Stroud had suffered from a bronchial condition which was aggravated by the cold dampness of the Scottish climate. He found it more congenial to spend his winters on the south coast of England or in southern Europe, and he spent much of each summer on holiday on the continent or in the Scottish Highlands. He came to work in his office at Anniesland only from May until

September, making special trips to attend board meetings. During the rest of the year he dealt with the technical matters relating to his inventions or the development of improved instruments by keeping up a regular correspondence with the firm's directors and technical staff, acting virtually as a senior consultant.[60] Dr Barr had taken the first of a series of extended holidays in Egypt in 1920, but he continued to devote much of his time to his work at Anniesland during the 1920s. He worked on projects which were of particular interest to him, such as the development of the optophone, and directed and advised the technical staff on other experimental and development work, while he continued to have

Dr Barr, with his wife, and members of his family on a visit to Egypt, 1920.

LARGE MIRROR HOLDER   SMALL MIRROR HOLDER   EYE HOLES
                                                          SMALL MIRROR HOLDER   LARGE MIRROR HOLDER

MIRROR LINK   RUBBER BUFFERS

RUBBER BUFFERS   CONNECTING ROD

CLIP   CLIP

MAIN STAY FRAME   CLAMPING SCREW

GRID SCALE   GRID PLATE

CLAMPING SCREW   CLIP

FINE ADJUSTMENT LEVER

WOODEN INSET   WOODEN INSET

                                                          2888

GRID PLATE FRAME   BASE BOARD CLIP   FINE ADJUSTMENT LEVER

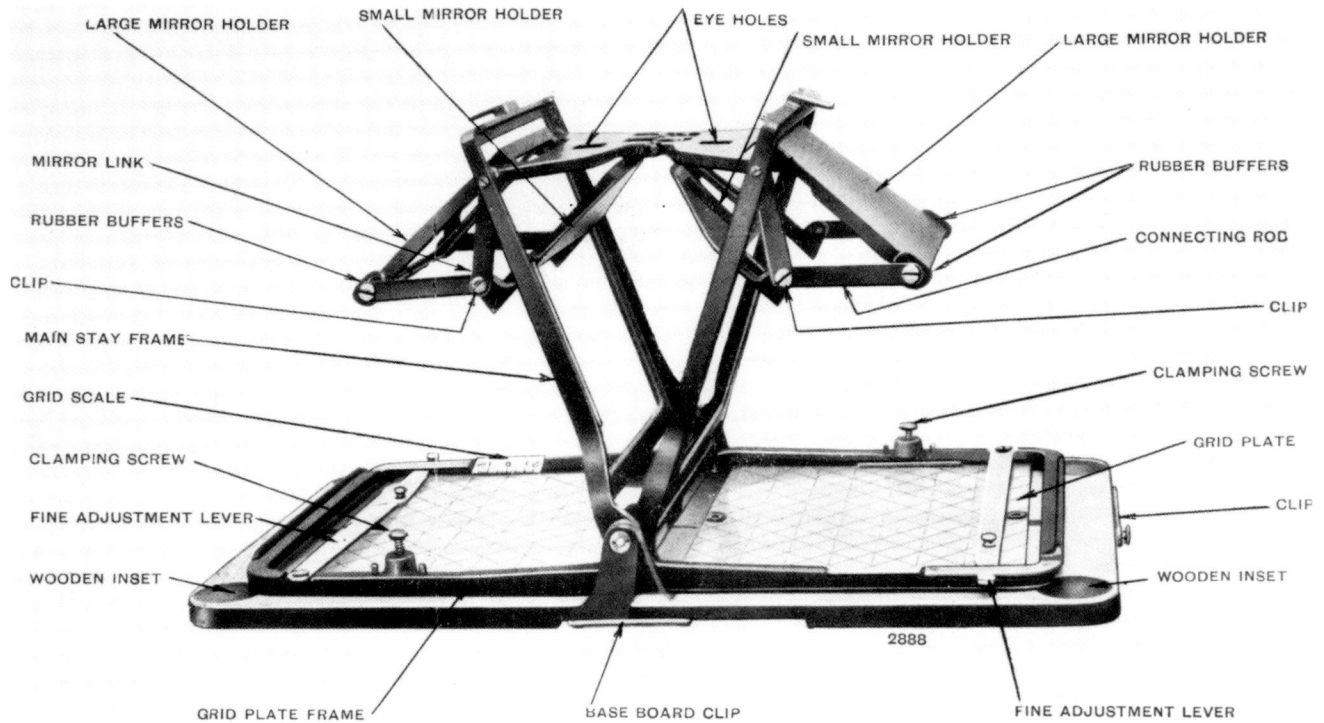

SIMPLE PORTABLE STEREOSCOPE, TYPE Z.D. 4

a decisive influence on board decisions affecting the direction of the firm's affairs. However, he began to suffer from periodic bouts of illness during the late 1920s and felt that it was time to hand over greater responsibilities to the younger directors.[61] This became even more vital after the death of Harold Jackson.

J. Martin Strang succeeded Jackson as Barr & Stroud's secretary in 1928, but the position of managing director was left vacant, and the executive functions divided between James French, Neil Maclean, Strang and Francis Morrison. As technical director, Dr French (awarded a DSc by Glasgow University in 1921 for his work on glass grinding and polishing) was in charge of research and development work, Maclean remained as works director, Strang assumed control of financial and general administrative affairs and Morrison, the London director, took greater responsibilities in the commercial field, as well as in the direction of the firm's growing investment portfolio.[62] Although Dr Barr and Dr Stroud continued to offer their advice on technical matters, and Dr Barr's advice on general business policy was valued highly, the founders' younger colleagues were left in charge of the day-to-day affairs of the firm, and had to shoulder the burden of responsibility for guiding Barr & Stroud through the difficult years of the Depression.

Barr & Stroud's recovery was set back by the onset of the worldwide recession which followed the Wall Street Crash and the collapse of the Austrian Credit Anstalt bank in 1929. However, the directors had already taken steps to trim their workforce and cut costs before the Depression began, and determined moves to convince the Admiralty of the need to place vital orders to keep the machine shop open at Anniesland, as well as success in improving the design and marketing of products for the civilian market, allowed Barr & Stroud to come through the depressed years of the early 1930s in better shape than many other Clydeside industries. One important new field, in which Barr & Stroud established an excellent

Archie Walker demonstrates the epidiascope, May 1928.

reputation, was in the manufacture of aerial survey instruments. The advantages of using aerial photographs in map-making had become obvious during the First World War, and the War Office Aerial Survey Committee was formed to help the British Army develop means of improving its expertise in this new technology. In 1925, Barr & Stroud were asked if they were interested in developing instruments for the British Army, and Dr Barr made aerial survey one of his own pet projects.

Barr & Stroud's most successful aerial survey instruments were their topographical stereoscopes, the first of which were ordered by the War Office in 1927. The instrument enabled an observer to view stereoscopically pairs of photographs taken from the air, so that the contours of the area under study appeared in relief. Grid nets were superimposed in the field of view, and could be 'raised' or 'lowered' until they appeared to be at the same level as a feature of the landscape, the height of which could then be measured.[63] To complement the topographical stereoscopes, Barr & Stroud began to manufacture mapping epidiascopes in 1929. These were instruments which provided a means of inserting new details from recent aerial photographs on to existing maps, by superimposing an impression of the photo on to the map and allowing the map-maker to trace the new features on to the latter.[64] The firm also manufactured four photogrammatic plotters for the War Office, for more detailed work than could be done using the topographical stereoscopes, as well as photonymographs, invented by a member of staff from the War Office Geographical Section. Using a photonymograph, a man could produce as much lettering for maps in one day as a skilled cartographer could produce in about six weeks.[65]

The epidiascope featured one of Dr Barr's more unusual innovations. He required reflectors to shield the light bulbs in the instrument from the eyes of the map-maker, but was unwilling to go to the expense of having them specially designed and manufactured in the works. His assistant was sent off to find a cheap alternative, and he returned from Woolworths with four butter dishes, purchased for the grand sum of 2 shillings (10p). The dish lids were silvered and painted before being fitted in the instrument, and proved perfect for the purpose. The firm promptly laid in a stock of Woolworths' butter dishes, which were integral features of the instruments sold during the 1920s and 1930s.[66]

Job security for Barr & Stroud's employees was further enhanced by the firm's successes in developing and marketing prismatic binoculars at the end of the 1920s. A new range of light-weight civilian binoculars was launched in 1929, backed by a strong advertising campaign and a more professional marketing operation organised by Francis Morrison in London. The lighter instruments, made of aluminium rather than brass, and supplied with a Bakelite prism box, proved highly popular and were sold in such exclusive retail outlets as Harrods in London. Barr & Stroud were manufacturing up to 1,000 civilian binoculars a month by 1939.[67] The firm also succeeded in capturing the market for binoculars for the Royal Navy. Trials of the firm's CF12 night glasses in 1921 had shown them to be superior optically to the others tested, but no orders had followed. Between 1928 and 1930, however, Barr & Stroud submitted improved 7x15 binoculars,

A photonymograph, 1932.

the CF15, for further trials at the National Physics Laboratory and the Admiralty Experimental Station, offering others to Royal Navy officers for comment.[68] J. Martin Strang was able to claim proudly that the CF15 was found to match equivalent Zeiss glasses in quality of definition, and to be superior in the brightness of the image transmitted to the eye-pieces.[69] In December 1930, the Admiralty ordered 250 CF15 binoculars and Barr & Stroud's glasses were adopted as the standard binoculars for the Royal Navy.[70]

The improved marketing of new products at the end of the 1920s was matched by greater success for Barr & Stroud in winning other orders from the Admiralty. The firm's efforts were assisted by government defence policy. Britain's submarine fleet was composed mostly of boats of First World War vintage, and the Admiralty was particularly concerned that the ageing submarines would be unable to conduct long-range operations in the Far East, should Britain be drawn into a confrontation with

A range of Barr & Stroud binoculars on display in the shop window of John Trotter Ltd, Gordon Street in Glasgow, November 1931.

Japan. During the late 1920s, work began on modernising the submarine fleet, and Barr & Stroud received valuable orders for periscopes for the new boats. The first new CK2 search periscopes and CH21 attack periscopes for submarines of the new 'O' class were delivered to the Royal Navy in 1928, and the manufacture of new periscopes for O, P, R and S class submarines kept the periscope department fully occupied during the early 1930s.[71] CK8 and CK9 search periscopes and CH51 and

CH55 attack periscopes were fitted in T and U class boats before 1939, by which time Barr & Stroud had delivered a total of 150 instruments to the Royal Navy. Eighty-five more were manufactured for foreign navies, including those of the USA, the USSR, Poland, Yugoslavia and Sweden, while optical parts were supplied to Société Française des Instruments d'Optique, which took out a licence to manufacture periscopes under Barr & Stroud's patents and which supplied about eighty instruments to the French Navy before 1939.[72] Barr & Stroud's periscope business provided continuity of employment for many men at Anniesland, and a welcome steady income during the Depression.

The growing threat posed to warships by carrier-borne and long-range aircraft encouraged the Admiralty to improve the anti-aircraft defences of British warships during the late 1920s, and provided Barr & Stroud with more valuable contracts. In 1927 the Admiralty ordered the first improved heightfinder, the UD3, and in 1932 the first UF1.[73] Later types featured larger optical parts to improve the light-gathering powers of the instruments, and the UK1, introduced in 1933 and operated by a rangetaker, a trainer, a layer, and a control officer, could be used to find surface ranges as well as heights, and came equipped with a pistol which fired the anti-aircraft gun.[74] The UR instrument, which was adopted by the Royal Navy on the eve of the Second World War, had an eye-piece fixed in elevation so that it remained in the same position no matter the angle at which the instrument had to be trained to 'find' the target.[75] In all, nearly seven hundred heightfinders were purchased by the Royal Navy before the end of 1939, and many

A Central Station Instrument Board manufactured for a Norwegian warship in 1923.

more were supplied to the Spanish, Swedish, Japanese, Turkish and Dutch fleets.[76]

Barr & Stroud's work on fire-control had continued during the 1920s, and Frank Gerstenberg had taken charge of the project to design the fire-control table devised by Dr Stroud and the firm's consultant, Admiral Mouton, before the war. The firm won an order to equip a Japanese battleship with a complete fire-control system, including the fire-control table which Barr & Stroud named the 'Central Station Instrument Board', in 1923.[77] In 1925, Central Station Instrument Boards were ordered for the British destroyers HMS *Amazon* and HMS *Ambuscade*, and others were made for trials on Italian, Swedish, Norwegian and Yugoslavian ships.[78] The 9-foot-long plotting board contained a complicated series of mechanisms and gears to produce a plot from the information on ranges, bearings and other measurements fed into it, and its manufacture provided a great deal of work for the machine shop.[79] Barr & Stroud hoped that the instrument would provide them with a profitable product for the future, but the Admiralty made no move to adopt it for the Royal Navy, despite its success in trials, and foreign navies were reluctant to place further orders for what was regarded as an experimental system. In 1932, the Admiralty informed Barr & Stroud that the Royal Navy would be equipped instead with an instrument developed by the service, the Admiralty Fire-Control Clock. Appreciating that Barr & Stroud had spent a great deal of money on the private development of their own plotting table, and that the decision to reject it would force Barr & Stroud to lay off many highly skilled men and hinder the firm's ability to take on intricate mechanical work for the Royal Navy in the future, the Admiralty sent drawings of the AFCC to Anniesland in 1932 and placed an order with the firm for eight of them. Barr & Stroud were able to retain the services of many men to work on the AFCCs, and the firm manufactured over 150 of the instruments between 1932 and 1945.[80]

The directors' successes in winning Admiralty orders, and in marketing their civilian products more effectively, helped the firm survive the Depression. Sales fell in value from £298,933 in 1928 to £221,081 in 1929, £218,710 in 1930 and £175,615 in 1931, recovered to £245,429 with the receipt of large payments for many of the Royal Navy's new submarine periscopes in 1932, and then fell to £147,697 in 1933.[81] Although after-tax profits were hardly spectacular during these years— the average was just over £48,000, or about 4 per cent on sales — they were achieved during years in which much of British industry was struggling to remain in business while recording heavy losses. The recovery in the British economy which began in 1934 was underpinned by greater spending on defence, as the nation's leaders took the first steps to rearm to meet the threat to peace formed by belligerent totalitarian regimes in Italy and Germany, and the increasingly aggressive foreign policy of Japan in the Far East. Barr & Stroud came through the Depression without

A CH46 periscope, manufactured for a Swedish submarine, 1934.

having to shed large numbers of skilled men, and with improved instruments which were to be in great demand when Britain began to re-equip and modernise her armed forces.

Dr Barr died on 5 August 1931, just as the firm appeared to be winning its fight for survival. Francis Morrison expressed the opinions of his fellow directors when he wrote on 11 August that:

> It has indeed been a shock to us. It was so unexpected. He retained his wonderful vigour until practically the end, indeed until about 10 days ago when he had to undergo an operation which would have been only a minor one for a younger man. But, alas, he failed to pull through; it proved too much for him at his age.[82]

Dr Barr was a remarkably successful professor. The number of students studying

Dr Archibald Barr, 1855-1931.

Engineering trebled during his short stay at the Yorkshire College of Science.[83] There were only thirty-nine students in his department when he returned to Glasgow in 1889, but the number had swelled to over two hundred by the time of his retirement.[84] He was remembered by his students as an excellent teacher who had an admirable talent for conciseness and clarity of expression, but his contribution to the life of the University did not lie solely in his teaching. Dr Barr helped set up the Faculty of Science in 1893 and campaigned successfully for the creation of a lectureship in Electrical Engineering. When the University decided to replace gas with electrical power in the buildings on Gilmorehill, Dr Barr was asked to report on the best means of carrying out the conversion and was convenor of the committee which took charge of the project. The greatest monument to his career at Glasgow University was the James Watt Engineering Building, opened by Lord Kelvin in September 1901, which housed what were considered to be the finest science laboratories in the kingdom. Dr Barr raised £40,000 from local industrialists, the Randolph Bequest, the Bellahouston Trust and the University Court to have the laboratories built, and they were furnished with £14,000 worth of the very latest in scientific equipment.[85]

Dr Barr acted as a consultant to many of Glasgow's engineering firms during his career at the University, mostly to test and advise on the construction of boilers. His most important work as a consultant was undertaken at the turn of the century, when he helped design the machinery for Pinkston Power Station, which was built to provide the power for Glasgow's new electric trams.[86] He enjoyed being involved in other engineering projects and keeping abreast with developments in the design of engineering plant, but he had many interests outwith industrial engineering. He was a prominent member of the Scottish Auto Club, and in 1901 he organised the first Motor Car Reliability Trials to be held in Scotland. A keen motorist, he purchased his first Argyll car at the turn of the century, graduating to an Albion and then a Delanney Belleville and a Straker-Squire before 1914.[87] After the war he became the proud owner of a brown Daimler, which was fitted in 1924 with what the makers called 'a device for flattening raindrops' — said to be the first windscreen wiper to be seen in Glasgow.[88] His interest in mechanised forms of transport was not confined to motor cars. Dr Barr helped form the Scottish Aeronautical Club in 1909, became its president, and was involved in promoting Scotland's first aviation meeting at Lanark in 1910, just seven years after the Wright Brothers made the first powered flight in history.[89]

Like most successful academics, Dr Barr was greatly in demand to act as an office-holder in learned societies. He was president of the Royal Philosophical Society of Glasgow (1901-04), a councillor, vice-president and then president (1910-11) of the Institute of Engineers and Shipbuilders in Scotland, through which he did much to foster even closer contacts between the universities and industrialists, and became president of the Optical Society and a Fellow of the Royal Society in 1923. His eagerness to promote co-operation between 'town and gown' led to his involvement in Glasgow's huge International Exhibition of 1901 and to his acting as a guarantor for the one which followed in 1911.[90]

Dr Barr left 'Royston' in Dowanhill at the West End of Glasgow in 1906, to settle with his wife, their three sons and their daughter at Westerton-of-Mugdock in Milngavie to the north-west of the city.[91] He enjoyed entertaining guests, and the family regularly held parties in the grounds of their new home during the summer. He was convivial by nature, and one of his successors at the University remembered him as a speaker whose wit was surpassed only by the famous Macneile Dixon, Professor of English. However, he continued to give serious consideration to every aspect of his firm's affairs, and resisted any temptation to sit

back and allow younger men to take charge of Barr & Stroud's research and development work. He devoted long hours to the design of new instruments, and earned the respect of even the most brilliant of his members of staff, by his ability to get to the root of any problem, and by the clarity and precision of the instructions and drawings he passed down to them.

More than any man, Dr Barr moulded the character of the firm. A time-served mechanical engineer himself, he insisted on and always showed his appreciation of a high standard of workmanship in the machine shop. He was a perfectionist in his own work for Barr & Stroud, and would not tolerate ill-conceived or shoddy design drawings. The high standards he set were retained after his death, for the men who designed and manufactured Barr & Stroud's instruments learned their trade under his benign, but critical, tutelage.[92]

The death of Dr Barr forced the directors of the firm to make further alterations to the divisions of authority on the board. Dr Stroud succeeded his old friend as Chairman of the firm, but he remained in semi-retirement and continued to spend only the summer months at Anniesland. James French was appointed Deputy Chairman and became, in effect, the firm's chief executive.[93] Barr & Stroud had to face many new problems without Dr Barr, most particularly in meeting the British armed forces' demands for new instruments once the government permitted limited rearmament programmes to commence during the mid-1930s. In 1936, the Admiralty asked Barr & Stroud to begin laying in stocks of glass and other materials which might be required to begin mass production of submarine periscopes.[94] The War Office and Air Ministry joined their colleagues at the Admiralty in placing the first of many large orders about this time, as the government asked them to accelerate their preparations for a possible war with the Axis powers.

Barr & Stroud had invented a 'bomb-dropper' sight during the First World War, and supplied some to the War Office towards the end of that conflict.[95] In 1927 the firm was presented with drawings of a new instrument, the 'Course Setting Bomb Sight', and the Air Ministry's steady flow of orders for the sights became a flood after 1935. About 5,000 of these complicated pieces of equipment were delivered to the RAF before 1939.[96] The Air Ministry were important customers for other sights, developed by Barr & Stroud themselves. A reflector gunsight, the GJ3, was designed by Barr & Stroud in 1924 for bomber plane gunners.[97] Thousands of sights were supplied to the RAF during the 1930s, when the belief that 'the bomber will always get through' encouraged the RAF to build a large bomber fleet which, it was hoped, would deter an aggressor by threatening massive retaliation for any attacks on British cities. The firm also developed a special ring mounting for bomber turret guns. The gunner sat within the ring, and an ingenious series of linkages caused his seat to sink lower in his turret as the angle of sight became greater, eliminating the discomfort of aiming the gun at maximum elevation. The firm was unable to begin mass production of the mountings during the late 1930s, owing to the heavy demand for its more established products, but the job was carried out by other firms using Barr & Stroud's drawings.[98]

Barr & Stroud were called upon during the

The Barr & Stroud GH2 ring mounting, with machine-gun and CJ3 reflector sight, 1934.

1930s to supply pilots' sights for fighter aircraft and the GD5 sight was patented by the firm in 1934. It fulfilled the difficult function of providing the pilot with a sighting mark free from distortion no matter from which angle the pilot looked through it, by incorporating a paraboloid metal reflector in place of a lens in the optical system which projected the mark into the line of vision.[99] The GD5 proved very effective, but the firm and the RAF foresaw problems in mass-producing the metal reflectors quickly in time of war. In consequence, Barr & Stroud developed the GM pilot's sight, the optical computing department designing a lens with a numerical aperture of F/0 0.68 for the complicated optical system. The GM2 system was patented in 1937, and it became the standard pilot's sight in service with

The GM2 reflector sight.

the RAF before the war began.[100]

Fear of the dangers posed by bomber attacks led the British Army to ask Barr & Stroud for a new, improved heightfinder during the 1930s. The UB7 and FQ25 instruments, with a base length of 15 feet and higher magnification and better light-gathering powers than the old UB instruments, began to reach anti-aircraft units in 1937.[101] To meet the need for an early air-raid warning system, the firm also developed sound-locators, large listening devices which could indicate the range and direction of incoming enemy aircraft, but these were rendered obsolete by the development of radar and the establishment of the 'Chain Home' network of radar stations along the south and east coats of England just before the war. Only a few sound-locators were sold, the majority to foreign governments.[102]

Barr & Stroud's sales dropped in value from £274,848 in 1934 to £174,323 in 1935, but rose steadily once Britain's rearmament programme was put into high gear. Sales worth £355,886 in 1936 were followed by figures of £420,649 in 1937 and £725,516 in 1938. They topped £1 million for the first time in 1939, when they amounted to £1,226,015. After-tax profits rose steadily during these years, exceeding £100,000 in 1937 for the first time since the First World War, and the firm was able to re-engage men laid off during the Depression.[103]

The important position held by the firm in the government's rearmament programme convinced the directors of the need to start work on a series of new extensions to the factory in 1937. A new three-storey building was built at the north-eastern end of the original factory site, to house the pattern shop, an extension to the glass-making shop, and floor-space for the erection and testing of reflector sights. Two storeys were added to the frontages on Crow Road and Strathcona Street, for extensions to the drawing office and optical shop, and areas for gun-sight assembly and the assembly and adjustment of binoculars. The West Works was extended to the north and west, to provide additional space for the assembly, adjustment and testing of large rangefinders, heightfinders and periscopes, and air-raid shelters were built beneath the western part of the site. These extensions gave Barr & Stroud a total floor area of 374,800 square feet at Anniesland by the time they were completed, shortly after the outbreak of the Second World War.[104]

Dr Stroud did not live to see the new factory extensions. He was still actively involved in attempting to devise an improved high-angle

Sinclair Reid, Barr & Stroud's head foreman from 1895 until his retirement in 1938, demonstrates an experimental sound-locator. 'Sinky' was one of the firm's best-known and respected figures.

Kilted Territorials demonstrate the VD5 sound-locator. This photograph was intended for a publicity brochure but was never used. A senior director feared that the Chinese, who had expressed great interest in the instrument, might gain the impression that the sound-locator was intended for female operators. He ordered new photographs, featuring soldiers in trousers.

rangefinder when, on 27 May 1938, he died while on holiday in Torquay.[105]   Dr Stroud's death might not have been unexpected — like Dr Barr, he was in his seventies when he passed away and had suffered from ill-health for some time — but his loss was felt keenly, nonetheless. He had continued to live at Ashwood Villas in Leeds after Dr Barr's departure in 1889, and his daughter remembered vividly the dark, dusty, study to which he retired whenever a new plea for assistance arrived from Byres Road.[106] He, too, had three sons and a daughter, and he took

his family to stay in a chalet in Ilkley in 1903. The Strouds finally decided to move north in 1909 and stayed briefly at The Ridge in Bearsden before settling at a new home, Bankell to the north of Milngavie.[107] Dr Stroud was able to devote far more time to the firm's affairs after leaving academia, and he shared an office at Anniesland with his old friend and partner.[108]

The years he spent at the Yorkshire College of Science were remembered with great affection by Dr Stroud, and the professor was held in esteem and regarded with great affection by his students, who appreciated the unique blend of humour and intellectual stimulation which he brought to his lectures.[109]   Like Dr Barr, Dr Stroud did not confine himself to the teaching side of academic life. After seeing a production of *The Mikado* in London in 1889, he 'came away enthralled' and became a devotee of Gilbert and Sullivan.   For many years he wrote Gilbertian verses for distribution to his friends at the end of each year, lampooning gently his students and colleagues and poking fun at the institutional eccentricities of the Yorkshire College of Science.   In 1895 he began to participate in student union theatrical and musical evenings, and his willingness to become involved in college social life, coupled with his modest and unassuming manner and his ability to appreciate a joke at his own expense as well as to 'rag' others, made him a popular figure.[110] His gesture in providing the funds for a building to house a Lads' Club for disadvantaged young men in Leeds was also greatly appreciated in the city.[111] Dr Stroud was a keen hill-walker, and his family spent many of their holidays on walking tours in Germany and southern France.[112] He inherited his mother's enthusiasm for playing chess, and he continued to read Latin classics

and his Greek Bible until the end of his life.[113]
He cared less than did Dr Barr for the social
scene in Glasgow and seldom entertained
guests on a lavish scale. He spent comparatively
little on luxuries, but he did purchase a new car
in 1906, some years after Dr Barr acquired his
Argyll. Dr Stroud was never so keen on
motoring as was his partner, and disliked
driving; it is said that he only bought a car
because the workings of automobile engines

fascinated his scientific imagination. He was
able to discuss the engine with a leading
authority, for one of the many eminent men to
visit the Strouds socially was C.H. Rolls, the car
manufacturer. Other guests included
Gugliemo Marconi and Sir Alfred Yarrow, who
shared Dr Stroud's interest in the latest
scientific developments in industry.[114]

With the death of Dr Stroud, the firm lost the
third member of the triumvirate of the scientist,

A pre-war Army Training photograph, showing a 3.7" anti-aircraft gun, a UB7 heightfinder, and a Vickers predictor fire-control instrument.

IMPERIAL WAR MUSEUM

Anniesland Cross looking north-east, just before the Second World War. Work is proceeding on extensions to the main factory on Strathcona Street and Crow Road, and to the West Works on Bearsden Road, opposite a new housing development. The virtual absence of parked cars in Crow Road and Caxton Street is now a thing of the past, while Anniesland Cross has become one of the busiest road junctions in the city.

the engineer and the business manager upon which Barr & Stroud's success was built. The breadth of Dr Stroud's scientific knowledge, and the inventive and imaginative way in which he applied academic learning to the complex practical problems encountered in devising new instruments, made him Barr & Stroud's greatest asset. Dr Barr believed in the maxim that, to be successful in business, one must 'first find a genius, then work him hard'.[115] Dr Stroud worked hard to provide his colleagues with a stream of ideas for new instruments and on improvements to existing models. These ideas formed the life-blood of the firm, and, after they were sifted by Dr Barr from the point of view of the practical possibilities of design, and by Harold Jackson from the standpoint of commercial viability, they provided the means by which Barr & Stroud maintained their position as leading manufacturers of advanced electrical, mechanical and optical instruments.[116]

James French became Chairman of Barr & Stroud after the death of Dr Stroud. He was the obvious successor to the firm's founders, after Harold Jackson's death in 1928, by right of his seniority in years of service as well as his undoubted talents as an engineer and scientist. However, if he had any plans of his own to redirect the firm's business activities, they had to be shelved soon after the new Chairman took office. On 1 September 1939, Hitler's army and airforce launched a ferocious attack on Poland.

Britain, which had been preparing reluctantly for war for several years, joined France in declaring war on Germany two days later. Just as had happened in 1914, Barr & Stroud were asked to lay aside their own plans and research and development projects, and to concentrate on producing the optical munitions most urgently required by the armed forces in their prosecution of a second Great War.

Dr William Stroud, 1860-1938.

'THAT LITTLE TOYSHOP IN ANNIESLAND...'1939-1954

Barr & Stroud were better prepared for war in 1939 than they had been twenty-five years earlier. The directors and many members of staff and of the workforce had experienced, during the Great War of 1914-18, all the difficulties which were likely to arise in running a factory and boosting output during a time of national crisis. The firm had already begun to step up production, to meet orders placed in connection with the rearmament programmes of the late 1930s, and factory extensions were well under way. Nevertheless, the sheer scale of the orders placed by Britain's military authorities during the first three years of the Second World War surprised everyone at Anniesland. Warfare had become even more highly mechanised and scientific since 1918, on land, at sea, and in the air, and tactics were ever more dependent on the availability of sophisticated optical instruments. In consequence, Barr & Stroud were deluged with orders and had to act swiftly to expand their workforce, extend their premises, and ensure a vast increase in their output.

The firm's workforce rose from about 2,000 in 1939 to a peak of 6,100 in 1944.[1] The problems of retaining the services of skilled men were less serious than they had been during the First World War, as the government and armed forces were fully aware of the damage which indiscriminate conscription had done to the munitions industries in 1917, and the authorities generally responded promptly to requests for exemptions from military service for essential workers. In the machine shop and optical shop, experienced men were able to train the newcomers, set up jobs, and supervise their work on the machines.[2]

Assembly, fitting and optical adjustment posed greater difficulties for the recruits, as they involved skills which took years to learn. The firm's solution was to break down jobs, which would have been entrusted in full to a skilled worker before the war into small parts, each of which could be learned quickly under expert tuition.[3] Such specialisation would have been impossible in peacetime, as there was not sufficient work to keep what was virtually a production line fully occupied, but the flow of orders during the six years of the war was more than sufficient to ensure that there were no periods of enforced idleness for the newcomers.

There was no great opposition, in the boardroom or on the shop-floor, to the recruitment of female labour during the Second World War. Attitudes towards the employment of women had changed markedly since 1914. Indeed Barr & Stroud had become one of the few engineering firms to employ significant numbers of women during the 1930s, and around five hundred of them were already employed by 1939, mostly on delicate work such as adjusting and optical assembly. Many of the women who started work for Barr & Stroud during the war were from local middle-class families, seeking to 'do their bit' in a way which would not have found favour in 'polite' society twenty-five years earlier.[4]

Even after the completion of the extensions to the Anniesland works, Barr & Stroud had insufficient room to deal with the wartime demand for their instruments. However, the firm was fortunate in being able to acquire more floor space, by occupying and converting other business premises and setting up 'shadow' factories to which much of the manufacturing and assembly work could be farmed out.

Another aerial view of Barr & Stroud's factory shortly before the war, looking east. Entrances to the air-raid shelters are ranged along the wall of the West Works facing Bearsden Road. Glasgow University would not permit the firm to anchor barrage balloons in the Westerlands playing fields, at the top of the picture. Sir James French feared that his works were vulnerable to dive-bomber attack, if they were not protected by barrage balloons. The University's Principal feared that the installation and maintenance of the balloons would damage the sports fields.

MacLehose's printworks, on the south side of Caxton Street, was used for the assembly of submarine periscopes; Knightswood Motors' garage nearby became a small machine shop; two floors above Callander's Garage in Kirklee, about a mile to the east of the factory, were converted to house a complete optical shop. With fourteen other shadow factories in the Glasgow area these provided Barr & Stroud with an additional 70,000 square feet of floor space for all kinds of machine, optical and assembly work. In addition, thirty-five firms worked for Barr & Stroud as subcontractors, supplying components.[5] The dispersion of men and machinery had its drawbacks in terms of the organisation and co-ordination of work, but it also had one very great advantage: by shifting employees and machinery to outlying factories, Barr & Stroud ensured that even a heavy air-raid on Anniesland, and the bombing of the works there, would not bring production of optical instruments to a complete halt.

Neil Maclean had retired as works director in February 1938, and Dr French took responsibility for introducing measures to boost productivity at the beginning of the war. He introduced a nightshift, extended the working hours for the day-shift to 9 p.m., and asked the firm's employees to work at weekends, but the increase in output which resulted from longer working hours failed to satisfy fully the needs of the armed forces. Neil Maclean was invited by the board to resume his duties as works director in 1942, to apply his proven talents for organisation and man-management to the problem, and he quickly made his mark. Maclean believed that employees were being asked to work excessively long hours, and that tiredness was affecting the speed and quality of production. He ended late working on Tuesdays and Thursdays for the day-shift, and cut overtime at weekends. The workforce, given longer periods in which to relax away from the pressures of work at the factory, responded as Maclean hoped they would by achieving greater levels of productivity and better standards of quality in their work.[6]

There was serious concern at the beginning of the war that Barr & Stroud would be

Neil J. Maclean.

designated a prime target by the Luftwaffe. Lord Haw-Haw, the Irish-American fascist who broadcast Nazi propaganda to Britain each day, was reported to have boasted that German bombers would destroy 'that little toyshop in Anniesland', and it was discovered after the war that the Luftwaffe had taken aerial photographs of the factory in 1938 and had it marked down with the nearby gasworks for attack.[7] Barr & Stroud had to paint over the glass roof of the main factory in camouflage colours and take measures to ensure that the blackout was

The Luftwaffe's photograph of the Anniesland area, probably taken from a German airship in 1938. Although the factory and the gasworks nearby must have been considered a prime target, German bombers failed to mount an attack on the Anniesland area.

rigourously observed during the night-shift.[8] As part of the government's Air-Raid Precaution scheme, air-raid shelters had been built beneath the West Works in 1938, with separate accommodation for men and women. When the factory received warning of approaching enemy aircraft, the employees filed calmly underground until the all-clear sounded. In the shelters, impromptu concerts and 'turns' helped while away the time and distract everyone's mind from the dangers above, although the air-raid alerts usually lasted for less than two hours and proved ultimately to be more of a nuisance than a worry.[9] Stray bombs fell on nearby Crow Road and in Kelvindale, but there was no attack on the factory itself as the Luftwaffe concentrated on larger targets on the banks of the River Clyde. However, German bombing did cause some disruption. Many Barr & Stroud employees lived in the Clydebank area, and suffered loss and damage to their homes during the horrific air-raids of 13 and 14 March 1941. They had to be excused from work for a few days while they recovered from the shock of their experiences and until public transport services were restarted.[10]

The fear of a bombing campaign was accompanied at the beginning of the war by the very real concern that the Germany Army, the Wehrmacht, might attempt to invade Britain or to launch commando raids on vital war installations. This fear became even greater after the success of the German 'blitzkrieg' on the Western Front in May 1940, and the evacuation of the remnants of the British and French armies from Dunkirk. In 1940, the government asked volunteers to enrol in a Local Defence Volunteer Force, later known as the Home Guard, to protect their homes and work places from enemy attacks, and 213 of Barr & Stroud's employees were enrolled in the firm's own unit by July.[11] The twelve members of Barr & Stroud's rifle club, formed in 1905, were able to provide their workmates with expert tuition in marksmanship, but although it proved relatively easy to recruit part-time soldiers to defend Anniesland, it was rather more difficult to find the weapons they would need to fight the enemy.[12] Barr & Stroud received only five rifles of First World War vintage, and fifty rounds of ammunition, while the unit was sent only five service caps after the firm asked to be supplied with uniforms.[13] There is no doubt that the men of Barr & Stroud's Home Guard unit were quite determined to face the might of any German invasion, but initial attempts to provide them with the means of doing so contained elements of high farce.

The armoured car and machine-guns promised to Barr & Stroud had not arrived by June 1940, and Dr French saw little hope of holding off an attack on his factory with just five rifles. Nevertheless, should the worse come to the worst, he was unwilling to surrender the works without a fight, and he proposed to the Secretary of the Ministry of Aircraft Production that contingency plans be laid for conducting a guerilla war against any insurgents who succeeded in fighting their way into the factory. He told the Secretary that:

> We have suggested...the establishment of a Pepper Corps, and we have actually laid in a stock of pepper. The likeliest routes from the various entrances to the works would be traced out and at intervals, at working positions, there would be available a number of pepper bags. The question arises as to whether or not people throwing pepper would require to be enrolled in some combative Corps [according to the terms of the Geneva Convention]. We have been told that as they are not attempting to take life it is unnecessary to do so.[14]

It is impossible to guess how hard-bitten German storm-troopers would have reacted to a determined attack by condiment-throwing irregulars from the machine shop, but Barr & Stroud were able to abandon this makeshift plan for a last-ditch defence when new, more conventional, weapons eventually appeared at the works. A Beaverette armoured car was delivered, carrying a Bren gun on a swivel mounting, and it was soon accompanying the men on patrols and training manoeuvres in the Anniesland area.[15] Dr French expressed his thanks to the Ministry of Aircraft Production for six Lewis machine-guns which arrived a little later, but asked politely that some of the missing parts, including the six magazines, be sent out to enable the men to fire these weapons. The missing components arrived a few weeks later.[16] Three machine-guns were mounted on the roofs of the factory building, and the others in specially built concrete pill-boxes, to cover every approach to the works. The machine-guns had been intended originally for the rear cockpits of two-seater fighters and came with aircraft mountings, but Barr & Stroud manufactured suitable new mountings in their own machine shop.[17]

Despite its 'Dads' Army' beginnings, Barr & Stroud's volunteer corps was moulded into an impressive body of fighting men. It became the A2 unit of 'A' Company of the 4th Glasgow Batallion of the Home Guard, and as most of the men were rather younger than the average Home Guardsman, A2 unit was one of the fittest and most combat-ready in the city. The battle patrols received extensive training in street fighting and conventional warfare, often using live ammunition, and won recognition for excellent marksmanship with the modern rifles which replaced their first five old .303s. The unit's pipe band played its part in boosting civilian morale in the West End of Glasgow, during the darkest months of the war, with

A concrete pill-box defends the camouflage-painted West Works, with its newly completed periscope tower and air-raid shelters, from any attempted assault along Bearsden Road. The photograph was taken in July 1940, just after six Lewis machine-guns were delivered to the firm to improve the factory's defences.

stirring renditions of Highland battle tunes on parade days.[18]

Barr & Stroud's main function during the war, as seen by the naval, air and military authorities, was to concentrate on the improvement and mass production of its existing range of products, leaving others to carry on research in new technologies. The firm supplied a total of 26,650 of the latest 1-metre-base FT37 rangefinders during the period 1939-44, most of them for the British Army, and these short-base field rangefinders were carried into action on many battlefields.[19] A British sniper told the firm after the war that, during the battle for Monte Casino in Italy in 1944, the Allied advance was held up by a concealed nest of German mortars. He went out in search of the nest, accompanied by a comrade armed with a rangefinder, and spotted the muzzle of a mortar at a range given by the rangefinder of 375.5 yards. The sniper set his sights and opened fire, hitting a pile of shells and setting off a series of explosions which destroyed the enemy position. He may have exaggerated slightly when he said 'it was a B & S rangefinder that won the battle for Casino', but his story illustrated the usefulness of the instrument in the field.[20]

In November 1940 the Director of Naval Ordnance asked Barr & Stroud to consider a Canadian proposal to begin the manufacture of rangefinders and heightfinders by Research Enterprises, a company set up with the Canadian government's assistance. The terms of a collaboration agreement were quickly worked out by representatives of the two firms, and Archie Ballantyne, a manager in the rangefinder shop, took several experienced men with him to set up a factory in Canada to help Research Enterprises to manufacture FT37 rangefinders and UR1 and UB7 heightfinders under licence. The Canadian venture proved very successful, and Research Enterprises won contracts to supply the US Army as well as the Canadian armed forces with rangefinders and heightfinders. US Army officers had tested the FT37 soon after Research Enterprises began to produce the instrument, and were impressed by its performance. In November 1942, the Ministry of Supply asked Barr & Stroud to send complete manufacturing drawings of their rangefinders to the USA, and in June 1943 to give the Americans access to the manufacturing techniques which had been introduced at Research Enterprises' works in Canada. The

Americans were supplied with all the information they requested to allow them to manufacture the FT37.[21]

The RAF relied on Barr & Stroud to supply tens of thousands of gunsights and bombsights for British warplanes during the war. The firm manufactured nearly 5,000 of the RAF's Mark I, II, VI and VII course-setting bombsights before the war, and nearly as many Mark IX sights between 1939 and 1942, until Bomber Command adopted the gyro-stabilised Mark XIV.[22] Barr & Stroud's GJ3 reflector sight for bomber turret guns was superseded in 1939 by another improved design from Anniesland, the RAF's Mark III reflector sight, which proved more compact and efficient than the GJ3. It became the standard sight for all turret and free-mounted guns in the aircraft of Bomber Command until a gyro sight was adopted in 1944, and the firm manufactured over 80,000 GJ3 and Mark III sights between 1936 and 1944.[23]

The Barr & Stroud GM2, designated by the RAF the Reflector Sight Mark II, was the standard pilots' sight for British fighter planes at the beginning of the war, and Hurricane and Spitfire pilots used them to deadly effect during the Battle of Britain in 1941. Barr & Stroud manufactured nearly 65,000 GM2 sights between 1937 and 1942, and it was adopted by the US Navy's 8th Air Force as the 'Illuminated Sight Mark 8' and by US Army fighter units.[24] Other companies, principally the Salford Electrical Instrument Co, were brought in to manufacture the GM2, and 700 of these sights were delivered by C.P. Goerz of Vienna, having been ordered in 1938 when Barr & Stroud were unable to keep up with large RAF orders. The sights were delivered to Britain before Austria,

as part of the Third Reich, went to war with Britain in September 1939.[25]

The GM2 provided the pilot with the means to fix on a target and measure its range, when the line of sight was the same as the pointing direction of the guns, but if the target was not flying on a steady and level course, then the pilot had to estimate for himself the amount of

A mortar team serving with the British Expeditionary Force in France, 1940. The observer on the left is taking the range of what appear to be enemy tanks.

An American gunner in a Boeing B-17 bomber draws a bead through a Mark III reflector sight. The donkey's role in aerial combat remains one of the mysteries of the war.

deflection required to hit it. A pilot learned how to 'aim off' to hit a target crossing his line of sight only through experience, and the RAF was eager to find a gunsight which could estimate the crossing rate itself, to improve the shooting of inexperienced pilots in dog-fights with enemy fighters.   The Royal Aircraft Establishment at Farnborough developed a predictor sight, the Gyro Gun Sight (GGS), to

meet these needs, and the electronics company Ferranti opened a new factory in Edinburgh in 1942 to begin manufacturing it. The GGS gyro set the reflecting mirror of the sight according to the rate of turn of the attacking plane as it followed its target, offsetting the line of sight to compensate for the distance the enemy would travel across during the time of flight of the bullets or cannon-shells fired at it.   The GGS Mark II sight was adopted by the RAF for British fighters in 1943, and the GGS Mark IIC became the standard gunsight for British bombers soon afterwards. Barr & Stroud stopped production of their bomber gunsights and the GM2 when the gyro predictor sights went into production at Edinburgh, although the firm manufactured 1,130 GGS sights, using drawings supplied by RAE and gyros sent to Anniesland by Ferranti, between December 1942 and the end of the war.[26]

As in 1914, Barr & Stroud were considered to be primarily Admiralty contractors, and the Royal Navy received the greatest amount of Barr & Stroud instruments during the Second World War. Naval rangefinder production continued to be one of Barr & Stroud's greatest priorities, but the optical rangefinder was already losing its central importance in naval fire-control before the war began.   In 1935, the British scientist R. Watson Watt had demonstrated successfully that RADAR — radio detection and ranging — could be used to 'find' and measure the range of a target at long ranges. Radar works by sending out pulses of radio energy, which are reflected by any object, such as a ship or aircraft, which crosses their path. By measuring the time which elapses between the transmission and the return of the reflected radio pulses, it is possible to find the distance of the object with great accuracy. In

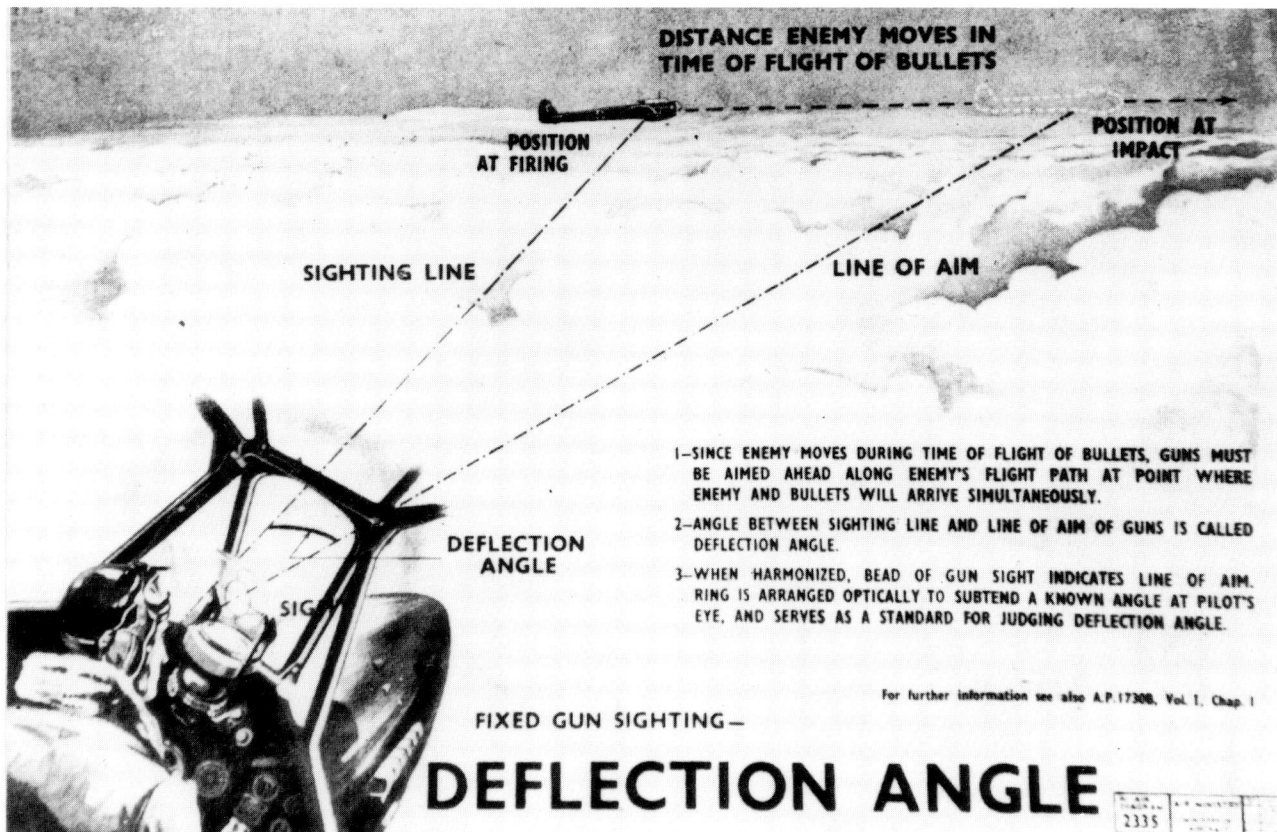

An illustration from an RAF training manual, showing how to 'aim off', when using a reflector sight, in order to hit a crossing target.

September 1939 the Royal Navy received Type 79 radar sets, which could detect aircraft at distances of over fifty miles, and work was proceeding on the development of the Type 284 sets, capable of ranging on surface craft at over ten miles.[27] The advent of radar signalled the end for naval optical rangefinders, as each new development in Britain, and in the USA and Germany, enabled operators to detect targets at greater distances and measure ranges with greater accuracy. However, the first instruments were prone to mechanical break-down and interference, while radar masts were exposed and vulnerable to blast-damage in action, and optical rangefinders remained in service with the British and other navies for the duration of the war, to confirm radar ranges and to provide a back-up service when radar equipment was out of service. British battleships each carried up to seventeen optical rangefinders and heightfinders into action, and the Barr & Stroud instruments proved their continued worth on a number of occasions.

On 24 May 1941, the battle-cruiser HMS *Hood* and the newly-completed battleship HMS *Prince of Wales* engaged the German battleship

Bismarck and the heavy cruiser *Prinz Eugen* in the Denmark Strait, off Greenland. The Type 284 gunnery radar aboard *Prince of Wales* had broken down, and she was refused permission to turn on her search radar on the grounds that it would interfere with *Hood*'s gunnery set. As heavy seas obscured the view of the operators at the 42-foot rangefinders in her fore turrets, and at the 22-foot duplex rangefinder in the fore Director Control Tower, *Prince of Wales* went into action

Sailors on HMS Sheffield *point out shrapnel damage to the cruiser's after-director, inflicted by the Bismarck during the Denmark Strait engagement. The crews manning the 15-foot rangefinders in the DCTs of British warships went into action with very little protection from enemy fire.*

relying on a 15-foot rangefinder in the after DCT for ranges. She succeeded in straddling the *Bismarck* with her sixth salvo, as the range closed to about 15,000 yards, before *Hood* sustained a number of hits and blew up. Coming under heavy fire from the two German ships, and with several of her 14-inch guns out of action due to mechanical breakdown, *Prince of Wales* was forced to break off the action. However, she had scored three damaging hits on the German battleship, causing an oil leak and putting one boiler out of action. *Bismarck* was forced to make for St Nazaire for repairs, at a reduced speed. En route, she was further slowed by hits scored by British torpedo-bombers, and finally sunk by the guns and torpedoes of the battleships HMS *Rodney*, HMS *King George V*, and other ships of the Home Fleet.[28]

The *Prince of Wales* was not the only British battleship which went into action relying on her optical rangefinders. The *King George V* had to switch to rangefinder control during the final action against the *Bismarck*, after her gunnery radar set broke down.[29] At the Battle of North Cape on Boxing Day 1943, the *Duke of York* opened fire on the battle-cruiser *Scharnhorst* using rangefinder ranges, as she feared that her radar would be unable to pinpoint the target accurately due to 'clutter' interference caused by heavy seas. From 12,000 yards, *Duke of York* straddled the *Scharnhorst* with her first salvo, and scored several hits before the German ship disappeared into the Arctic gloom and the guns were put on to blind fire using radar control. *Duke of York*'s good shooting at the beginning of the battle succeeded in damaging the enemy battle-cruiser, helping to slow her down so that the British battleship and her accompanying cruisers and destroyers were able to hunt down the *Scharnhorst* and sink her with gunfire and torpedoes later in the day.[30]

The importance of optical rangefinders as components in the fire-control systems of British warships made it essential that the instruments were maintained in a state of battle-readiness at all times. A flying squad of expert fitters and adjusters was formed by Barr & Stroud at the beginning of the war, to travel to any port in which a ship was reported to have a damaged or faulty rangefinder or heightfinder.[31] Most of Barr & Stroud's naval heightfinders were installed in High-Angle Control Towers in British warships during the war. The HACT was manned by a rangetaker, layer, trainer and control officer, and in some models a rate officer to select future targets, and they transmitted information on the range, height, speed and bearing of enemy aircraft to the anti-aircraft fire-control station. Barr & Stroud were themselves invited in 1936 to manufacture HACTs for British destroyers, and they delivered 142 to the Royal Navy before

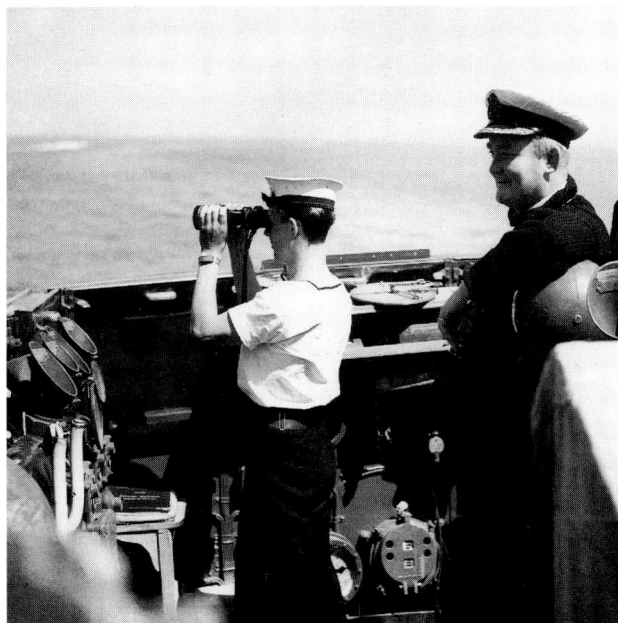

Barr & Stroud binoculars scan the horizon from HMS Sheffield, the shadower of the Bismarck.

1941.[32] The most common naval heightfinders in service during the Second World War were the UK, UL and UR instruments, which could be used as ordinary rangefinders for low-angle gunnery control against surface targets. British destroyers rarely carried a standard rangefinder, and the heightfinder in the HACT was often used to find the initial range of enemy ships at the beginning of the war, in successful actions such as those fought by British destroyers during the battle for Norway in

The 5.25" director on HMS King George V, *the rangetaker's face buried in the rubber face pad of his rangefinder.*

1940.[33] However, optical heightfinders suffered from a serious drawback: the temperatures of 'layers' of air lying over the earth's surface often differs, causing light refraction, and this adversely affected the heightfinder's ability to measure distance.[34] In 1942, the Admiralty Signals Establishment supplied British destroyers with a high-angle radar set which was coupled to the HACT for elevation and bearing, improving the accuracy of the information transmitted to the anti-aircraft fire-control station. The set could also be used for low-angle work, although the heightfinders were retained in the HACTs for the duration of the war to provide essential back-up for the radar system.[35]

Barr & Stroud manufactured binoculars solely for the Admiralty during the war. The firm delivered over 75,000 standard CF41 and CF42 7x50 binoculars during the war (the CF42 having a graticule to aid measurement of the deflection of fall of shot) as well as about 600 special GK5 prismatic binocular sights for rangefinder director towers and about 500 high-magnification CN stereoscopic spotting

HMS Kelly, *the famous but ill-fated British destroyer commanded by Earl Mountbatten during the war, from a painting now hanging in the foyer at Barr & Stroud's works. The director control tower on British destroyers, just forward of the mast on HMS* Kelly, *was usually equipped with a UK or UR rangefinder, which could also be used for high-angle work.*

telescopes, on special anti-vibration mountings, which were used to observe the fall of shot at extreme ranges.[36] Dr J. Martin Strang (who was awarded a DSc by Glasgow University in 1933 for his work on the effects of heat on optical rangefinders) remembered after the

CN15 Spotting binoculars.

war that a senior British naval officer congratulated him on the quality of the firm's 7x50 binoculars, and told him that their excellent performance in dark conditions had proved invaluable during the night battle of Cape Matapan in 1942, when a British Battle Squadron surprised and sank three Italian cruisers and two destroyers.[37] Still greater praise of the Barr & Stroud binoculars came from Admiral Sir Geoffrey Oliver. He told the naval historian Arthur Marder that he attributed 'whatever success we had in night operations for the first few years of the Second World War to our familiarity and confidence in working at

night, engendered by intensive preparation in peace training. This would certainly not have been achieved without the Barr & Stroud night glasses.'[38] Marder himself believed that 'the admirable Barr & Stroud 7x50, in general issue by the 1930s, were probably the equal of the Zeiss at night.'[39] There were many at Barr & Stroud who, remembering the results of the Admiralty trials in 1930, might have objected to the word 'probably'.

Submarines played an important role in British naval strategy during the Second World War, and the 215 boats which served under Submarine Command between 1939 and 1945 were all equipped with Barr & Stroud periscopes.[40] Unlike German U-Boats, which were built primarily as ocean-going commerce raiders, British submarines were usually deployed to patrol shallow waters close to enemy bases, lying in wait for warships, troopships and convoys of merchant vessels. Except on the rare occasions when small, unescorted and poorly armed targets were found, they attacked with torpedoes while submerged, relying on their periscopes to locate and find the range of the enemy. During the war, Barr & Stroud were able to introduce important improvements in their submarine periscopes which greatly increased the effectiveness of the 'silent service' raids on Axis shipping.

Just before the war, Dr French, Dr Strang and members of technical staff began to study the possibilities of producing anti-reflection coatings on glass surfaces by high-vacuum techniques, and a high-vacuum laboratory was set up. John Rupert Davy, a physicist who came to the firm in 1937 from the Mazda company, was put in charge of the project.[41] A submarine periscope usually contains over twenty air-glass

Lieutenant Maydon RN at the search periscope on HMS Umbra, *July 1943.* Umbra *sank the Italian cruiser* Trento *and damaged the battleship* Littorio *in a torpedo attack in June 1942.*

surfaces and, since light suffers a transmission loss of around 5 per cent when it passes through an air and ordinary crown glass surface, the image suffered from severe loss of brightness at the eye-piece.   A solution to the problem involved depositing a thin layer of transparent salt, usually magnesium fluoride, on the optical surfaces.   The anti-reflection coating required was only a two-hundred-thousandth of an inch thick, and had to be deposited at a very low pressure, in an ultra-high vacuum.   By 1940, Barr & Stroud had perfected the technique, and in 1941 the Admiralty ordered that all British submarine periscopes be 'bloomed', as the process was found to increase light transmission by about 60 per cent.[42]   After 1943, Barr & Stroud introduced a 40-foot bi-focal attack periscope with a limited sky-search facility, and began to produce a 40-foot long, 9.5-inch diameter bi-focal night search periscope.   They also developed an air blast technique, to clear the top window of the CK search periscope when it was 'blinded' by sea spray.[43]

Barr & Stroud's periscopes helped British submarines to sink 493 enemy merchant ships and damage 109 during the war, and submarines proved particularly effective in disrupting supplies of men and equipment being carried across the Mediterranean to Rommel's Afrika Corps before the Battle of El Alamien in 1942. Six cruisers, sixteen destroyers, thirty-five submarines and 112 other warships also fell prey to British submarines, and two battleships, two destroyers, six submarines and thirty-five other warships were damaged in torpedo attacks.[44]

One particularly daring submarine operation carried out during the war involved small boats equipped with special periscopes by Barr & Stroud.   In September 1943, six X-craft, midget submarines each with a crew of four men and carrying two explosive charges, were towed to Norway to attack the battleship *Tirpitz*, the battle-cruiser *Scharnhorst* and the pocket battleship *Lutzow* as they lay at anchor in Altenfiord.   Only three X-craft finally made the attack, two of which managed to drop their charges beneath the *Tirpitz* and inflict damage which the Germans took six months to repair.[45] Barr & Stroud had supplied a specially designed periscope, the CL8, which was 9 feet in length with only a 0.6-inch external diameter top tube, for the X-craft.   The Chief of the Admiralty Submarine Service wrote in October to congratulate the firm on the success of the CL8 during the raid, one of the most daring naval operations of the war.[46]   Lieutenants Donald Cameron and Godfrey Place received Victoria Crosses for their bravery in Altenfiord, and they visited Anniesland after the war to describe the raid and the performances of the special periscopes to Barr & Stroud's technical staff.

Barr & Stroud's role in equipping the armed forces during the difficult early years of the war did not go unnoticed in government circles, and the New Year's Honours List of 1941 contained a knighthood for the firm's Chairman, James French.   Sir James was an autocratic Chairman, not always popular with his subordinates, but his talents as an engineer, and especially in research and design, as well as his single-minded devotion to the firm's interests and his energetic if sometimes unsuccessful efforts to improve efficiency in production techniques, were recognised by all.   He was involved in the supervision of every aspect of the firm's affairs, from arranging for the creation and training of Barr & Stroud's Air-Raid Precautions and Home Guard units to organising the setting up of the

An XT1 midget submarine, HMS Extant, *in Holy Loch, February 1944.* Extant *was one of thirty-two X-craft that served with the Royal Navy during the war.*

shadow factories, while he continued to work on important research and development projects.[47] His personal contribution to the war effort was not confined within the walls of the factory. Sir James and his wife did much voluntary work for the Free French forces, setting up a printing press in the basement of their home to produce propaganda leaflets which were dropped in France by the RAF, organising a flag day in Glasgow for the Free French fighting forces, and entertaining many important French refugees. Sir James was delighted to play host to the famous General De Gaulle, when the French leader visited the factory during the war. De Gaulle towered over Sir James, who was little more than five feet tall. Showing a sense of humour seldom revealed to his employees and members of staff, the Chairman looked up at the general, smiled, and was heard to say that he was pleased that the Free French had come to meet the Wee French![48]

Barr & Stroud's excellent public image, founded on service to the nation during the two World Wars, was tarnished by an unseemly but fortunately brief dispute with the Admiralty, which came to public attention in the summer of 1942. A report by the House of Commons' powerful Committee of Public Accounts, published in July, criticised the firm for failing to supply government departments which placed orders with Barr & Stroud with free access to financial records dating back to 1938. The firm insisted that the collation of detailed figures demanded by the Admiralty, on behalf of all the government departments, would divert the directors and senior members of staff from their duties and disrupt production of vital optical munitions. The Committee of Public Accounts was unimpressed by this argument, and stated that if Barr & Stroud did not meet the Admiralty's demands for information voluntarily, then statutory powers would be invoked to force them to do so.[49] The whole sorry episode stemmed from the senior directors' failure to appreciate just how politically sensitive was the issue of war profits, and it is unlikely that Dr Barr and Harold Jackson would have been so undiplomatic in dealing with the reasonable requests of important customers. However, the directors acted quickly, after the appearance of the

Sir James French.

report, to prevent further damage to their relations with government departments and to their public image. Information on costs was rushed to the Admiralty, and Sir Henry Markham, Permanent Secretary at the Admiralty reported in October that 'the firm had been quite co-operative, [and] nothing had been withheld.'[50]

The bad publicity generated by the Admiralty dispute was soon forgotten, and Barr & Stroud were free to concentrate on what they did best, manufacturing optical instruments for the armed forces. The efforts put into boosting production during the war yielded some

spectacular results. Each month, Ian McKenzie's department turned out up to 2,000 binoculars, and the West Works, under Ian Garvie's management, despatched up to 500 FT37 rangefinders, mostly to the British Army.[51] Glass production surpassed all previous records, and the firm supplied the Air Ministry, War Office and Admiralty with nearly half of their requirements for optical glass each year.[52] Few British servicemen at the end of the war had not become acquainted with the rangefinder, gun and bomb sights, periscopes, binoculars and other optical instruments manufactured at Anniesland.

The value of Barr & Stroud's sales topped the £1 million mark during each of the seven calendar years of the Second World War, 1939-45, and surpassed £2 million for the first time in the firm's history in 1944.[53] However, profits did not soar to match these sales figures. The government was concerned to ensure that inflation was kept firmly under control during the war, rather than be allowed to disrupt the economy as it had done during the First World War. As part of its programme of financial controls, the government introduced measures intended to limit government contractors' profits to a maximum of 4 per cent of capital employed, which was reckoned to be the 'real' return. This was done by awarding contracts on a costs plus percentage basis, and by reintroducing an Excess Profit Tax to reclaim a high proportion of profits made on large contracts. Barr & Stroud had made excellent annual after-tax profits of up to 20 per cent on sales during the late 1930s, but in 1940 their profits amounted to only £67,783 — just over 4 per cent on sales that year. The firm's overheads virtually doubled during 1941, amounting to

£731,000, as the bills for heating, cleaning, equipping and maintaining the shadow factories had to be met, new workers had to be paid, and the Scientific Department's budget rose from £22,000 in 1940 to £86,000, to meet the cost of vital research and the development of improved instruments and facilities such as the high-vacuum department for periscope 'blooming'. The firm's annual after-tax profits did not rise above 4 per cent after 1940, and Barr & Stroud paid no Excess Profits Tax in 1942 and even received a small tax rebate the following year.[54] The firm's reservoir of capital, which had increased substantially during the most profitable years of rearmament, 1937-39, grew little during the war as the firm ploughed its limited profits into expanding production capacity. By the time the Japanese surrendered to the Allies in September 1945, the directors sensed that hard times lay ahead once more for the firm.

Barr & Stroud knew from bitter experience that distinguished service to the nation in wartime provided no guarantee of prosperity in peacetime. As had happened in 1918, many orders were cancelled at the end of the Second World War. The firm had to tighten its belt on the assumption that there would be a steep fall in demand for military instruments for several years, as the Labour government elected in 1945 concentrated its energies and the nation's resources on creating the National Health Service and on other social programmes. To make matters worse, improved radar equipment had rendered the optical rangefinder, Barr & Stroud's staple product since 1895, virtually obsolete by 1945 except as an infantry instrument. Countries which began to re-equip their fleets after the war discarded

rangefinders and procured the latest radar technology. Inevitably, there were redundancies at Anniesland, and Barr & Stroud's workforce fell from a wartime peak of 6,100 to just 1,500 in 1948.[55] The directors were

A Barr & Stroud heightfinder, probably an FQ25, somewhere in Britain, c. 1940.

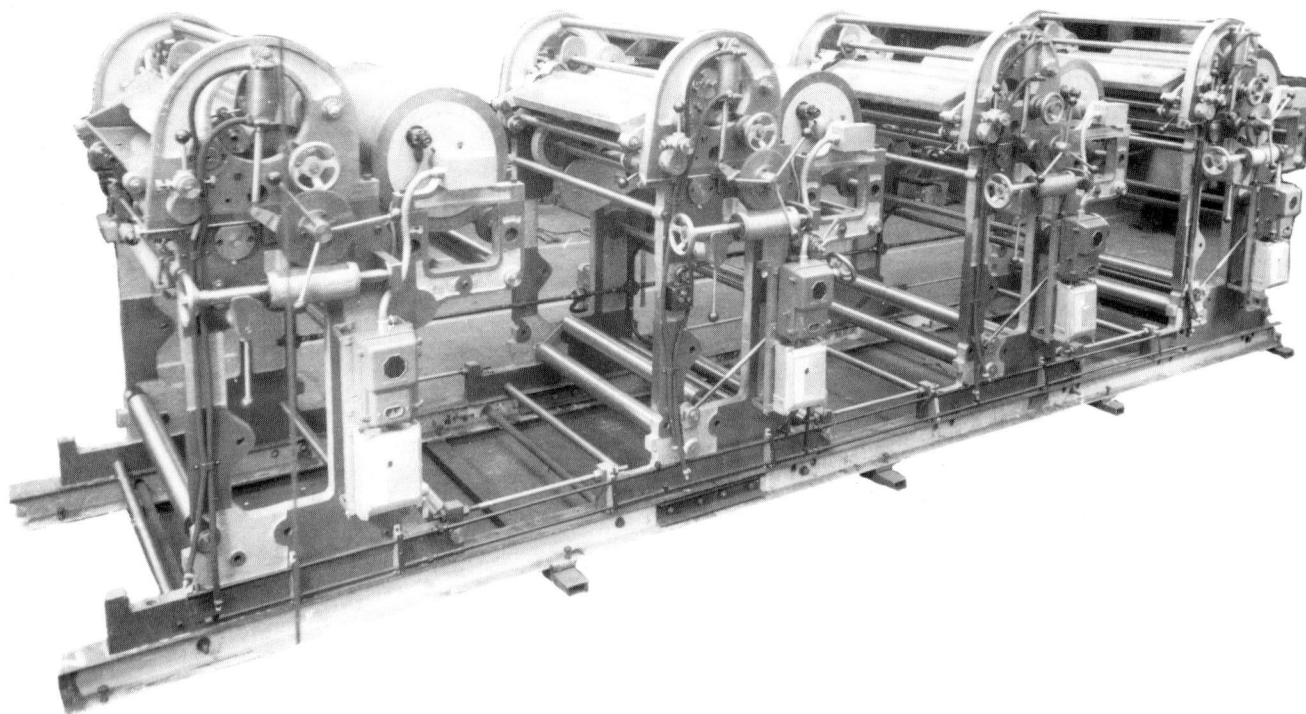

*One of the many types of machines manufactured by Barr &
Stroud to order during the late 1940s: a colour printing machine
for Halley, 1948.*

faced with the problem of finding work for the
'survivors', while endeavouring to master new
technologies and to begin developing the next
generation of instruments for the defence
markets of the future.

The directors' first step was to contact firms
which were in need of new machinery to resume
mass production of consumer goods given a low
priority during the war. Envelope making, pan
loaf moulding, bread slicing, cigarette cutting,
book stitching, offset printing, pen nib
grinding, and paper gumming machines were
among the many manufactured to order at
Anniesland.[56] They were all highly complex
machines, requiring a great deal of
sophisticated gear cutting, and their

manufacture provided regular employment to
skilled machinists and fitters and a regular
income to the firm. The optical workers were
kept busy at first making prisms and lenses for
other optical instrument makers, and for the
range of civilian binoculars marketed by Barr &
Stroud soon after the war.

The development of a new range of civilian
products was also given a high priority, to
provide the firm with more options to choose
from should subcontracting work fail to
materialise in the near future and while work
continued on new defence equipment. Smoke

indicators were optical instruments which were installed mostly in ships' boiler rooms, a relatively simple reflector system transmitting an image of the smoke in the uptake of a boiler to a viewing screen. The image on the screen provided a visual means of determining the density of the exhaust from oil-fired boilers, and therefore of assessing if the level of air inflow to the burners was correct for maximum fuel efficiency. Barr & Stroud began to manufacture smoke indicators for the Admiralty in 1946. They improved on the design they were given, making the instrument cheaper and more effective, with a view to winning orders from merchant shipping companies concerned to improve oil fuel consumption control in the years of shortages which followed the war. Hundreds of Barr & Stroud smoke indicators were manufactured for the Royal Navy and for British and foreign merchant ships, and some were even installed in British factories after the

Ian Mackenzie with an FP4 dendrometer. The instrument was one of several produced using Barr & Stroud's vast experience in optical rangefinder design and construction.

passing of the Clean Air Act of 1956.[57]

In 1947, the Mensuration Officer of the Forestry Commission asked Barr & Stroud if they could supply a dendrometer — 'an instrument for measuring the diameters and heights of standing trees'— to help ascertain the trees' growth rates. The Swedish Liljenstrom dendrometer, invented twenty years earlier, consisted of a telescope with an angle grid and stand, but the Forestry Commission sought a less cumbersome instrument, capable of measuring a tree's diameter to within 0.1 inch at 30-40 yards. Seeing an opportunity to exploit their expertise in rangefinder design and to manufacture for civilian markets, Barr & Stroud produced a suitable design and, in 1953, their first models. The dendrometer was just 8 inches in length, weighed only 5 pounds and, working on the coincidence principle, measured trunk diameters of between 1.5 inches and 200 inches, as well as the heights of trees. Instruments were ordered by the authorities in charge of large tracts of forest in countries such as Canada, the USSR and China, and the dendrometer sold steadily until the 1970s, when the decision was taken to discontinue production.[58]

Two other projects undertaken just after the war provided less work for the factory, but confirmed Barr & Stroud's reputation as leading optical engineers and boosted the morale of the workforce during those difficult times. In March 1945 Sir Giles Gilbert Scott, the architect entrusted with supervising the rebuilding of the bomb-damaged House of Commons chamber, wrote to Barr & Stroud for assistance. He was 'anxious to know whether it would be possible to provide a periscope to enable the ventilation control engineer to see how many Members and Strangers are in the chamber at any moment, and where they are grouped, so that the ventilation can be adjusted accordingly'.   The firm set out to design an instrument with an optical system of about 85 feet, with several 'bends' to carry the light from a window in the roof of the chamber to the eye-piece in the basement. The periscope had to be incorporated in the structure of the building, which required that the firm worked closely with the consulting engineers.   A proposal design was finally submitted in August 1946, and an order received in July 1948. The new periscope was constructed at Barr & Stroud's factory, and installed in the House of Commons in the spring of 1950.[59]

Barr & Stroud were also approached at the end of the war to replace the old camera obscura on Castle Hill in Edinburgh.   The original instrument, installed in the nineteenth century, consisted of a rotatable mirror and one objective of 5 inches in diameter. However, only half a dozen people could sit in the upstairs room where the images of the city were projected on to a viewing table, and Barr & Stroud were asked to find a way of projecting the images through a hole in the floor to a more spacious downstairs room. Dr Strang set to work with enthusiasm. In 1916 he had helped design a camera obscura, which the firm considered might prove valuable for observation purposes in the trenches on the Western Front.   The patterns for the prototypes of this original instrument were broken after the Armistice in 1918, but Dr Strang was able to adapt his original design for the new instrument. He spent three months on the computations and calculations for the various lens systems, before a design was produced in September 1946. The new camera

obscura, weighing 257 pounds and costing £550, had a range of over sixty miles, almost twice that of its predecessor.   Since it was installed in 1947, hundreds of thousands of tourists have been able to see more of the Athens of the North (on a clear day!) than was possible before.[60]

The House of Commons periscope and Edinburgh's camera obscura were interesting projects, and the subcontracting work obtained after 1945 kept the reduced labour force in full employment, but Barr & Stroud could only return to pre-war levels of profitability by returning to what they did best — inventing, designing and manufacturing advanced electrical, mechanical and optical instruments. The firm had had to concentrate its energies on mass producing its established lines during the war, and had fallen behind its competitors in many areas of the latest military technology as government-assisted   research   and development work on innovations such as radar was placed elsewhere.   The board seemed unsure of what direction to take during the late 1940s, preferring to wait for invitations from government departments to take on new projects rather than to instigate its own development of novel defence systems. Fortunately, the Admiralty had not forgotten Barr & Stroud's contribution to the war effort, and offered every encouragement to the firm to become involved in updating the Royal Navy's equipment.

The Admiralty Signals Establishment invited Barr & Stroud to design a combined radar and optical periscope in 1945, and placed a development contract with them in March of the following year.   The firm succeeded in accommodating a radar aerial within the

An engineer at work on Edinburgh's camera obscura.

diameter of the periscope tube, by devising an aerial with a dialectric lens through which the radar beam was transmitted. During trials in 1947, it was found that the experimental periscope radar could operate at over twice the specified 8,000 yards, and a contract for prototype radar ranging and optical periscopes was placed with the firm in 1948. The prototype satisfied the officers who tested them at sea, and the radar ranging device became a standard feature of Barr & Stroud's periscopes after 1950.[61] The development of a 'telescopic high frequency and very high frequency aerial system', also known as a main mast assembly and begun in 1948 at the Admiralty's request, was also completed successfully, and all British submarines were equipped with the firm's main mast assemblies after 1952.[62]

At the end of the war, Close Range Blind Fire Directors were introduced to supersede HACTs as the control centres for defence against enemy torpedo and dive bombers. In the CRBF, a radar or an optical sight could be used to find and follow the target, the change of range rate was measured using a tacheometrical box incorporating a gyro control, and allowances for windspeed, humidity, and other conditions which affected the flight of projectiles were calculated. A sight spot was lined up on the target, the whole anti-aircraft gun system following the sight automatically, and the guns were laid and fired by remote control. Barr & Stroud made some components for the Admiralty CRBF until 1948, when the main contractors for the system switched to other products and orders were placed at Anniesland for the fully assembled and fitted units. Despite the complexity of the electronic and mechanical work involved in manufacturing the

CRBF units, Barr & Stroud proved highly proficient in this line of work and received a stream of orders during the 1950s. Barr & Stroud's CRBFs were installed mostly on aircraft carriers, and on cruisers such as HMS *Belfast,* but the Admiralty also ordered many to go into store, intending to install them on merchant vessels which might have to travel in convoys vulnerable to air attacks during any future war. The firm delivered up to one new CRBF each month to the Royal Navy until 1957, and made several CRBF skeletons for two years afterwards, to provide control stations for ship-borne Seaslug missiles.[63]

These first introductions to the latest in modern electronic technology were made at a time when the post-war lull in defence spending in Britain was coming to an end. The shock of the revelations that the USSR had successfully tested an atomic bomb in 1949, and what appeared to be the further evidence of the aggressive intentions of Russian-backed regimes provided by North Korea's invasion of South Korea in June 1950, persuaded the Labour government that Britain needed and must find the money to pay for a massive rearmament programme. Expenditure on military equipment had risen to £200 million in 1949, but in January 1951 the newly re-elected Labour government decided to go further and announced a three-year rearmament programme to cost £4,700 million. Although defence spending was cut from this emergency level by Winston Churchill's Conservative government after the election in October 1951, as the Korean War settled into stalemate and the perceived Communist threat receded, the priority given to the development of new weapons and defence equipment was maintained. Barr & Stroud were given the opportunity to make major contributions to the re-equipment of the British Army and Royal Navy.

Barr & Stroud's income from sales dropped from just over £1 million in 1946, when the firm's last war contracts were settled, to around the £500,000 mark in each of the years 1947-50. Although the firm received tax rebates totalling £129,054 during this period, after-tax profits were low.[64] Nevertheless, Barr & Stroud suffered far less from the post-war slump during the late 1940s than they had done during the early 1920s, and in 1951 sales amounted in value to £803,984. Government contracts, mostly for defence equipment such as submarine periscopes, naval gun sights and fire-control instruments, accounted for 39.7 per cent of this sum; sales to foreign and colonial governments accounted for 6.8 per cent and civilian sales for 53.5 per cent. Two-thirds of the civilian sales were to firms such as Ferranti and consisted of components required to complete their own government contracts.[65] Barr & Stroud seemed to be in danger of slipping into the role of a subcontractor for defence systems manufacturers, now that their own complete system, based around the optical rangefinder, had been superseded by new technology. However, events in 1951 encouraged the directors to believe that the firm could again become a leading defence systems contractor in its own right.

The Admiralty was anxious to ensure that Barr & Stroud's expertise in precision engineering and optics, and their excellent research staff and facilities were put to greater use than simply providing components for other companies to order. The greatest advances in military enabling technologies were in electronics, a field in which Barr & Stroud had already gained some experience in manufacturing special periscope masts and CRBF directors, and the Admiralty encouraged the firm to concentrate more of their resources in this area. In 1951, Dr Strang and Francis Morrison met with the Controller of the Admiralty and the Chief of the Naval Scientific Service and were persuaded to make greater efforts to catch up with developments in electronic technology. Dr Strang, Francis Morrison, and John Davy visited Haslemere, Witley, Portsdown, Eastney and Portland, where Admiralty research establishments were involved in advanced electronic research and development work and where experts explained to them the latest methods and prototypes under development.[66] Sensing that there could be valuable contracts to be won in the future, and that the firm could only ignore the Admiralty's proddings at its peril, the directors determined to broaden the areas of expertise already existing at Anniesland.

By 1951, many changes had already taken place at Anniesland. Four new directors had joined the board in May 1949. Andrew Alison, manager of the Commercial Office, Claud Foster, chief designer and manager of the Drawing Office, Ian Garvie, works manager, and Frank Gerstenberg, manager of the Optical Shop, had accumulated a total of 167 years' service with Barr & Stroud.[67] They brought to the boardroom first-hand experience of the managerial and technical problems which had to be faced in reorganising the factory to meet the challenges of working in new areas of technology. With the arrival of the 'new boys', Sir James French and Neil MacLean felt able to announce their retirements, Dr Strang and Francis Morrison becoming joint managing directors after MacLean announced his retirement in 1949 and alternate chairmen on Sir James's departure in March 1950.[68]

Neil Maclean's contribution to Barr & Stroud's success, since his arrival at the factory as works manager in 1904, was recognised by all at Anniesland. He was widely respected, by managers and employees alike, and his love of the firm and his affection for the men who worked for him in the factory were responsible for his decision to purchase eight acres of ground at Netherton, to the north-west of Anniesland, after the war. Two football pitches, a cricket pitch and a bowling green were laid out on the land, and a groundsman's cottage built, and Maclean presented the new sports ground to the Barr & Stroud Amateur Athletic Association in 1947. Ten years later, Barr & Stroud financed the construction of a pavilion at the sports ground, and Netherton remains the home of Barr & Stroud AFC, one of the most successful amateur soccer clubs in the West of Scotland.[69]

The rejuvenation of the board was accompanied by a drive to recruit new talent to work on the anticipated research and development projects of the future. Young men who had recent training in the latest developments in science and engineering were required to work alongside the talented but over-burdened managers, such as John Davy and Ian McKenzie, who would head the firm's drive to develop new products. The recruitment campaign was aided by one of Barr & Stroud's unexpectedly vital assets. The firm owned a number of flats in the West End of Glasgow, purchased as investments and rented out to members of staff. A chronic housing shortage existed in Britain after the Second World War, and young men just out of university, or newly demobilised from the armed forces, had great difficulty in finding homes. Some of the newcomers, such as Tom Johnston and David Ritchie, found the offer of a company flat to be an important consideration when deciding on their future careers, and the firm recruited several other young men who might otherwise have taken their talents elsewhere.[70]

The years 1939 to 1954 were immensely difficult ones for Barr & Stroud. Directors, staff and employees were under great pressure during the war to maintain high levels of output at Anniesland, to meet the needs of the armed forces. They had then to face several years of worry and uncertainty, as the firm contracted due to the loss of traditional lines of business and the difficulties of breaking into new areas of enterprise during the late 1940s. Fortunately, Barr & Stroud were able to retain the services of a team of scientists and managers of the highest calibre, who proved capable of grasping the revolutionary developments in science and technology made during the war. By 1954, they had already begun to explore the potential applications of opto-electronics and infra-red materials to defence equipment, while work continued on the development of a new range of civilian products. The directors realised that the structure of Barr & Stroud must be altered to meet the changing economic and fiscal environment, and to enable them to exploit to the full the products of the firm's revived zest for innovation. At an extraordinary general meeting on 8 June 1954, they agreed to increase the share capital of the firm to £500,000, by capitalising the General Reserve through the

Barr & Stroud's works in 1948, showing the extensions completed during the war.

creation of 150,000 new 6 per cent cumulative preference shares and 150,000 ordinary shares of £1 each.[71] New Articles of Association were adopted, Barr & Stroud becoming a public company under the Companies Act of 1948, and consequently it became possible for shares to be traded on the open market.[72]

There were several motives for turning Barr & Stroud into a public company. Dr Strang and Francis Morrison, the senior partners, held the bulk of the firm's shares, and there were worries that, in the event of both men dying, their families would have to sell the firm in order to meet large death duties. By creating a market in the shares, the firm had the opportunity of broadening its shareholding base, and raising additional capital to finance new business ventures. In addition, the directors, the existing shareholders of Barr & Stroud, would be able to obtain a realistic market valuation of the business, allowing them to calculate accurately their exposure to death duties and to make the necessary provisions.   To achieve these objectives, many of the new shares were sold by the directors shortly after the company went public.

By taking this bold decision, the directors were inevitably opening the company to new influences and to greater scrutiny by outsiders of their business affairs. However, Dr Strang and Francis Morrison maintained their control of the firm, through their ownership of the majority of the ordinary shares. Barr & Stroud's efforts to exploit new enabling technologies during the 1950s would depend upon the drive and vision of these two men.

NEW OBJECTIVES: 1954-1964

The decision to convert the very private business of Barr & Stroud into a public company in 1954 was taken at a time when the whole system of international defence, on which the firm had depended for its market since 1888, was about to be replaced by totally new concepts with the advent of thermonuclear weapons. Strategic thinking developed over two centuries was abandoned almost overnight, as military theorists tried to envisage the likely impact of these new weapons. In Britain the traditional role of the Royal Navy in defending the country's vital sea lanes during a protracted conflict was now considered to be impractical in the nuclear age. On land it was reckoned that battlefield 'tactical' nuclear weapons would be vital in checking a Russian advance in Western Europe. Apart from aircraft, the principal means of delivering weapons either nuclear or conventional would be by rocket. The belief that war would quickly escalate into a nuclear exchange made it unnecessary to maintain large reserves of either men or equipment and diverted attention away from the development of conventional arsenals. Although this fundamental change in defence thinking was to rob many long established naval and military contractors of their market, it brought new opportunities to suppliers like Barr & Stroud who manufactured technically advanced devices. Even in a much reduced armed service there was an urgent need to modernise equipment by incorporating the new technologies being developed as fast as possible by both the USSR and the United States of America.[1]

Like many of their competitors at the time the board of Barr & Stroud, led by Francis Morrison and Dr Strang, was composed of

Francis Morrison, alternate chairman and joint managing director of Barr & Stroud from 1949 until 1965. From 1919 he represented the company's interests in London.

ageing men who could recall only too clearly the consequences of investing in new technology in the depressed years after the First World War. However, the directors realised that if Barr & Stroud were to be anything more than very skilled jobbing engineers, it was essential to explore, even if tentatively, recent advances in optics.   Accordingly new laboratories were constructed in 1954 and 1955 to encompass not only mechanics and optics but also physics and electronics.   As part of this commitment to research and development, a plant was installed at the same time to enlarge the companies high vacuum capabilities for coating lenses.[2] Since all gunnery direction gear was controlled by

mechanical computational equipment, the board placed considerable emphasis on the quality of the company's gear cutting, purchasing new machine tools for the production of gears of 'super-precision quality', particularly intricate spiral bevel gears.[3]   In making these substantial investments the board was encouraged by the award of a number of military development contracts.   Some of these, like the re-engineering of the periscope to meet new service requirements, were in areas familiar to the company, others like the guidance test console for the 'Firestreak' air-to-air missile provided the first practical applications for infra-red technology emerging

The newly constructed electronics laboratory in 1954 designed to take the company into new enabling technologies.

from the laboratory.[4] The expertise gained by the management and their departments in the execution of these commissions provided the foundations for the future of the company.

By the early 1950s the British Navy's submarine fleet was rapidly becoming obsolete. Although all the wartime vessels still in service had been improved by fitting the Dutch Schnorkel system, developed by the Germans, that allowed for higher underwater speeds, they lacked sufficient power to exploit the full potential of this device.[5] Their hulls, designed for surface operations, were ill-suited to the long underwater patrols that were now possible.[5] Recognising that the construction of new vessels would require considerable research and development in every aspect of submarine design and equipment, the Admiralty chose in 1951 to refit and in some cases rebuild the existing 'T' and 'A' class fleet of thirty-three vessels. The hulls were streamlined and the bridge structure replaced by a sail or fin. All the external rigging was removed to reduce the risk of collision when coming to periscope depth.[6] No sooner had this programme started than watchkeepers began to report problems with the periscope due to higher speeds and the excessive vibration caused by the much larger unsupported length that now protruded from the hull. There was no simple solution to this problem and Barr & Stroud were invited to co-operate in redesigning the periscope, using the converted 'T' class submarines for their experiments.[7]

It was soon discovered that, due to vibration, it was not possible to follow the image using bronze tubes at speeds of over seven to eight knots. Bronze was replaced by austenitic stainless steel. Since the joint between the two tubes had to withstand greater stresses than before, new welding techniques were

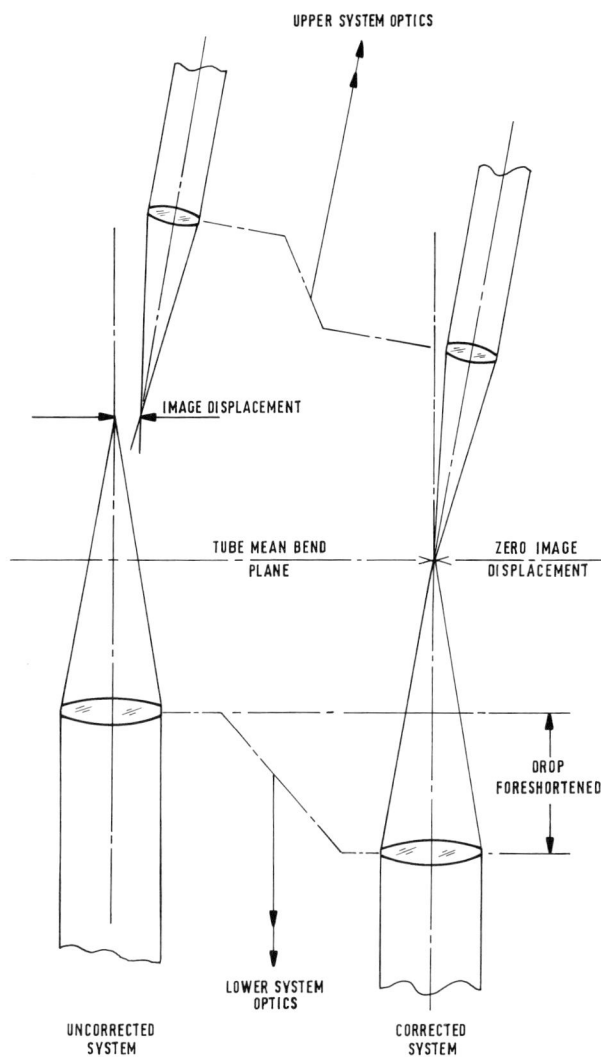

A drawing of the anti-vibration system for periscope tubes, illustrating the method of reducing image displacement.

developed. The elimination of vibration was much more difficult. On investigation it was found that at high speeds, when the Attack periscope was raised, eddy-shedding effects made it almost impossible to use the Search periscope positioned behind.   After many abortive factory experiments, a simple solution was conceived based on careful scrutiny of the way the raised periscope flexed under vibration, in the region where it enters the hull

through the submarine's sail or fin. However great the vibration, the upper and lower halves of the periscope effectively remain straight. Barr & Stroud proposed to the Admiralty that the inner periscope optical frame holding the lenses should be designed in two parts, the upper mounted in the unsupported section outside the vessel and the lower within the fin. To prevent loss of vision in vibration as the upper section moved, an optical hinge was formed by placing a focal plane between the two sections. As a result, the amplitude of the image movement was substantially reduced to the extent that the eye could follow it without loss of definition whatever the forces on either periscope.   To seal the window and the joints between the top of the periscope and the main tube, the rubber gaskets were replaced by the newly developed precision 'O' rings.   This made periscopes far more watertight than they had been before.[8]

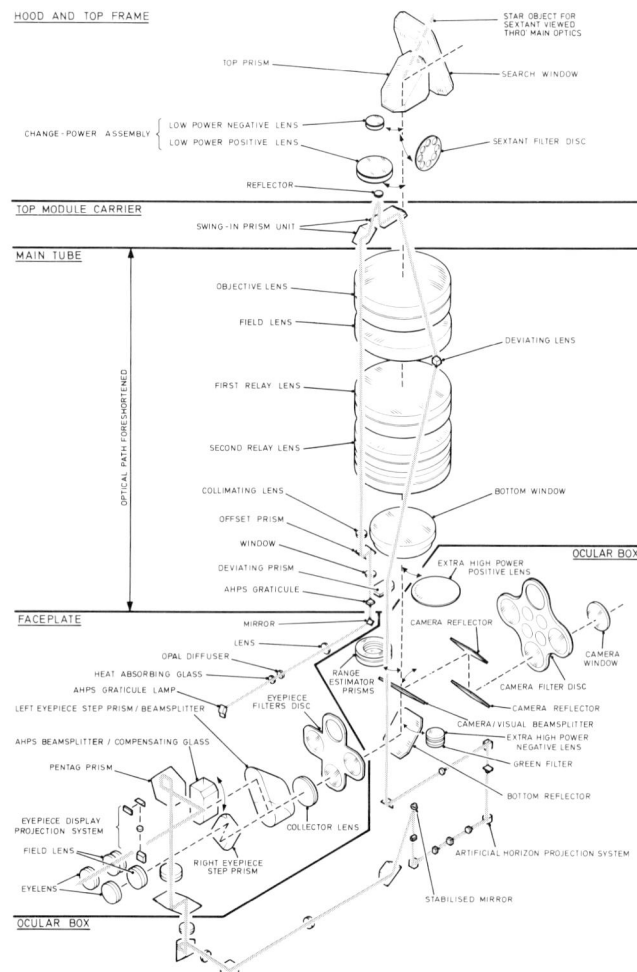

The long underwater patrols to be undertaken by the new generation of submarines made the development of the periscope sextant essential for navigation purposes.   Attempts to provide an artificial horizon from which to calculate the exact position had been less than successful.   In collaboration with the Admiralty Compass Observatory, Barr & Stroud produced a remotely controlled mechanism for elevating an upper sextant sighting prism in accurately known steps of elevation. It was agreed that the best position for the artificial horizon gyro was at the bottom of the periscope near the meta centre of the hull where acceleration forces were least severe. Such a position could only be effective if a means could be found of calculating the error caused by flex in the

Figure labels:
HOOD AND TOP FRAME
STAR OBJECT FOR SEXTANT VIEWED THRO MAIN OPTICS
TOP PRISM
SEARCH WINDOW
CHANGE-POWER ASSEMBLY
LOW POWER NEGATIVE LENS
LOW POWER POSITIVE LENS
SEXTANT FILTER DISC
REFLECTOR
TOP MODULE CARRIER
SWING-IN PRISM UNIT
MAIN TUBE
OBJECTIVE LENS
FIELD LENS
DEVIATING LENS
FIRST RELAY LENS
SECOND RELAY LENS
COLLIMATING LENS
OFFSET PRISM
BOTTOM WINDOW
WINDOW
DEVIATING PRISM
AHPS GRATICULE
OCULAR BOX
EXTRA HIGH POWER POSITIVE LENS
FACEPLATE
MIRROR
LENS
CAMERA REFLECTOR
OPAL DIFFUSER
HEAT ABSORBING GLASS
RANGE ESTIMATOR PRISMS
CAMERA WINDOW
AHPS GRATICULE LAMP
EYEPIECE FILTERS DISC
CAMERA FILTER DISC
LEFT EYEPIECE STEP PRISM / BEAMSPLITTER
CAMERA REFLECTOR
CAMERA/VISUAL BEAMSPLITTER
AHPS BEAMSPLITTER / COMPENSATING GLASS
EXTRA HIGH POWER NEGATIVE LENS
GREEN FILTER
PENTAG PRISM
BOTTOM REFLECTOR
EYEPIECE DISPLAY PROJECTION SYSTEM
COLLECTOR LENS
FIELD LENS
ARTIFICIAL HORIZON PROJECTION SYSTEM
RIGHT EYEPIECE STEP PRISM
EYELENS
STABILISED MIRROR
OCULAR BOX
OPTICAL PATH FORESHORTENED

Typical search periscope. with sextant optical system.

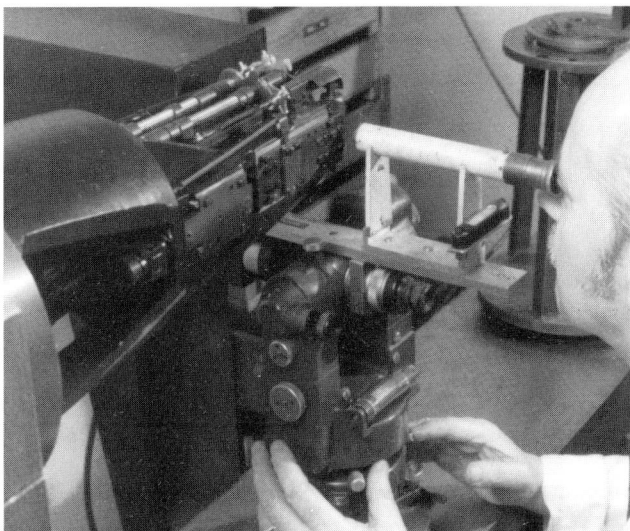

The highly skilled task of calibrating the early version of submarine periscope sextant with natural and artificial horizons in the early 1960s.

optical train which, because of the way in which it is magnified in the lower telescope system, could cause disproportionate errors in the final readings. Barr & Stroud contrived an elegant optical compensation measure; the Admiralty Compass Observatory devised the artificial horizon using a gyro-mounted mirror and a pendulum dampened in a silicone liquid.[9]

While these improvements were being made to the periscope, Barr & Stroud was also working on a Torpedo Control Calculator (TCC). A pilot batch of twelve was ordered during 1954 to be manufactured to the design of the Admiralty Gunnery Establishment. The equipment comprised the TCC, a complex assembly of gears and electronics, to compute the gyro angle for setting the run of the torpedo and Gyro Angle Re-Transmission Unit (GARTU) to convey the information to the torpedo positions. When the first models were

tested at Anniesland they fell far short of the estimated accuracy. A review of the design concluded that substantial modification was required and Barr & Stroud were asked to carry out a rigorous enquiry. The company, with its expertise in precision gear cutting, had no difficulty in locating the problem and recommended improvements which made the TCC accurate to within $\pm 1°$.[10]

In May 1955 representatives of the Flag Officer Submarines, the Naval Equipment, Construction, Electrical and Ordnance Departments, the Admiralty Compass Observatory, the Gunnery, Signals and Radar Establishment, and Barr & Stroud met at the Admiralty in Bath to review progress in the modernisation of the periscope and its associated equipment.[11] Commander Lane, who was responsible for liaison with the company, explained that answers had been found to most of the technical problems. These included the greatly increased turning torque which he had solved himself with the invention of an electrically powered roundabout which allowed the observer to remain seated, controlling the movement by pedals.[12] Known as the Lane Roundabout, it was to be incorporated by Barr & Stroud in a prototype of the new periscope. This was completed within six months and installed in HMS *Taciturn*. Sea trials matched expectations, with clarity of vision using the anti-vibration optical system at speeds of well over ten knots, and the sextant giving sighting readings using the natural horizon as good as those obtained from a hand held sextant.[13] It was to be another four years before the ACO was satisfied with the artificial horizon for star sights.

With all these issues still unresolved when the

The internal arragement of the Torpedo Control Calculator System Mark III (a) showing the complex gearing for working out the torpedo setting and (b) the Gyro Angle Re-Transmission Unit, a similar elaborate assembly of gears and dials used to convey the information to the torpedo positions.

1954/5 defence estimates were compiled, no further modifications of submarines in service were carried out until the outcome of all the trials were complete and the performance of the new periscope in the first experimental high speed submarine, due to be completed in 1956, was assessed.[14] The design of this vessel, HMS *Excalibur* was based on the surrendered German U-1407 and incorporated turbines driven by burning diesel in decomposed hydrogen peroxide. With an underwater speed of 25 knots, HMS *Excalibur* soon demonstrated the efficiency of the Barr & Stroud re-engineered periscope and associated

facilities.[15] Although this achievement coincided with a severe pruning of defence spending, Harold Macmillan's Conservative government agreed to press ahead with the refitting of the remainder of the submarine fleet. Over thirty sets of periscopes were supplied by Barr & Stroud during 1957 and 1958 for this purpose, in addition to the five sets already ordered for the new 'Porpoise' class which were shortly to be commissioned.[16] The company could also take comfort from the announcement in April 1957 that substantial progress had been made in the design of Britain's first nuclear-powered submarine, already named HMS *Dreadnought* after the similarly path-breaking battleship completed in 1905.[17] Apart from the British Admiralty, the Netherlands, Denmark and Norway, Italy and the countries purchasing the Oberon class submarines, placed orders over several years for the fitting of periscopes incorporating upgraded features.[18]

From 1958 the new periscopes also featured wire-heated windows that prevented the image

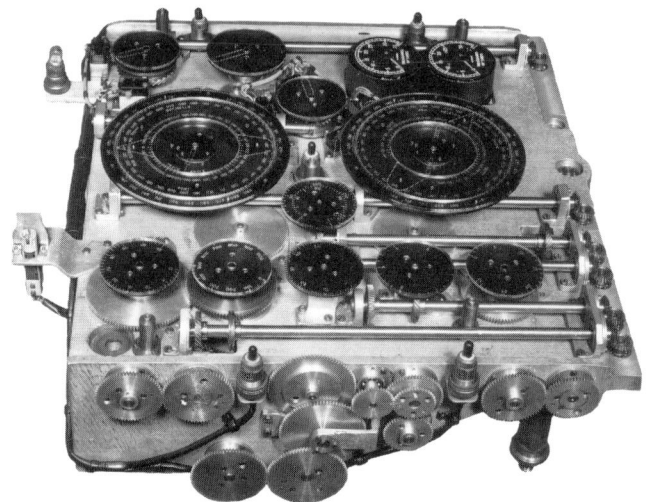

misting or freezing over. This problem had long troubled Barr & Stroud, but it was not until the mid-1950s that 'laminated glass', with heating wires sandwiched between, was commercially available. Assessment of early samples in the company's laboratories soon revealed that even the relatively low power loadings in the heating wires caused distortion, rendering them useless for quality optics. Undaunted, research continued to find the cause of the loss of definition in the image as heat increased in the laminated glass. By mid-1956 a suitable inter-layer material had been found which did not result in any loss of clarity, even under a loading of 1200 watts per square foot in an optical system giving a 15x magnification. So that the view would not be interrupted by criss-crossed heating wires, these were made from wire as fine as human hair. Techniques, protected by patent, were devised to lay the wires between the inter-layer materials. After exhaustive tests under all sorts of climatic conditions, from tropical heat to the severest Arctic weather, the Admiralty placed orders early in 1957 for fitting windows to the optical gunsights on vessels still in service. It took another year to produce a laminated glass that satisfied the much higher specification for periscope top windows. From 1958 wire-heated windows became standard in all Barr & Stroud's submarine periscopes. The United States Navy, unable to find an American manufacturer, had to turn to Barr & Stroud for windows for their submarine periscopes.[19] Subsequently, in 1972 a licence agreement was signed with Kollmorgen, the American periscope builders.

In the reshaping of British defence policy in the mid-1950s, considerable importance was attached to the development of British air-to-air and surface-to-air guided weapons using technology developed by the Germans during the war.[20] Amongst these missiles was the successful air-to-air Firestreak missile, which was guided on to the target by an infra-red system that detected hot plumes of air emitted from the exhaust of enemy aircraft. Although the continuation of the visual spectrum into the longer wavelengths, known as the infra-red, had been discovered in 1800, little practical research had been undertaken on its properties until the Second World War. Britain's investigation was abandoned shortly after the outbreak of war as effort was concentrated on the perfection of radar for detecting enemy ships and aircraft. In Germany and America, however, interest in infra-red intensified. By the end of the war a variety of experimental active and very near passive infra-red devices for detecting and ranging on enemy targets were being tested by German forces. Parallel developments by the United States National Defence Research Committee had resulted in a reliable infra-red image tube using active illumination for night sight by snipers. When the Allies discovered the extent and success of German use of infra-red at the end of the war, research was rekindled in Britain.[21] It was natural that the Radar Research Establishment (RRE) should approach Barr & Stroud, as leading military optical engineers, to help investigate the potential of infra-red.[22] One of the difficulties of harnessing the power of infra-red radiation is that glass is opaque to wavelengths greater than 2 microns. New materials had to be sought for manufacturing optical parts capable of transmitting and receiving infra-red radiation in the two atmospheric window bands of 3 to 5 microns

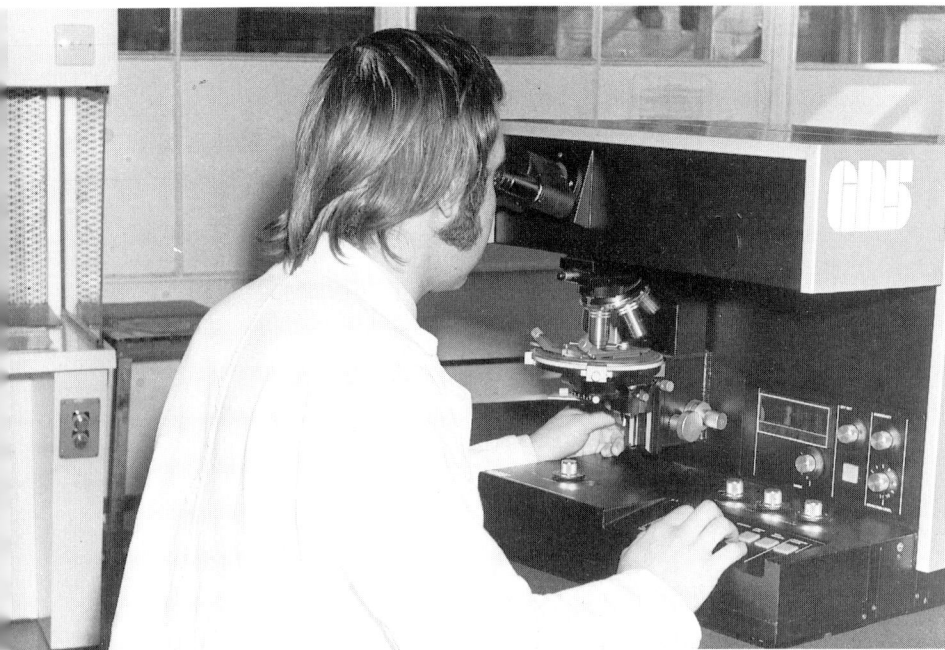

The upgraded GN5 version of the integrated microdensitometer, first designed by Barr & Stroud in the mid 1950s to distinguish between cell-types by measuring light absorption. This was Barr & Stroud's first venture into the market for medical intsruments.

and 8 to 13 microns.

In pace with American advances some such materials were being made in Britain by the end of the war, particularly arsenic trisulphide produced by ICI. When that company ceased its manufacture for the government in the late 1940s, all the stocks were transferred to Anniesland, and Barr & Stroud became solely responsible for smoothing and polishing this difficult and toxic substance. Working closely with the physicist, Professor R.V. Jones of the University of Aberdeen, the Company's laboratories began to attempt to grow large single crystals of other less dangerous infra-red transmitter materials such as quartz and germanium, using high-vacuum equipment.

The interest shown in these large crystals, termed 'boules' when they were first displayed at the Physical Society in 1954, led the board to approve a wider programme of research in November of the following year.[23]

The company's proven expertise in infra-red radiation led RRE towards the end of 1956, to support and extend research at Anniesland into the creation of new types of infra-red transmitting materials, to solve the problem caused by the absorption of infra-red by water vapour in all the existing substances. These new materials were to be tailored to suit different applications in the three regions of infra-red (near infra-red, the infra-red and far infra-red). Barr & Stroud soon developed the very effective calcium aluminate to replace arsenic trisulphide in missile nose-cones. Apart from the difficulty of growing the boules, the company's laboratories had also to pioneer methods of cutting and polishing the materials and coating the finished lenses with anti-reflective layers. The RRE was so impressed with the results of this project that it was continued, and Barr & Stroud received orders for the supply of many infra-red components, particularly missile sensor heads.[24] Knowing that Barr & Stroud were engaged in these studies, the Ministry of Aviation, during 1954, invited the company to design, originate and manufacture the Guidance Test Console for Firestreak. This instrument was to contain a precision infra-red optical system to inject infra-red radiation into the sensing head of the missile, and a complex electronic system to measure the resulting signals which controlled the movements of the missile. In carrying out this research dozens of new optical cements had to be devised to attach the nose-cones to the missiles. Delighted with the prototype console systems, the Ministry placed contracts for very large numbers with the company over the next five years, for Firestreak and later Red Top missiles.[25]

If infra-red stretched the company's optical capabilities, two other related contracts awarded in 1954 gave entry to the rapidly advancing world of electronics. Within weeks of the placing of the order for the Guidance Test Console, the company was invited to take over from R. & Y. Pickering of Motherwell in Lanarkshire the manufacture of test gear for the 'Blue Study' bomb-aiming device being built by Ferranti in Edinburgh. Barr & Stroud acquired equipment and technical staff from the Lanarkshire company as part of the deal. The personnel included a number of skilled electrical engineers, of which Barr & Stroud were badly in need.[26] The arrival of the newcomers was followed shortly afterwards by a more significant joint project with Ferranti to develop a broad band microwave homing device, known as 'Video Homer', to be installed in the Navy's new Buccaneer aircraft to detect enemy radar. This was one of the first pieces of equipment which had transistorised circuits to be fitted in an aircraft. The transistor had been invented as recently as 1948 and had only become commercially available within the last three years.[27] These joint projects with Ferranti, which were successfully completed, took Barr & Stroud into new territory, and a contract for production models followed. The expertise in electronics gained as a result came precisely at the time when microcircuitry was about to replace the cumbersome mechanical calculating devices for which the company's gear cutting department was renowned.

Despite the breadth and volume of the military research and development undertaken by Barr & Stroud in the late 1950s, it could not immediately generate sufficient contracts to keep the workshops fully employed. The loading on the expensive precision gear cutting machine was maintained by continuing to seek orders, albeit selectively, from other engineering companies, for the construction of

The Barr & Stroud high-speed CP5 camera which could take photographs at the rate of between 50,000 and 8 million per second. The only previous experience the company had in making cameras was a 7-lens instrument for aerial photographs produced during the 1930s.

sophisticated equipment such as numerical ticket printing, envelope making, toffee wrapping and cigarette making machines. The dendrometer and smoke indicator developed in the late 1940s and 1950s, brought employment for the optical capacity. Nevertheless, there was a continuing search for new products for the civilian market that could draw on the company's existing expertise.[28] Attention was focused on the medical market, the requirements of colour television manufacturers and the nuclear power industry.

A microdensitometer was developed in conjunction with academics for use in pathological laboratories to distinguish between cell types by measuring light absorption. When cells are coloured in a certain way, the amount of light absorbed by the stain is directly proportional to its mass. The microdensitometer measures the light absorbtion very precisely, allowing medical staff to distinguish between healthy and abnormal cells. This was vital equipment in diagnosing malignant disorders.[29]

In the knowledge that Barr & Stroud had been investigating interference and colour separation filters as an extension of their wartime development of anti-reflection coatings, the American firm Colorvision, had invited the company in 1953 to consider making dichroic coatings for plates in colour television cameras. Nothing came of this enquiry beyond a preliminary study by Dr Hope in the physics department, but in 1956 Barr & Stroud began work on the development of thin film dichroic coatings for prism assemblies and interference filters which had now replaced plates in colour cameras. These films, which are controlled by interference effect, permit the transmission of one colour and the reflection of all others. The first dichroic coating splits off a proportion of white light and the next two the primary colours, blue and red, leaving green to be transmitted straight through. The individual colour characteristics are then trimmed, using very precise optical interference filters. Each of these consists of a stack of individual films, deposited under high-vacuum conditions with every layer being a fraction of a wavelength of visible light in thickness. The first Barr & Stroud dichroic coatings were supplied to the Marconi company in 1959 and could be adapted for closed circuit, broadcast and telecine applications, and for converting colour into monochrome. Other orders followed, bringing good returns to the company for about ten years, when the system was superseded by other technology.[30]

Growing concern at Britain's overseas trade deficit in the early 1950s, coupled with the National Coal Board's inability to guarantee sufficient supplies to meet the nation's electrical energy needs, prompted the initiation of a nuclear power programme in 1955 which it was reckoned would save large amounts of foreign exchange that would otherwise be spent on oil. The Suez crisis of the following year exposed the vulnerability of Britain's oil supplies, leading to an expansion in the programme. With their experience in building a high-speed camera for the Admiralty-Research Laboratory at Teddington, Barr & Stroud were ideally placed to manufacture yet more powerful cameras designed by the Atomic Energy Authority to record very precisely the process of nuclear reaction. The contract for the Admiralty camera had been placed in 1948, but it had taken six years to develop a prototype capable of taking 50,000 exposures every second.[31] Two models were subsequently devised for the Atomic Energy Authority, one giving a frame shot and the other a streak, both depending for their successful operation on an extremely high-speed rotating mirror. In the framing camera, the reflected light from the rotating mirror passed through a series of lenses, which relayed the image on to the film to produce a sequence of circular pictures at the rate of between 50,000 and 8 million pictures per second. In the streak camera, the beam of light entering the camera was first focused on an adjustable slit and then passed through a relay lens on to the rotating mirror. The reflection from the mirror was focused on to the film recording the event as a continuous streak or smear. Critical to the operation of both cameras was the engineering of the mirror, which had to rotate at a maximum speed of 333,000 revolutions per minute. To ensure that dust particles did not scratch the mirror at this very high velocity and to reduce drag, the whole mirror assembly had to be enclosed in a heavy walled vacuum-tight casing. Due to problems with the ballraces and the prisms which required the mirror unit to be repaired at Anniesland after every thirty runs, the whole assembly was redesigned, extending the intervals between services to 5,000 operations.[32]

As a result of these initiatives and the other commercial jobbing work, Barr & Stroud were able to maintain their 1,500 strong workforce. At a time of little inflation profits remained buoyant, rising from £108,000 in 1954 and 1955, to £144,000 in 1958, allowing the directors to maintain a programme of re-equipping the factory with the most advanced

The gear cutting department after it had been re-equipped with the latest machinery during the mid-1950s. Barr & Stroud's high reputation for gear cutting brought in many outside contracts for complex instruments.

tools. Prudently they chose to preserve the company's investment portfolio of some £300,000, valued at £500,000 by the end of 1958.[33]

At the beginning of that year, on 1 January, the board was reconstructed by the appointment of five new directors drawn from the ranks of the senior managers who had been the architects of the company's technical achievements since the war. The new directors were John R. Davy, Ian H. Mackenzie, David S. Ritchie, Montague C. Timbury and W. Guthrie Strang. John Davy had joined Barr & Stroud in 1937 as a physicist, working at first on the use of high-vacuum techniques in coating lenses. Ian Mackenzie had been with the company since his graduation from Glasgow University in 1929. He had specialised in optics, becoming skilled in the final adjustment of instruments and rising to become manager of the optical department. Montague Timbury had come to the Anniesland works in 1911, just seven years after they were built, and since 1945 taken charge of the machine shop and foundry with the responsibility for winning outside commercial contracts. W. Guthrie Strang, the son of the managing director Dr Strang, had begun work in 1939 in the design office. David Ritchie, a Cambridge graduate, was the youngest of the five and the most recent recruit, only coming to Barr & Stroud after war service in the Navy and then taking charge of developments in the periscope.[34]

Although the existing directors Francis Morrison, Dr Strang, Andrew Alison, Ian Garvie and Frank Gerstenberg, clearly expected the five recruits to the board eventually to succeed them in the overall direction of the enterprise, they were not prepared, like many of their contemporaries in other British companies, to allow them to change their management style. This remained as it had been in the day of Dr Barr and Dr Stroud, autocratic, with Francis Morrison, based in London, and Dr Strang at Anniesland ruling with an iron rod. The board met largely to confirm decisions already taken and discussed matters like the award of individual pensions and allowances. There was no formal strategy for research and development. The individual directors were left more or less to run their own departments in a loose federation under the watchful eye of Dr Strang.[35] Such an approach was characteristic of much of British industry at the time.

However frustrated some of the new directors may have been by their lack of executive power, Francis Morrison and Dr Strang were committed to research and product development, particularly in optics. They were less confident in approaching the rapidly advancing field of advanced electronics

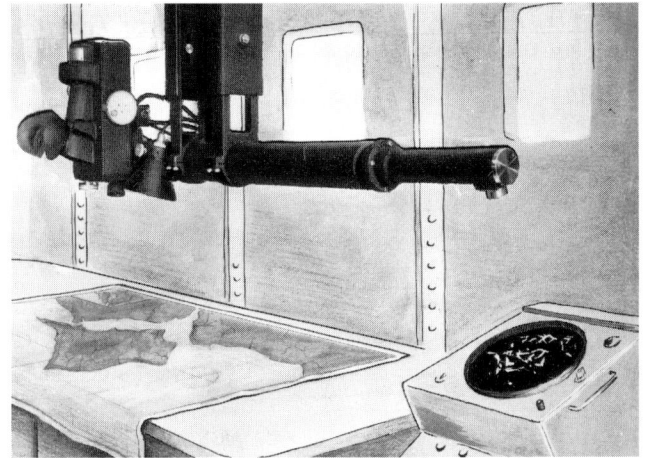

A radar navigational chart comparison unit designed to combine a radar with a chart image so that direct comparison could be made by navigators. This product was designed for both civilian and Admiralty customers.

except in so far as devices of proven reliability could be used as components in optical instruments. In the immediate future the much enlarged board was confronted with a marked change in government policy following the appointment of Duncan Sandys as Minister of Defence in January 1957. Encouraged by the new Prime Minister, Harold Macmillan, he had carried out a fundamental review of Britain's defence policy by early April, recommending a massive reduction in expenditure as part of an overall programme to reduce government spending to bring it into line with Britain's lacklustre economic performance.[36] There was no time to cancel existing contracts, but for the next two years Barr & Stroud remained uncertain as to how the stance of the Minister of Defence would affect the business. The directors warned in their 1958 annual report that the company was 'engaged largely on highly specialised Naval and Military work and the results are therefore influenced by government policies, British and Foreign'.[37] They were fortunate that the Government placed a high priority on research and development. Duncan Sandy's White Paper *Defence — Outline of Future Policy* in 1957 declared unequivocally 'If the weapons and equipment of the armed forces are to be kept up to date, adequate efforts on research and development are to be continuously maintained.'[38] This commitment was repeated regularly in subsequent reviews over the next seven years of Conservative government. In 1960 the annual *Report on Defence* stated explicitly — 'In all defence work the government's research and development establishments play a large part...The maintenance of the strength of these establishments is a vital feature of our defence plan.'[39]

Despite these assurances, Barr & Stroud did not escape unscathed from the defence cuts. By early 1960 the directors were forced to admit that the decline in work in progress during the previous year, from £1.6 million in 1958 to £1.2 million in 1959, was entirely the result of government policy. Their response was to 'continue to pursue the policy of broadening the scope of the company's products'.[40] After the delivery of the successful prototype integrated microdensitometer to the University of Glasgow during 1958, orders were received from hospitals and university medical research institutes in Britain and overseas.[41] During 1959 the contract was signed with the Atomic Energy Authority to start production of the ultra-high-speed camera. Before this could begin in earnest an extension had to be built to the West Works at a total cost of some £100,000,

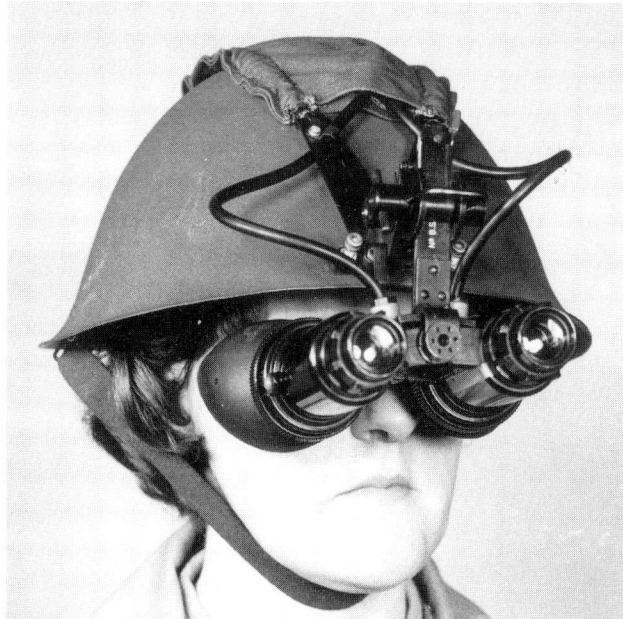

Have I got to wear this hat? The Ministry designed active common-user infra-red binoculars modelled by one of Barr & Stroud's employees. The infra-red searchlight was separate from the helmet.

to provide 'clean room' conditions for the assembly of the mirror units.[42] As part of the diversification programme the potential of existing civilian markets was reviewed. An opportunity was identified to build on the company's reputation for cartographic equipment by automating some of the processes previously carried out by highly skilled draughtsmen. With W.H. Dobbie McInnes (Electronics) Ltd, who made plotting tables, Barr & Stroud developed a system for projecting complete names from an automatically controlled projector mounted on to a numerically controlled co-ordinate plotting table. A projector similarly mounted, for drawing lines by moving a projected spot of light, was devised and patented at the same time. Although Dobbie McInnes subsequently withdrew from the project, Barr & Stroud persevered with the development of production models which were widely acclaimed.[43]

These forays into the civilian market, however accomplished, could not protect the company from the effects of continuing cuts in defence expenditure. Profits after tax collapsed to under £66,000 in 1960, just 6 per cent on turnover. At the July board meeting in 1960 David Ritchie, one of the new directors, called on his colleagues 'to consider new lines for discussion at a further board meeting'.[44] By the turn of the year there was a consensus that something needed to be done but no agreement on a course of action. Dr Strang and the senior directors, taking heart from public pronouncements about the centrality of research to defence procurement, hoped that salvation would come through further government contracts. They urged the staff to

make a 'good impression, particularly on the scientific side e.g. physics laboratory and electronics department' when the Minister of Technology, Lord Hailsham, visited the works in February.[45]

Any expectation that defence contracts would be forthcoming was quickly quashed when, in the early summer of 1961, the government was overwhelmed by a massive balance of payments crisis. The International Monetary Fund imposed a tough deflationary package leading to another round of cuts. As well as robbing Barr & Stroud of government business, these measures depressed demand throughout the economy, making it difficult to secure jobbing work and to sell those products aimed at the civilian market. To improve the marketing of existing lines, the sales organisation in NATO countries was reviewed during 1961. Several directors went on foreign tours and the network of agents was extended to give comprehensive coverage throughout

The Lister auto truck used to transport completed periscopes around the works.

Western Europe and North America.[46] There was concern amongst the directors that the company's failure to sell its goods and services might be due to other causes. In February the board had agreed to make 'preliminary enquiries...with a view to employing' Associated Industrial Consultants to investigate binocular production.[47] Although this radical proposal was not pursued, it heralded a fundamental alteration in the management of the company. At the end of October the board, in reflective attitude, decided to channel the 'development of new instruments into a few specific lines' such as 'medical, laboratory and printing'.[48]

With the nuclear power programme little affected by the cuts, demand for high-speed cameras was so strong that the company could not make them fast enough for the Atomic Energy Authority's laboratories. To ensure that this should not happen in future, shop orders were issued for ten framing and five streak cameras to be held in stock.[49] At the same time, John Gunn was instructed to consult hospitals and academic medical departments with a view to raising sales of the integrated microdensitometer and to finding new products.[50] The range of binoculars was reduced and the design modified to bring down the cost of production. All these efforts could not halt the decline in profitability from the company's manufacturing activities, which dropped below £33,000 in 1961, £2,000 less than the income from the company's investments.[51] In declaring this poor result, W. Guthrie Strang, who had succeeded Andrew Alison as secretary in July of that year, blamed a variety of causes:

Dr J.M. Strang signs the laser agreement with Hughes in November 1963. On his right is John Davy, and on his left Ian MacKenzie. The signing of the agreement was a momentous occasion in the company's history, confirming the long-held commitment to exploiting the very latest in enabling technologies.

1. The rise in wage rates introduced at the end of 1960. This loss, of course, increased the cost of all products and in many cases it has not been possible to increase selling prices owing to foreign competition.

2. The introduction by the Government of a pension scheme which involved a serious increase in overhead costs.

3. The heavy cost of developing new products and bringing them to a marketable state.

4. The general deterioration in the profit margins throughout industry.[52]

Valid as these reasons were, they could not disguise the fact that Barr & Stroud, like many other engineering companies, were in trouble.

To add to the board's problems, the results of the search for other medical products was not encouraging. After taking preliminary soundings, the potential of fibre optics for use in the diagnosis and treatment of disease was explored in detail. The possibility of transferring light by means of glass fibres had been known since at least 1920, when the Scottish television pioneer, John Logie Baird, had experimented with them to transmit pictures. He had been unsuccessful because of the loss of light from the sides of the fibres. This problem was not overcome until the 1950s, when American and Dutch scientists discovered that by sheathing each fibre with a glass of a lower refractive index the walls could be made to act like mirrors. It was now feasible to transmit light and possibly images through bundles of fibres made up into cable.[53] The medical profession were excited by the prospect of illuminating the inside of the human body to examine the various organs, particularly the stomach, without resorting to potentially harmful X-rays. Attractive as the idea was, it took many years to realise. Aware that fibre optics was a natural extension of Barr & Stroud's current business, the board authorised laboratory trials of the manufacturing process. Early in September 1962 John Davy and Francis Morrison's son

Gordon, who had become a director a year before on the retirement of Andrew Alison, were sent to ask the view of R.W. Cook of the Supplies Division of the Ministry of Health. When he confirmed that demand for such equipment from the medical profession was likely to be strong, the board decided to embark on a more ambitious research project.[54] Since no commercial products could be expected to result for some years, efforts were made through American consultants to obtain manufacturing rights for existing medical

Not just a black box, but a common-user active infra-red periscope sight for drivers of the Chieftain tank.

The Firestreak missile for which Barr & Stroud made the guidance test console using their newly acquired infra-red know-how.

A wire-heated window devised in the late 1950s by Barr & Stroud to prevent the periscope image misting or freezing over.

instruments. These efforts were fruitless. The only immediately practical new device to emerge from all this intensive scrutiny of the medical field was the rapid cassette changer for X-ray cameras. Developed in collaboration with the West of Scotland Neuro-Surgical Unit at Killearn Hospital, it enabled standard X-ray equipment to take a series of rapid exposures for such procedures as cerebral angiography.[55]

Although the Director General — Weapons, Rear Admiral R.E. Washbourn, made it clear during a visit to Anniesland on 2 July 1962 that his department had no work 'in sight' for Barr & Stroud, Dr Strang was still convinced that the defence market, both at home and abroad, offered the best opportunity for recovery and future growth.[56] In endorsing this assessment the board could take heart from a shift in government economic policy during July away from the deflationary stance of the previous summer towards a mood of expansion. This had important consequences for defence contractors, preventing any major disruption to development and construction programmes. For Barr & Stroud the end of the financial emergency brought the confirmation of further orders for periscopes for the Oberon class of submarines, which had succeeded the Porpoise class from 1960. Four of these submarines were to be delivered during 1962, and orders had been placed for an additional six to replace the obsolete 'T' class.[57] Reliance on nuclear weapons at all levels of military thinking over the past five years had closed the eyes of British defence experts to rapid advances in conventional weapon systems for the ground forces and their air support. Perceiving this widening gap in the country's armour, Barr & Stroud returned to the military

application it knew best, and began investigating the use of lasers for finding ranges.

Laboratory work on the laser started late in 1961, just a year after the first successful device had been built. The name was an acronym standing for Light Amplification by Stimulated Emissions of Radiation, which described the way in which a flash tube was used to excite a ruby rod to a high energy level which was released suddenly, emitting very short and very intense flashes of light in a narrow parallel beam. This laser light beam was not only very bright, but was also potentially intensely powerful, capable of cutting anything from the toughest to the most delicate material with great accuracy. Very rapidly, military strategists and medical researchers started to look for possible uses for this new invention.[58] Some predicted lasers could be used as powerful weapons to destroy enemy missiles and aircraft. As practical engineers, Barr & Stroud realised that the laser could be employed as an optical radar, without the same risk of detection and false echoes as normal radar. Experiments in measuring ranges by bouncing laser beams off a target began at Anniesland in September 1962 under the direction of John Davy, and within six months the Board authorised the design and construction of a prototype.[59]

Shortly thereafter Barr & Stroud were approached by the American owned aerospace corporation, Hughes International, who had recently opened a factory at Glenrothes in Fife. Hughes International were the overseas group of the parent company Hughes Aircraft Company, the first in the world to demonstrate a working laser. This company was also developing a laser rangefinder named, appropriately, 'Colidar' and was keen to collaborate, using private funds, in the design of an artillery model for NATO forces. The laser rangefinder was to be carried by observers to a forward position and the ranges relayed back to the guns by radio.[60] At the end of May, Ian Mackenzie and John Davy were sent off to visit the Glenrothes plant as a prelude to formal discussions. On receiving their favourable report at the end of June, Dr Strang moved quickly calling a board meeting and cabling the Hughes head office at Culver City in the United States to enquire about the patents position. Directly the reply arrived four days later, the board met again and on 5 July took the momentous decision 'to enter into a licensing agreement with Hughes whereby each company would make its technical know-how available to the other'.[61] Although the Barr & Stroud directors grasped the potential of the laser for rangefinding, it was a much more difficult task to persuade the War Office. The Barr & Stroud board was so convinced by the performance of the prototype that it was agreed in November 'to proceed forthwith with the production of six portable laser rangefinders regardless of whether or not a contract was received from the War Office'.[62] While this artillery model LF1 (Laser Finder) was being manufactured as a private risk venture, the company was invited to become involved in the competition for the design of tank sights incorporating a laser rangefinder.

Barr & Stroud had briefly manufactured a Ministry design 4-foot optical rangefinder for the ill-starred Conqueror heavy tank in the mid-1950s. Before this tank was abandoned, because of the damage its excessive weight caused to German roads, the rangefinders were removed, as the vibration upset the mechanism and rendered them useless.[63] The first requirement of Fighting Vehicle Research and Development Establishment (FVRDE) was to design a periscope for the driver which would allow him to observe his route and the target without the need to open his hatch. This was not a difficult task, and in June 1964 an order was placed for 600 drivers' wide-angle periscopes for the existing fleet of Churchill tanks, which were nearing the end of their useful service. The single-sight, named the Common User (CU) sight, was supported by an active infra-red searchlight to provide enhanced night vision.[64] FVRDE was busily engaged in designing a new and more powerful tank, the Chieftain, which would bear the brunt of a conventional attack in Western Europe. Since the Warsaw Pact's armoured divisions would always outnumber those of NATO in Europe, the Army was determined that the Chieftain would be provided with sights and rangefinders that ensured a rapid response and a high hit ratio. It was no longer possible to use the traditional method of ranging with tracer bullets fired from a machine-gun which could only travel 1.5 kilometres, because the gun on the Chieftain would be accurate up to 3 kilometres. Faced with this dilemma, FVRDE sought a radical alternative, inviting studies into ways of integrating a laser rangefinder into the sight, and inviting competitive tenders from GEC, Plessey, and Barr & Stroud. This was a critical contest for the future of the enterprise and the board was delighted to win the contract against such powerful adversaries.[65]

The new generation of tanks could only be deployed effectively on the battlefield if protected by a mobile, short-range ground-to-air missile system. The army had initially

Barr & Stroud height and stagger gauge which measured the height of the overhead electric wire above the rails and the amount of offset or 'stagger' of the wire above relative to the centre of the track. Between 1959 and 1977 the company manufactured eighty-seven of these instruments which were adapted from the coincidence rangefinder.

An intricate logarithmic gear cutting gear used for calculating ranges machined in the department in the 1950s.

A group of optical components manufactured by Barr & Stroud in the 1960s. The filters standing on edge in the centre have dichroic coatings. Two pentangular prisms are on the left and the rest are an assortment of lenses, all for 1-metre-base optical rangefinders.

The top stem of an attack periscope for an Oberon class submarine being reconditioned and upgraded at Anniesland early in 1988.

chosen to design its own system, the PT428, but this had been cancelled during the 1962 financial crisis in favour of the American Mauler missile. Undeterred by this decision, the British Aircraft Corporation (BAC) had proceeded in 1961, independently of the Government and at private risk, with a project to develop its own system, known at first as ET316. During March 1963 BAC invited Barr & Stroud to collaborate in the origination of the optical heads. It emerged that the servo-optical head would have to be a complex assembly, with a periscope sight incorporating accurate mechanisms for the transmission of signals to the computer-element of the tracker that controlled the flight of the missile. Development work, under the direction of Ian Mackenzie, proceeded steadily to evolve a prototype which would satisfy the exacting specification. The electrical circuits connecting the optical tracker to the computer were so intricate that forty-five slip rings had to be integrated into the periscope. In the foundry, techniques had to be evolved to make die castings of suitable quality. Numerous mechanical and optical problems had to be resolved, not least to ensure that the servo-optical head would be robust enough to stand extremes of temperature and hard treatment in transit over rough terrain.[66]

Barr & Stroud's ability to tackle a project as complex as the design and the development of the sensors for the ET316 and Seacat Dark Fire missiles involving advanced computer technology, stemmed from the long established expertise in optics, combined with new-found skills in electronics. Since 1959 the electronics department had been collaborating with scientists from the Natural Philosophy department at the University of Glasgow to put together one of the first digital computers. At the time the University, through the work of Professor Ivor Dee and Dr John Gunn, was reckoned to be far ahead of most other British institutions of higher education in its computer know-how. It took four years to complete the computer, named SOLIDAC. Although a pioneering achievement, the company turned aside from entering the computer business. Like the laser rangefinder, the work on the SOLIDAC computer and the ET316 tracker could not be expected to bring work immediately to the shop floor. SOLIDAC gained popular acclaim for its musical capabilities. Barr & Stroud's chief mathematician, T.H. O'Beirne, programmed the computer to play bagpipe music and produced a long-playing record of thirty-six examples of Mozart's Dice-composition music. Requests for copies of this record were received for many years.[67]

Apart from the orders for periscopes for the driver's sight in the Churchill tank, and for the Oberon class submarines, Barr & Stroud were engaged between 1962 and 1964 in the construction of periscopes to meet the most demanding conditions. During 1960 the company had responded to an urgent plea from the Atomic Energy Authority to supply a periscope within twenty-four hours to inspect the inside of the reactor at Dounreay in the far north of Scotland, which was behaving abnormally. With great presence of mind, a periscope for an X-class midget submarine was lengthened and adapted at break-neck speed to improve the field of view. It was flown to Dounreay, in time to beat the deadline. This wholehearted response to the emergency earned further orders for periscopes from the Atomic Energy Authority, including one for the experimental 'Hero' reactor installed in 1962. During the year Barr & Stroud submitted a successful tender for the supply of the periscope to the European 'Dragon' reactor being built on Winfrith Heath in Dorset. This was to be used to view the inside of the pressurised core chamber of the reactor, where the temperature could rise to 750° centigrade, and also inside the connecting transfer chamber. The image was to be presented on a low-light television monitor situated in the control room 80 feet below. Since the top of the periscope was to remain permanently in the reactor, Barr & Stroud hoped to guarantee that the total leakage rate would not exceed 1 cubic foot of helium gas in ninety years. In planning the installation the company chose a combination of two separate viewing periscopes, with the television cameras situated well down the periscope tube where there was no chance of irradiation and temperature distortion. Special stabilised glasses was used throughout the optical system. The television cameras to Barr & Stroud's own designs were amongst the first to be fully transistorised. The complete periscope was fully operational by the end of 1963. Further orders from the Atomic Energy Authority and RAE followed for a variety of special purpose periscopes.[68]   At the same time, so heavy was the loading on the submarine periscope department that in the spring of 1964 two additional long-bed periscope lathes were installed.[69]

The revival in defence spending between the summer of 1962 and the autumn of 1964, the final two years of the Conservative government, restored Barr & Stroud's profitability. This upturn did not close the management's eyes entirely to the difficult question of controlling production costs.   Rising wages and falling productivity were problems that afflicted the whole of British manufacturing industry at the time.   In January 1963 the board considered 'the serious effect of the high cost of manufacture' and, after some discussion, Gordon Morrison, Montague Timbury and W. Guthrie Strang, were delegated to 'see if an outside consultant engineer could be found to examine the rate fixed times in the machine shop and if possible the fitting shop'.[70]   They selected Associated Industrial Consultants Ltd, who had been proposed two years before to investigate the binocular department.   Their report was received in July. Instead of accepting the findings and authorising a reorganisation of production, the board, after considerable debate, simply noted them 'for future use'.[71]

Not all the directors were happy with this outcome, but there was little they could do. Their misgivings were echoed the following year at the shareholders annual meeting in May 1964 when R.S. Waddell, representing Barclays Nominees, subjected the chairman, Dr Strang, to a cross-fire of questions. He wanted to be told 'the main field in which the company does its business' and 'how much of the turnover depends on defence expenditure by the

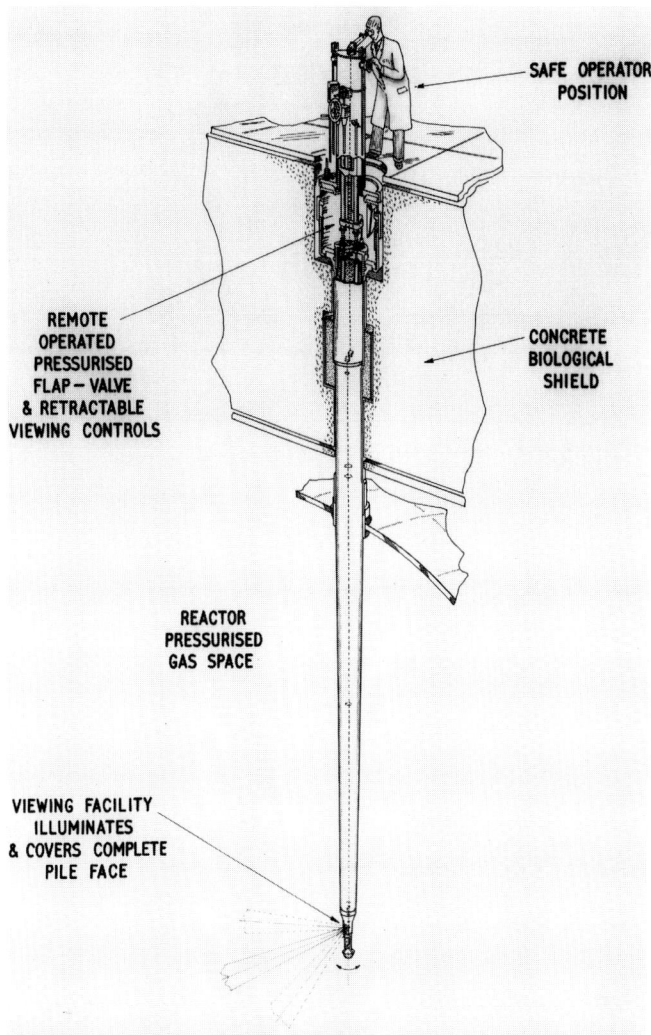

A drawing of the special periscope designed and manufactured by Barr & Stroud for inspecting the inside of the pressure vessel of the gas reactor at the Barclay nuclear power station in Avon, 1960. This was the first standard periscope for such purposes to be produced by the company.

Government'.   Less than satisfied with Dr Strang's refusal to answer, he pressed on, criticising the low rate of return on turnover and accusing the board of misleading

Fitting a CU9 driver's sight into the Chieftain tank, which succeeded the Churchill as Britain's main battle tank. In 1964 Barr & Stroud were invited to tender for the development of a laser rangefinder for this tank.

shareholders into believing economies had led to increased profits 'because on a strict comparison they had actually fallen'. His last query referred to the company's investments held in readily realisable securities, valued at £846,000 and representing almost £2.50 per share. Lying behind those questions was the decline in popularity of the Conservative government and the likelihood that the Labour party, committed to a policy of arms reduction, would win the forthcoming election.[72]

Despite these problems, Dr Strang, Francis Morrison and their fellow directors could take pride in the transformation of the company over the last decade. Older products had been updated and a range of new products created stemming from innovative developments such as infra-red, lasers, fibre optics and computers, together with the necessary enabling technologies. New skills had been acquired in the manufacturing and processing of advanced types of glass and in electronics. All of these were a tribute to the board's determination to be in the forefront of technology and its commitment to providing the necessary resources.

Since 1954 a coherent plan for widening the product base had begun to emerge together with a new corporate management style suited to the changing business environment. In ten years Barr & Stroud had won a reputation second to none in highly specialised areas of advanced technology most suited to military products. It remained to be seen if the Labour government elected in October 1964 would set as much store by the latest technology as had its predecessor.

THROUGH A GLASS DARKLY: 1964-1977

The election of the Labour government in October 1964 came at a time when the Ministry of Defence was in the throes of a massive reorganisation implemented the previous spring by the outgoing Conservative minister Peter Thorneycroft, and Lord Mountbatten, the Chief of Defence Staff. The crux of the changes was the replacement of the three service ministries with three Ministers of State within the Ministry of Defence responsible for each arm of the three services. Although the service chiefs protested loudly at the loss of independence, there was general agreement that co-ordination in research and development was essential if costly mistakes were to be avoided. This was to be achieved through the formation of two committees, the Defence Research Policy Committee and the Weapons Development Committee, which were to match new projects to available resources.[1] Under Labour these resources were set to fall once more as the Secretary of State for Defence, Denis Healey, struggled to hold spending at £2,000 million per annum at a time of rising costs. The most notable victim of this further round of spending cuts was the cancellation in April 1964 of the multipurpose TSR-2 plane.[2] Luckily for Barr & Stroud, Labour policy emphasised the need to continue improving NATO's conventional capability to lessen dependence on the nuclear deterrent. There was, however, no question of abandoning nuclear weapons altogether, despite a manifesto commitment to the contrary. To meet these twin objectives, Denis Healey had no alternative but to replace outmoded equipment with the best modern technology could provide. This led him to confirm the well-advanced preparations to buy from the

The LF1, one of the earliest laser rangefinders. Completed in March 1965, it was widely praised for its accuracy at ranges of up to 10,000 metres.

United States the Polaris strategic missile, to be launched from five nuclear-powered submarines for which orders had already been placed. The only concession to economy and the anti-nuclear lobby was the cancellation of one vessel.[3]

So as to fulfil Britain's role in the defence of Europe, work on the design of the Chieftain tank, the next generation of main battle tank was maintained. The change of government came precisely at a time when Barr & Stroud was seeking to finalise the development contract for

Installing a laser rangefinder gunner's sight in a Chieftain tank. The development of the first successful tank laser rangefinder by Barr & Stroud in the late 1960s made it possible for whoever fired the first shot in a tank battle to win an exchange.

the laser rangefinder for the Chieftain. The Ministry of Defence (Army) was not willing at a time of a further review of spending to guarantee the award of the first production orders immediately. Undeterred, the board agreed to press ahead with design and development of the artillery version to be used by forward observers. This was to be financed at the company's own risk and expense, on the same basis that research into the potential of laser rangefinding had been undertaken with Hughes Aircraft Co. The first prototype LF1 was completed in March 1965, and three months later it was demonstrated at an exhibition of new military equipment in Paris, where it attracted considerable interest. The British Army conducted their own trials in October on Salisbury Plain, which showed that laser range-taking was practicable. The minimum range of the LF1 was 300 metres and the maximum, depending on weather conditions, 10,000 metres, with an accuracy of plus or minus 10 metres. The weight of this equipment, designed to be carried into advanced positions, was 30 pounds with power pack, but excluding the tripod. The LF1 was placed on the market in March, and was the first commercially available laser rangefinder.[4]

By the time the LF1 was completed in March 1965, the Ministry of Defence (Army) had finally given authority for the production of six prototype (LF2) laser rangefinders for the Chieftain tank. Barr & Stroud had already proposed that, to make laser rangefinding as simple as possible, the LF2 should be incorporated within the armour shell of the tank and integrated into the gunner's sight. The design concept recognised the need always to maintain accurate alignment between sight and rangefinder. Although it complicated the design there was sufficient space within the hull of the Chieftain to accommodate the equipment. Working in close co-operation with the Fighting Vehicle Research and Development Establishment (FVRDE), it took the company more than two and a half years to develop the tank laser rangefinder. The first version was delivered for evaluation in November 1967 and fitted to one of the new Chieftains which had only just come into regular service. Exhaustive trials conducted at the tank firing range in Kirkcudbrightshire in April 1968 were outstandingly successful. After some modifications to improve the usefulness of the LF2 to the tank gunner, the contract for the first 200 laser rangefinder production models was placed towards the close of the following year.[5]

Winning this major production contract in a new technology was a considerable achievement for Barr & Stroud, the outcome of an amalgam of management awareness and skills not previously co-ordinated. Having identified the potential of laser rangefinding, the board, with courage and determination, had committed large funds and resources to a private risk venture and to fostering the relationship with Hughes International. After the prototypes had been successfully demonstrated, Barr & Stroud had won through difficult political and commercial negotiations to secure their first production contract — a milestone in the company's development. The enthusiasm it stimulated at all levels amongst the staff and workforce laid the foundations for entry into the larger and more complex electro-optical systems business both in the United Kingdom and overseas. In addition to the technical accomplishment, the development of the tank laser rangefinder represented a return to the marketing strategy summed up by Harold Jackson in 1904 in the phrase 'what the customer wants'.

Barr & Stroud were able to claim in 1969 that the LF2 was the first fully engineered tank laser rangefinder in production on the market. As intended from the outset, it combined 'the function of a laser rangefinder with the well established design of the tank gunner's sight'. Since the characteristics of optical sighting were retained, the only additional operation that the gunner had to perform was to press the laser flash button. The range could be read through an eyepiece positioned so that as little head movement as possible was needed. The combined unit was connected to the barrel by a parallel linkage, causing it to elevate or decline at the same time. As the LF2 was mounted inside the gun turret, it naturally moved in

An observer using the SOGs to guide the Rapier's surface-to-air missile on to the target. The missile launcher of this highly successful system is in the distance on the left.

azimuth with the gun. Both sighting and adjustment of the sight system simultaneously corrected the transmitting and receiving apparatus of the rangefinder. The top prism assembly could be replaced from inside the vehicle in the event of damage during action.[6] Although it was developed for the Chieftain tank, both Barr & Stroud and FVRDE were keen to emphasise that the LF2 could be fitted into any tank with sufficient space in service with

NATO forces and other friendly countries. Export orders quickly followed.

The introduction of the laser rangefinder into main battle tanks was the start of a new era in tank warfare. Range information until then had always been the prime variable in predicting the correct super-elevation to hit the target. Consequently it was accepted practice that several shots had to be fired before expecting to hit the target. Laser rangefinding gave, for the first time, unambiguous accurate range information out to all ranges achievable by tank guns, making it possible to strike the target with the first shot. Tactical thinking in warfare changed overnight to take on board the probability that whoever fired the first shot was likely to win an exchange. As a result, tank

Testing Rapier Servo Optical Groups (SOGs) at Barr & Stroud's Anniesland works before delivery.

commanders became increasingly anxious to make the interval between sighting a target and firing a shell as small as possible.

While research and development work into laser rangefinding was proceeding apace at Anniesland, Barr & Stroud did not neglect their interest in new vision technology, and in the design of the servo-optical tracker device for the British Aircraft Corporation's ET316 missile. In pursuing this work the Barr & Stroud board was encouraged by the cancellation during 1963 of the American Mauler missile programme, which held out the possibility of large orders for BAC's much more straightforward ET316 missile that was being developed as a private venture. The first test firings had just taken place with successful results.[7] Armed with the results of these tests, Ian Mackenzie, the director responsible for the ET316 project at Anniesland, pressed ahead with the perfection of the servo-optical head for tracking the aircraft and guiding the missile. It took a further four years' research and experimentation to achieve sufficiently robust equipment for service requirements.[8] When finally developed, the whole ET316 system comprised three parts, a fire unit, an optical tracker, and a generator, all towed by Land Rovers. After the missile was launched, the operator used a joystick on the optical tracker to guide the missile on to the target. As the British Aircraft Corporation had intended from the outset, the system was almost foolproof against low-flying aircraft and helicopters, it was in fact a 'hittile'. Officially christened 'Rapier', it soon became the principal surface-to-air missile (SAM) of the British Army and Royal Airforce.[9] Orders for Rapier Servo-Optical Groups (SOGs), as they were termed, flowed into

SHORTIE, a short-range thermal imaging equipment developed during the late 1960s and brought into production in 1971-72. It was at the time the best military thermal imager available in the western world.

Anniesland from 1970 onwards.

During the summer of 1964, to enhance Barr & Stroud's infra-red capability, a VIA induction furnace was installed for the vacuum melting of production infra-red glass for rocket cones. The Ministry of Aviation which, despite the formation of the Ministry of Defence, remained responsible for aircraft and rocket development, placed a contract in 1964 for test collimators or 'general purpose near infra-red test equipment' for the evaluation of various types of infra-red instruments.[10] Taking heart from the successful collaboration in laser production, the board discussed with Hughes International and the British EMI company the possibility of a joint infra-red research venture.

It was proposed that a separate factory for the project should be established at Hillington, an industrial estate to the west of Glasgow. This ambitious plan came to nothing and Barr & Stroud continued their investigations independently.[11] During 1965 experiments began at Anniesland into 'automatic optimisation' using digital computers to design new optical systems performing in the infra-red. The first trials were conducted on a Ferranti Sirius computer at Yarrows, but this soon proved too small and the work was transferred to the KDFG computer at the University of Glasgow.[12]

The drawback of the infra-red products that had been devised up to the mid-1960s for military purposes was that they worked in the near infra-red and required the active illumination of the target. As these could be detected by an enemy they were as unpopular with the troops as the Mekometer instruments had been during the Boer War. The development of efficient image-intensifier tubes working in the visible spectrum in the early 1960s offered the opportunity for the design of a passive sight for night vision. These comprised a specially designed large lens to gather photons in conditions of low light and a tube which converted the photons into electrons and accelerated them using high voltage on to a phosphorescent screen. The resulting image could be viewed by the observer through a conventional optical eye-piece. Barr & Stroud investigated their potential through the development of a small number of passive sights, exploring particularly their application in periscopes where normal vision was limited in the hours of darkness.[13] By 1965 a method had been developed for fitting the large lens required for image intensification near the top of the main tube in the attack periscope. This greatly enhanced visibility in starlight and moonlight conditions where there was light available in the scene, but did little to improve visibility in overcast skies at longer ranges, when there was little or no light. The intensified image, as well as being presented through a conventional eye-piece, could be relayed by television to a screen remote from the base of the periscope. Television recording of the view above the water markedly reduced the length of time the periscope needed to be raised. It was no longer necessary for the scene to be surveyed and assessed by the human operator, now the recorded image could be examined at leisure when submerged. These innovations brought orders to Barr & Stroud for retrofitting in the twelve 'O' class submarines and for the periscopes for the new Resolution class of nuclear submarines that carried the Polaris deterrent. Altogether over fifty sets were ordered by the British and other friendly navies, including those of Italy and later Sweden.[14]

Building on this achievement, Barr & Stroud concentrated their research effort on the next generation of night vision equipment, using thermal imaging techniques. In 1965 the first thermal image scanning head was assembled for the Royal Armament Research and Development Establishment (RARDE) at Fort Halstead for missile tracking. The device was designed to form an image from the infra-red emissions from objects in the field of view, normally in the band 8 to 13 micrometres, as compared to the infra-red band of 3 to 5 micrometres of hotter aeroplane exhaust gases. This was a major advance allowing television pictures to be created from heat emissions

The control room of a Royal Navy Valiant class submarine, equipped with periscopes fitted with torque assist motor and rotating wave guide coupling, in the late 1960s.

which could be detected even on very dark nights when the existing image intensifier would have been able to record next to nothing. For the first time it was practical to think in terms of 24-hour surveillance of enemy targets.[15] In creating an effective system Barr & Stroud extended research into the growing of large germanium boules and the development of suitable anti-reflection coatings to maximise the capture of the infra-red.[16] Three prototypes were developed from 1966 before the production in 1971/72 of IR4, named SHORTIE, a short-range thermal imager. SHORTIE, although bulky and heavy by subsequent standards, was the best military thermal imager available anywhere in the western world at the time.[17]

Although laser and infra-red imaging equipment carried Barr & Stroud into uncharted territory, there still appeared to be a military demand for the company's more traditional skills. Early in 1965 the Admiralty Compass Observatory at Slough proposed the

Dr J. Martin Strang who was sole chairman and managing director of Barr & Stroud from 1965 until his retirement in May 1968. He was awarded the CBE in 1966 in recognition of his contribution to the British defence industry and to the Boys Brigade.

joint design and manufacture of a magnetic compass test table which incorporated a 16-inch turntable and optical components demanding a high standard of engineering. This device was reported to be urgently required for the evaluation of marine magnetic compasses to conform to the stringent specification laid down in the recently issued recommendations from the International Standardisation Organisation. The design and manufacture of the equipment was not without its problems. The castings and other materials had to be carefully chosen and their non-magnetic qualities and durability thoroughly assessed. The electric motors for the turntable drives had to have closely contained magnetic fields. The Compass Inspectors needed to have a clear, accurate and full-size overhead view of the compass under test and a precise master reference graticule had to be optically super-imposed on the image of the compass. By May 1966 the Admiralty Compass Observatory was sufficiently pleased with the development work to negotiate a contract for production modules. The prototype was modified during the following year to improve its performance and provided the basis for the production specification issued in July 1967. As this equipment for testing marine compasses began to be delivered, Barr & Stroud adapted and simplified the design for evaluating aircraft and hand-held compasses. Unfortunately for the company, after conquering the very difficult technical problems of making the test table, the market for the equipment did not materialise as the new International Standard failed to gain acceptance.[18]

The redesign of the compass test table to find a wider market that was not necessarily military was indicative of a quickening of effort to find other civilian products, particularly in the medical field. Early in 1964 the Ministry of Health enquired whether Barr & Stroud would be interested in joining with the Genito Urinary Manufacturing Co in making medical endoscopes incorporating fibre optics.[19] Despite the rejection of this proposal, the board decided to devote additional resources to investigating techniques of assembling fibre optic bundles. Within eighteen months the directors were confident enough to enlarge the scope of fibre optic manufacture by the creation within the Anniesland works of an air-conditioned 'clean' department. When fully operational in 1966, this housed drawing furnaces for making the fibres and laminar-flow clean air benches and other equipment, all designed by the company, for bundling the fibres.[20] The first products were light guides supplied with a high intensity light source for use principally by dentists who require hand-held cold illuminators for their work. Technically the device performed well, but dentists were reluctant to buy them in sufficient numbers to make the product viable.[21] The medical application of the laser was also investigated in collaboration with ophthalmologists at Glasgow University, who were interested in its use for the treatment of detached retinas. In this procedure the retina is welded back into place by using a very fine laser beam. In the laboratory at Anniesland, a laser was fitted to a commercially available ophthalmoscope and successfully used by an eye surgeon to perform such an operation at a local hospital. A few trial models were made available to Glasgow doctors, but it rapidly became apparent that further refinement was necessary before commercial production could be contemplated. With competitors beginning to market fully developed equipment, Barr & Stroud decided to abandon this venture, concentrating their laser expertise on defence projects.[22] An attempt to create a medical thermal imaging system (videotherm) met a similar fate.[23] Discouraged by these failures, the directors were reluctant to spend money on upgrading the integrated microdensitometer which was in danger of being made obsolete by a competitor's equipment.

With confidence drawn from their past sales record, Barr & Stroud were persuaded to invest in improvements to the automatic drafting projector and control for the Norwegian Kongsberg Vapenfabrikk, which was instrumental in enabling them to become one of the world's leading manufacturers of mapping systems. The first four upgraded PS5 systems were delivered in 1968 and by 1970 over twenty-seven had been supplied. The PS5 system was an integrated package for use with digitally controlled drafting tables, providing the automatic exposure on photosensitive material of a wide variety of high quality lines,

Pressure testing a radar dish in the large pressure vessel in the West Works at Anniesland, one of the many tests carried out by the Quality Control Department since its formation in 1968.

The Vale of Leven factory, acquired in 1970 to provide clean-room conditions for the production of crystals and optical fibre.

symbols and alpha-numeric characters for cartographic and general drafting. The performance of the system in carrying out even the most difficult mapping operations, such as the drawing of parallel lines to represent roads, was greatly admired and proved a profitable and continuing product with sales to cartographic establishments around the world.[24]

Despite increased loading on the shop floor in 1964, Dr Strang and his colleagues on the board remained concerned about the high level of costs in the workshops. The reaction of Montague Timbury, who was the director responsible for production in the mechanical engineering shops, was to seek more jobbing work in an effort to distribute the costs more widely, rather than to search for means of reducing costs by organisational improvements.[25] Such a response was commonplace amongst British engineering management at the time and it usually took a takeover by a larger company to impose new production methods in the context of realistic financial forecasts. Although the problem remained unresolved, the Barr & Stroud board decided to spend £200,000 from the company's reserves by adding two additional floors to the single-storey building fronting Bearsden Road, adjoining the central tower of four storeys. The 46,000 square feet of additional floor space was to be used for the fitting and testing of precision instruments in clean conditions and for high vacuum deposition.[26] Before this was completed towards the end of 1966, advanced machinery had also been purchased for the Optical Department and the machine shop. These included one of the recently introduced tape-controlled drilling machines.[27] The introduction of new technology on to the shop floor was essential if Barr & Stroud were to possess the skill to manufacture the equipment that was under development in the laboratories. During 1968 an Environmental Test laboratory was established to assess the performance of products, particularly the Rapier SOG systems, under every climatic extreme. It contained a variety of sophisticated equipment, including hot and cold chambers fitted with vacuum facilities to simulate rapidly changing altitude, an electromechanical vibration system with a range from 5 to 5,000 cycles per second and bump and shock machines.[28]

The decisions to make these investments in new plant and equipment were taken by a reconstructed board of directors. After fifty years with the company, Frank Gerstenberg, the director in charge of the Optical Glass and Components Department, died in February 1965. He was replaced on the board by Eric Brash, who had first joined the firm in 1937. Francis Morrison stood down as alternate chairman and managing director in 1965 after fifty-five years of service, of which nearly fifty had been as a director. Dr Strang, now in his mid-seventies, decided to perform the duties of chief executive and chairman, instead of appointing a new managing director. During

July 1965 Tom Johnston who, since his recruitment in 1951, had specialised in manufacture including all the new devices emerging from development, was made a director. In a new role building on this experience, he was to be responsible for supervising the various projects under development in an effort to co-ordinate progress on the company's ventures into new technologies.[29] Dr Strang's contribution to the defence industry was publicly recognised in 1966 by the award of a CBE. After three years in sole charge of the business, he retired in May 1968. His son, W. Guthrie Strang, and Gordon Morrison, the son of Francis Morrison, took over their fathers' responsibilities of alternate chairmen and managing directors.[30] David Ritchie resigned his post to pursue other

Up periscopes! The five masts of an Oberon or Porpoise submarine. From left to right, the snort exhaust and induction, the ESM mast and the search and attack periscope.

business interests, but remained as a consultant.[31] The other directors pressed for changes, especially the appointment of a managerial team within the company which would be responsible for day-to-day administrative problems, leaving the board free to concentrate on wider issues.[32] This was agreed and a team appointed in June. For the first time senior managers were given job descriptions and titles which denoted their area of responsibility.

As in many long-established engineering concerns at the time, perhaps the greatest concern of the newer directors was the shape and effectiveness of the company's marketing arrangements. Since 1893 overseas sales had been negotiated through specially appointed agents with knowledge of defence procurement in their own countries. By the late 1960s there were some twenty-five agents in twenty-two different countries. With the introduction of so many new products during the last twenty years directors had periodically visited the company's agents to explain technical developments and describe operating features. The increasing availability of reliable intercontinental air services made such personal contact much simpler and more regular. Towards the end of 1968 the board decided the time had come to call an agents' seminar at Anniesland. Scheduled for April 1969, invitations were accepted from agents in countries as far apart as Australia, Austria, Denmark, France, Germany, Holland, Israel, Italy, Japan, Norway, Sweden and Switzerland. The programme included a comprehensive tour of the works and lectures and demonstrations of Barr & Stroud equipment for both military and civilian markets.

Prominence was given to recent introductions, notably fibre optics, lasers, optical and electronic filters and infra-red material. Throughout the three days of the seminar the directors were at pains to emphasise the company's roots in the long tradition of Scottish engineering. The agents were taken on a tour of the local countryside and were given a chance to sample another quintessentially Scottish product at a distillery. Pathbreaking as such a meeting was, it could only be of benefit in a fiercely competitive world market if Barr & Stroud could continue to innovate and manufacture their products at the right price.[33]

Within the boardroom there was disagreement about the future direction of the enterprise. Some favoured a more coherent approach to research and development and a greater emphasis on new technology, particularly electronics. John Davy was keen to advance into new areas of research, particularly in the field of telecommunications. He was resisted by those who considered that work on the lasers and thermal imagers should be consolidated before other projects were initiated. Disappointed, he fell ill and was away from work for six months, returning as a non-executive director.[34] As at other times in the last decade there was concern that costs were escalating and even in danger of running out of control. Against a background of general wage and price inflation which the Labour government was unable to control, there was a tendency to blame the company's problems on external factors rather than to take measures to cut costs.[35] However, with the Ministry of Defence demanding a more detailed breakdown of costs before settling accounts,

A B0105 helicopter with a Ferranti-Barr & Stroud IR18 heliball.

the issue could not be ignored.

One of the chief difficulties confronting the management in addressing the problem of cost control was the advanced nature of many processes, and the insistence by the Ministry of Defence on ever more exacting standards. From 1959 the company had been responsible for the quality control of their British defence contracts, within the so-called 'Approval Scheme'.[36] Barr & Stroud had been awarded development contracts since then by the various government research establishments because quality control was assured. This had led to the formation of a Quality Control Department in 1968 to monitor each stage of the manufacture of every product. The new department, managed by Robert Bell, had an extensive remit, requiring offices and workshops.[37] The factory at Anniesland was rapidly becoming congested and extra space was badly needed for making fibre optics and special glass, particularly for infra-red lenses. The directors, appreciating the need for investment in new enabling technologies, approved the expenditure of £80,000 on plant in the autumn of 1968. Some of this allocation was employed by Montague Timbury to purchase high-speed tools for machining aluminium that was to be used for many of the components of the new generation of products.[38]

Apart from the demands of the new Quality

The thermal imaging sight for the Swingfire missile system, designed to extend the usefulness of the weapon into the hours of darkness.

Control Department, additional house room was also required for a very large prospective order for Rapier SOGs from Libya and contracts for laser rangefinders promised by the British Ministry of Defence. There were two choices — either to extend the Anniesland works yet again or obtain, at less cost and trouble, a ready-made modern factory capable of conversion to a clean room environment. After only a short search an ideal factory was found on an industrial estate in the Vale of Leven, 13 miles to the west of Anniesland, near Loch Lomond. Previously used for the manufacture of watches, it was already fitted with filtering and air-conditioning plant. Unfortunately, this proved to be less than adequate for the very clean conditions needed for the manufacture of fibre optics and growing crystals. A totally new plant had to be installed, providing a clean room of almost 5,500 square feet. The transfer of production proved to be a much more difficult task than had been originally envisaged. The special glass furnaces could only be moved after the electrical supply had been upgraded to provide sufficient voltage. Fibre optic manufacture had to be maintained at Anniesland until the day of the removal so that there was no interruption. The Strathleven factory, as it was named, did not become fully operational under the supervision of Eric Brash until September 1970.[39]

By this time Barr & Stroud, like most other British engineering companies, was facing a serious crisis. Since the election of the Labour government in 1964, profits had remained steady at almost exactly 10 per cent of turnover. This had risen from £1.6 million in 1965 to a little under £2.3 million in 1968.[40] The first hint of trouble came the following year when turnover jumped by 18 per cent, but profits retreated. As in 1964, it was the annual meeting of the shareholders which sought to discover if this was due to an increase of productivity or rising costs. The chairman had to admit that costs had grown but added, by way of mitigation, that a major factor was 'the long-term nature of some large contracts, particularly periscopes', which were taken into the accounts in the year in which they were completed.[41] The board was, however, seriously concerned at 'its continual and accelerating increase in costs'.[42] Urgent action was taken to try to solve the problem. Unbeknown to the outside shareholders such a tightening of management was essential, for in February 1969 the company had been approached with a view to takeover by the American International Telephone and Telecommunications Corporation. The directors rejected this unwelcome bid, but were no doubt thankful that they had taken the precaution just the year before to alter the Articles of Association so as to prevent the company falling into foreign hands.[43]

Within a month of the ITT offer, measures had been taken to bring some degree of co-ordination to development work through the formation of an Instrument Development Department under Ian Mackenzie, who had almost single-handed supervised the work on the Rapier servo-optical group.[44] With the additional responsibility for the Electronics and General Physics Departments, Ian Mackenzie quickly found his new role too demanding. He

The highly successful IR18 thermal imager with x6 telescope which went into production at Anniesland from 1978.

became unwell and was forced to resign from the board in the summer of 1970. At much the same time, Montague Timbury retired as production director after fifty-nine years with the company. To fill the gap left by Ian Mackenzie, David Ritchie was recalled to the board as technical director with overall supervision of all the company's technical activities, from research and development through to the start of production.[45] Tom Johnston took over as production director, a natural progression from his job as projects director, where he had been responsible for ensuring that timetables were adhered to. In assuming Montague Timbury's role he also took charge of the company's labour relations.[46]

These changes were critical, not just because the company was in a tight financial corner, but also because the newly elected Conservative government was engaged in a fundamental review of the procurement of defence materials with the principal purpose of getting better value for money. Tom Johnston immediately consolidated cost-saving initiatives and took the important decision to stop taking on precision engineering subcontract work. He could do this because the products evolved over the past five years had started to come on stream. By not taking on outside work, he was able to prevent damage to his sophisticated tools caused by machining cast iron. Freed of the necessity of spending much of his time as Montague Timbury had done, searching for such outside business, Tom Johnston devoted his energies to the problems of manufacturing defence equipment.[47] David Ritchie, encouraged by W. Guthrie Strang, began to streamline research and development, discontinuing projects that had little chance of yielding commercial results. He called a halt to the recruitment of specialist staff, seeking to make more effective use of existing resources through the creation of clear co-ordinated project structures with delegated management. He won authority from the

Burglars or chimney-sweeps? Caught red handed by the IR18.

board to investigate the potential of computers to the company's operations.[48]

These reforms did not come in time to prevent Barr & Stroud slipping into the red during 1970. Gordon Morrison made no secret of the fact that this outcome was entirely 'due to increased costs'. Some of these were largely outside the company's control - notably rising wages, material prices and interest rates. Others had been incurred from a conscious decision by the board to invest the company's own money in developing the new military products, taking them a stage further than government funding permitted. With an overdraft that had increased tenfold in a year, from £31,000 to £317,000, Gordon Morrison emphasised that the board had taken action to steer the company back to profitability.[49] The casualties of Tom Johnston's campaign to reduce costs in 1971 were the closure of the glass foundry established during the First World War and the discontinuation of the manufacture of civilian binoculars in the face of mounting Japanese competition. The glass foundry was badly in need of modernisation, but costly new investment could not be justified as high-quality optical glass made using the novel flow line techniques was readily available from a number of suppliers.[50] While these necessary measures were being pushed through, it was considered prudent to defer planned investment in new equipment until priorities had been reassessed.

In charting the future of the company, the directors had to adjust to the Conservative government's reorganisation of defence procurement. Although the report on government organisation for defence procurement and civil aerospace by Derek

Rayner of Marks & Spencer had stressed the importance of production contracts following a development programme, it recommended that research and development could be made more cost-effective by obliging companies to share some of the risk.[51] This stimulated more

A fibre optic display.

effective control of research and development through the introduction of project management techniques by the Ministry of Defence and its contractors. At Barr & Stroud there was a general conviction that this new approach to technical management would allow the company to take more advantage of government sponsored research and development initiatives.[52] The first opportunity to test this assumption came early in 1971 when Decca Ltd invited Barr & Stroud to collaborate in the design and development of an Electronic Support Measure (ESM) mast for submarines. The purpose of the ESM mast was to detect, passively, radar transmissions from enemy search aircraft and helicopters before they could locate the submarine as a target. It was not sufficient just to detect radar but to distinguish between different types of signals to discover if the source was friendly or hostile. This was to be achieved through the installation of a computer library giving the parameters of all known radars, both friend and foe, military and civil. The mast was also to be used to gather electronic intelligence (ELINT) from hostile sources. Like the periscope, the ESM mast had to be raised and lowered, but since the ESM antennae were omnidirectional, there was no need for the whole mast to rotate. In developing the mast Barr & Stroud was to contribute its expertise in making periscopes and Decca Ltd its skill in radar technology.[53] This project, along with other MOD research and development contracts in hand, was to be conducted within more stringent budget limits.

This constraint also applied to the substantial re-engineering of the Rapier SOG system for installation complete with launcher in a tracked vehicle. No sooner had the early Rapier models become available during 1970, than the British Army was calling for a more mobile version. The original three-part system towed by Land Rovers took fifteen minutes to manhandle into position. The operator had then to commence his surveillance, either visually or later with Blindfire radar equipment. This all took time, which could have been saved if the whole assembly was fitted to a tracked vehicle. This was easier said than done as the SOG had to be refashioned to make it robust enough to withstand the shock of the missile launcher mounted close by. Oddly, the chief impetus for this upgrading of Rapier did not come from the requirements of the Ministry of Defence, but from the prospect of substantial orders from friendly countries in the Middle East. During the mid-1970s BAC secured a large contract from the Shah of Iran for Rapier systems installed on modified American M578 tracked cargo carriers.[54]

At the height of the changes at Barr & Stroud, Ian Garvie, the senior director, died at the age of seventy-nine in February 1971 after sixty years with the company. Although an old man, his counsel had been invaluable to the younger directors in meeting the company's current difficulties.[55] His place on the board was filled by John C. Gunn, the company secretary. When John Gunn came to prepare the next annual report and accounts for the year 1971, Barr & Stroud were in considerably better fettle than a year earlier, with profits of almost £120,000.[56] The company was, however, not out of the wood. The overdraft had climbed sharply for the second successive year to over £635,000 largely to finance an increase in work in progress, notably overseas orders for Rapier components and CU driver's sights for tanks.

Casting nickel-bronze for periscope components in 1972. Barr & Stroud's foundry opened in 1905.

Despite the liquidity problems the go-ahead was given for the expenditure of £85,000 on additional machine tools, which it was hoped would raise productivity.[57] Matters improved steadily during 1972 with a further recovery in profits to over £300,000 as costs were brought firmly under control. Stronger financial management allowed the overdraft to be paid off and further investment in new plant and equipment. At the end of the year Barr & Stroud were in the fortunate position, in a climate of very high interest rates, of holding a cash balance at the bank of £184,000.[58] This achievement in reshaping the company's fortunes in the two years following the 1970 crisis, provided the framework for future technical development.

Although the directors were all too conscious that their business was vulnerable to sudden swingeing cuts in defence expenditure due to a domestic economic crisis, they believed that, come what may, there would be demand for their technically advanced military and naval products. They appreciated that this assessment would only prove correct if their equipment continued to incorporate the latest technology without sacrificing Barr & Stroud's reputation for reliability and durability. In keeping with the streamlined research and development strategy, effort was to be concentrated on integrating new facilities, particularly thermal imaging, with the existing core products, the periscopes and the laser tank rangefinder. There were great risks in such a policy for a small specialist company if the technology could not be made to perform to specification. The naval authorities were not convinced that it was practical or useful to incorporate a thermal imaging device into submarine periscopes, on the grounds that the spray and mist would be too great to give an acceptable image on a dull night or in conditions when normal visibility was obscure. They also doubted that it would be possible to contrive a window of infra-red transmitting material that would be strong enough to withstand the full diving pressure and the corrosive effect of seawater.[59]

Despite the lack of Admiralty support, David Ritchie persuaded his colleagues at Barr & Stroud to persevere with the investigation at their own expense. A solution to both the criticisms raised by the Admiralty was found through the use of germanium of suitable shape to ensure compressive stresses only, and coated with a special ultra-hard coating. Improvements in the multi-element detector and cooling systems along with elegant mechanical/optical means of scanning the detector arrays all contributed to providing compact infra-red sensors which gave thermal imaging pictures comparable to a standard television. The image, like that obtained through the image intensifiers, was presented direct to the observer through the eye-piece at the foot of the periscope and to a monitor mounted at one side of the control room. The scanner was the Alpha module borrowed from missile systems. This development was accompanied by investigation of the remote control of the periscope from the monitor, using the recently introduced rotational assist facility. This operated on the same principle as power steering in a motor car, making it much less exhausting for the operator to rotate the periscope during long watches. By 1977 the first experimental version of the thermal imaging periscope, giving a 90 per cent overhead coverage as well as 360° in azimuth was sufficiently far advanced for sea trials.[60]

The further development of the laser rangefinder and a lightweight thermal imager for use in tanks was also undertaken with significant private-venture commitment from the company. The original laser work had started as a stand-alone application using ruby as the host material. In the early 1970s the possibility of integrating the rangefinder with a GEC computer to provide an Improved Fire Control System (IFCS) was identified. Barr & Stroud began work on an electronically driven aiming mark display powered by the computer developed by the GEC subsidiary MSDS. This was to replace the complicated ballistic graticule which had been steadily evolved since the turn of the century to take account of every type of shell. When fully developed the IFCS could interpret all the variables likely to affect the trajectory of a shell, such as the wind speed and direction, external temperature, and the gun trunnion angle. Full production began in 1975.[61]

During that year the company began to explore alternatives to the ruby as the host material for the laser. They finally settled on neodymium doped rods, which used yttrium aluminium garnate (Nd:YAG) as the host material. Nd:YAG had significant advantages. It proved ten times more efficient for rangefinding than ruby and also required considerably less power and much simpler circuitry thereby creating a significant saving in space and increase in reliability. Although the Ministry of Defence was unable to fund the investigation of the Nd:YAG lasers, the Barr & Stroud board was so confident in the potential that the the project was financed entirely as a private risk venture.[62]

At the same time the company was actively progressing from the successful SHORTIE thermal imaging system by winning development contracts for prototypes catering for the needs of all three services. A helicopter scanner, LOFTIE, of compact design was highly praised after trials in combat conditions between 1972 and 1974. This was one of the first thermal imaging devices to give a real TV rather than a banded line scan presentation. To protect the instrument from vibration, it was mounted on a stabilised platform.[63] Apart from this government sponsored research into thermal imagers, the Barr & Stroud board, from its experience with the laser, pushed ahead with the design of its own lightweight thermal imager at its own expense. Named Type IR18 it was intended to be mounted on various weapon platforms. Work began in 1974 and took several years to complete with many experiments using better quality detectors as they became available. The resolution of the thermal image improved rapidly so that it was soon possible to obtain an almost perfect picture of the ground under observation. As this work on thermal imaging advanced, serious thought was given during the mid-1970s to the possibility of combining laser and thermal capabilities with microcomputers to provide a 24-hour integrated fire-control system.[64] Barr & Stroud, with its background and awareness of these two important technologies, had an excellent chance of winning the contract to devise such a system when the MOD was expected to go to tender in the early 1980s.

In the meantime, British Aerospace (BAC's successor) invited Barr & Stroud to make a thermal imaging sight to enhance the performance of the Swingfire missile, the Army's main long-range anti-tank guided weapon. Although the concept of this wire-controlled weapon was outmoded, it was effective and could not be jammed by enemy electronic interference. The thermal imaging device was intended to enlarge the potential of Swingfire, allowing for use at night and in poor visibility. This was urgently needed because it had become apparent that the Warsaw Pact countries had an overwhelming superiority in tanks in Europe. The first production contract was placed during 1977.[65]

The Barr & Stroud board was not so

committed to these two major defence projects to neglect the potential of the civilian market for its expertise in thermal imaging and laser technology. In May 1971 the company called in the Department of Marketing at Lancaster University to identify suitable areas for the commercial expansion of the company. The board, on receiving the report, resolved to devote attention to medical instruments, establishing a Medical Instrument Development Group for the purpose. A search was instigated to locate products that could either be sold under agency agreements or, better still, manufactured under licence.[66] After a fruitless enquiry, Thomas Collier & Associates of Los Angeles were commissioned in July 1973 to continue the hunt. They did no better, largely because most of the products identified would not readily translate from the United States to Britain.[67] Disappointed, the Barr & Stroud directors redoubled their own scrutiny, deciding in the summer of 1974 to carry out a detailed study to arrive at a 'specification for a range of instrumentation applied to the diagnosis and monitoring but not treatment of the arterial blood system including the heart'.[68] The outcome was a recommendation that Barr & Stroud should enter the field of patient monitoring with a range of equipment from a single channel ECG recorder to a complete modular multi-bed system for intensive care units. Closer examination, however, raised concern at the financial implications of diversification on this scale, into such a competitive market.[69] Consequently, in March 1975 it was announced that the company would limit medical product development to thermal scanning equipment currently being tested.[70] A successor to the videotherm system, the design of the equipment to be used mostly for breast cancer screening, had been taken over from the Atomic Weapons Research Establishment in 1973. It proved troublesome in development and an effective prototype was not completed before the middle of 1977.[71]

The Medical Instrument Development Group reviewed other possibilities. They returned to the potential of fibre optics for diagnostic and surgical applications, following an agreement in 1970 with the Medical Supply Association to design and manufacture medical light guides and light sources. Although prospects seemed hopeful, and Barr & Stroud managed to produce instruments that satisfied a stringent new British Standard, the recession that started in 1973 killed the market and MSA lost interest in the sales drive.[72] This unhappy experience made Barr & Stroud reluctant to become involved in the development of coherent fibre optic bundles for use in endoscopes, when invited to do so by the Department of Health and Social Security in 1975 and 1976.[73] Equally unsuccessful was an attempt to design a contact mattress in collaboration with the Scottish Western Regional Hospital Board. On the advice of Dr C. G. Caro, whom the group turned to for advice about possible products, a non-invasive heart function measuring instrument was devised during 1974, based on a servo-linked development of the sphygmomanometer. Named the Caro Cuff or TOPSI, this instrument took a further three years to bring to field test stage. Dr Caro, acting for Peat Technologies, also tried to persuade Barr & Stroud to manufacture their Apnoea radar-based movement detector.[74]

Despite all the Medical Instrument Development Group's initiatives to find new products, Barr & Stroud were left in 1977 with only the two medical instruments that had been first introduced more than ten years before, the rapid X-ray cassette changer and the integrated microdensitometer. Neither of these sold in great numbers and could at no stretch of the imagination compensate for any sudden loss of defence work.[75] Like other non-specialist companies that ventured into the medical market at the time, Barr & Stroud had found it almost impossible to come to grips with the fragmented procurement structure of the British National Health Service and had been discouraged by the reluctance of medical men to agree on the features and facilities of new instrumentation. The company lacked the financial strength and size to mount a large private risk development programme in addition to its commitments to defence projects or to seek overseas involvement.[76]

As the 1970s unfolded the Barr & Stroud board became increasingly concerned about the slimness of its resources and the consequent difficulty of responding to international marketing opportunities. Like all their competitors in Britain, the Barr & Stroud board found the going rough in the mid-1970s as inflation soared. Although the company was fortunate to have a strong order book swelled by demand for laser rangefinders, Rapier SOGs, and periscopes, it was almost impossible for Tom Johnston as works director to hold costs in check. Each year the chairman's statements in the annual report complained bitterly of the difficulties that surrounded them. In 1975 W. Guthrie Strang declared: 'In line with many other companies we have battled throughout the year with liquidity problems', and went on to explain that healthy demand for the company's products had only exacerbated the financial predicament. The board was forced to seek help once more from their bankers, borrowing £500,000 at the currently very high rates of interest which simply served to cut profits. This, combined with dividend restraint imposed by the Labour government that came to office in the autumn of 1974, depressed the share-price, reducing the market value of the company to below the value of its investment portfolio.[77]

With no indication that the Government would do anything to remove dividend control, the directors started to think seriously about seeking shelter from the storm through a merger with a larger partner. Such ideas were fashionable at a time when a few large conglomerates were being formed out of the amalgamation of numerous small enterprises. The Barr & Stroud directors, led by W. Guthrie Strang, Gordon Morrison and Tom Johnston, who had been promoted to the new post of assistant managing director in 1975, were determined not to capitulate to an unwelcome predator so easily. There had been other offers since the bid from ITT in 1969, for example from Negretti and Zambra in 1973, and many tentative expressions of interest.[78] Rather than simply responding to such an approach, the Barr & Stroud board determinedly set about finding a partner, whose existing business complemented their own. Given the company's origins in optics, it was logical that the directors should have selected Pilkington Bros of St Helens in Lancashire, the world's leading glass manufacturers.[79]

Barr & Stroud had a long and amicable

association with Pilkington and its subsidiary, Chance Brothers, in the supply of special glass. They shared a common auditor in the accountants Coopers & Lybrand, who opened the negotiations. When Pilkington expressed interest, the financial details were hammered out by the London merchant bankers, Robert Fleming & Co, which had originated in Dundee.[80] Throughout the discussions it was acknowledged by Pilkington that the existing directors, management and research of Barr & Stroud would be retained and there would be no redundancies as a result of the merger. Furthermore, Barr & Stroud made it a condition that the company would be able to preserve its own identity, carry out its own trade union negotiations, and that there would be no wholesale transfer of work from Anniesland to other parts of the Pilkington Group.[81] On Tuesday 22 March 1977 the merger was made public, giving Barr & Stroud access to Pilkington's world-wide sales organisation, its financial strength and its management methods. In accepting Pilkington's terms at the beginning of their ninetieth year of trading, the Barr & Stroud directors had no doubt that they had made the right choice in securing the future of their business and employment for the workforce at Anniesland. However much they may have wished they were free to negotiate their own future, the directors' decision was subject to the scrutiny of the Office of Fair Trading which was required by law to scrutinise the bargain in the light of public interest. If there was any doubt the matter could be referred to the Monopolies Commission. After a month of nervous anticipation, the Department of Prices and Consumer Protection gave its blessing to the deal on 25 April 1977.   Four days later Barr & Stroud became a subsidiary of Pilkington Brothers Ltd. The board looked forward to a partnership that would carry the company forward towards its second century.[82]

In giving up their independence, the directors could congratulate themselves on having navigated their business since 1964 with such skill through one of the most difficult periods that British enterprise had ever experienced. At great risk they had exploited new technologies to generate new products for the company's traditional defence customers. They had made a determined effort to find an outlet for Barr & Stroud's skills in civilian markets, but had drawn back from winning such business at any price. They preferred to apply resources to private ventures associated with defence projects, sensing early on that the government would increasingly expect defence contractors to display such commitment. Writing to Gordon Morrison on the day the merger became public, Sir Alastair Pilkington assured him that Pilkington Brothers recognised the quality and distinction of their new subsidiary: 'We wish your company to maintain its identity and expect great things from you in the future. I believe we have much to contribute to each other's success.'[83]

SIGHTING THE FUTURE: 1977-1988

In deciding during 1977 to merge their business 'with that of a larger partner', the Barr & Stroud board was following a path that had been well worn since the beginning of the century by West of Scotland shipbuilding and engineering companies. Critics of such amalgamations believed that, whatever assurances were given at the time, they were simply a recipe for the eventual closure of factories and the transfer of work to other locations, either in England or overseas. This opinion, held by many people, provided easy scapegoats for the profound problems of Clydeside engineering in the late 1960s and 1970s. It ignored entirely the determined efforts by new owners to improve the quality and performance of management, and to raise often abysmally low levels of productivity. The Barr & Stroud directors were determined to preserve their identity by learning new ways of controlling the enterprise from their new owners.

Pilkington could trace its origins back 150 years to 1827 when the St Helens Crown Glass Company was formed in the town of that name in Lancashire. The Pilkington family had been involved in the business ever since, enlarging the original plant at St Helens and taking over competitors both in the United Kingdom and abroad.[1] The foundation of the modern success of the company was the invention in the early 1950s of the float glass process for producing clear flat glass. Although this process had taken over a decade to develop, Pilkington had persevered, reaping rewards, largely through licence agreements, from the late 1960s. Following the appointment of the inventor of the process, Sir Alastair Pilkington, as chairman in 1973, the management structure was modernised to devolve responsibility and authority from the main board to profit centres at home and overseas. In pushing through his reforms, Sir Alastair sought to streamline Group activities and to identify areas for development when the returns from licensing the float glass process began to fall away. The manufacture of optical and ophthalmic glass was selected as offering the potential for high earnings.[2]

Since the takeover of Chance Brothers of Smethwick in 1951, Pilkington had been major producers of ophthalmic glass. Six years later the optical sides of both companies had been combined in the new Chance-Pilkington works at St Asaph in North Wales. The venture was the brainchild of Dr Lawrence Pilkington, who was keen to foster this side of the enterprise and eventually take the Group into the grinding and polishing of lenses, and the production of optical systems. This strategy was frustrated by the need to deploy all the Group's available resources to finance the development of the float glass technique. It was not until 1966 that the first step in this direction was taken, through an agreement with the American Perkin Elmer company. A new jointly owned company, Pilkington Perkin-Elmer (now Pilkington PE) was formed, with premises at St Asaph to design camera and copier lenses and other simple optical devices. The market for these products proved hard to penetrate in the face of competition from Japan and West Germany. Perkin Elmer withdrew in 1972, leaving Pilkington as sole owner. Like Barr & Stroud, Pilkington PE started to investigate military applications of visual image intensifiers, particularly for use in aircraft.[3]

As this research was progressing, an opportunity arose during 1975 for Pilkington to merge with UK Optical and Industrial Holdings

Ltd, manufacturers of ophthalmic lenses. In Pilkington's view, an amalgamation would make for an efficient enterprise, combining their expertise in the production of glass blanks and UKO's skill in grinding and polishing lenses.[4] The proposal was referred by the Department of Prices and Consumer Protection to the Monopolies Commission in September 1976. While their investigation was proceeding, Pilkington received the enquiry from Barr & Stroud, whose business fitted with Pilkington

An array of infra-red transmitting lenses and in the top right a missile nose-cone. One of the reasons that Pilkington was enthusiastic about a merger with Barr & Stroud was the company's skill in grinding and polishing special lenses.

PE's interest in visual image intensification. Dr Lawrence Pilkington was enthusiastic at the prospect of Barr & Stroud joining the Group. Two days after the proposed merger with Barr & Stroud was made public, the Monopolies Commission reported on 24 March 1977 that the takeover of UK Optical and Industrial Holdings would not be in the public interest.[5] Bitterly disappointed, the Pilkington board waited anxiously to see if a similar fate awaited this more limited scheme to take the Group into new territory.

After the acquisition of Barr & Stroud in the spring of 1977 Pilkington, perhaps because of the bruising experience of the Monopolies Commission inquiry, were anxious not to take any hasty actions. There were novel features for the Group in the terms agreed with Barr & Stroud which ensured a far greater degree of independence than was the case with previous acquisitions. For the first time a substantial amount of research and development would be undertaken away from St Helens. During June 1977 two Pilkington executives, D. Cail and A.J. Milne, joined the Barr & Stroud board, but it was not until the autumn that any structural alterations were made in the management of the company. These changes were brought about in part by the death of the secretary, John Gunn, in September and the retirement the following month of W. Guthrie Strang as a joint managing director. He continued to serve as executive chairman with Gordon Morrison as his alternate and joint managing director. The vacancy for the other post of joint managing director was taken by the assistant managing director, Tom Johnston. Hugh Kelly, the accountant responsible for the finance department since 1956, was given the job of company secretary, the

Now you see it, now you don't. (a) A normal night scene of a jumbo jet at Prestwick airport and (b) the view through the IR 18 thermal imager night sight with the aircraft clearly defined.

first person with a commercial background to occupy the post.[6]

These promotions were followed towards the end of October by the overhaul of Barr & Stroud's marketing. Charles Lindsay, with a background of commercial negotiation and sales, was appointed to the new post of commercial director with overall responsibility for sales and marketing. At the same time, two new senior executive positions were created: that of projects manager and defence marketing manager.[7] As part of the campaign to improve marketing, it was decided to replace the entrance hall with one that would do justice to the company's image as a leading high technology company. The work was completed in July 1979 to coincide with the visit of Rear Admiral R.R. Squires, Flag Officer Submarines.[8]

The need for strengthening and streamlining the company strategy had been recognised for some time by the Barr & Stroud board. The merger with Pilkington provided additional stimulus to bring about reforms, principally because the directors began to participate in the management of other Pilkington companies, broadening their perspective and widening their experience. Reforms included the revitalisation of the Management Committee, established in 1969 after Dr Strang's retirement.

At the same board meeting that approved prominence to be given in future to marketing, the Management Committee was reconstituted to meet once a month with the twin objectives of implementing board policy and formulating proposals to the board. The committee comprised Tom Johnston, David Ritchie as technical director, Bill Walker as production director, Charles Lindsay as commercial director, Hugh Kelly as company secretary as

well as the design manager, components production manager, projects manager, defence marketing manager, and the Strathleven works manager.[9] One aim of this reorganisation was to impose greater financial and commercial disciplines in all areas of the company's activities. This was made manifest by the introduction of target annual budgets for all departments coupled to monthly accounting with results to be with the division within six days of the end of each month.[10] The delegation of executive power to such committees and the introduction of improved financial control was common at the time and in the case of engineering companies involved, like Barr & Stroud, in the design and development of complex equipment provided a focal point for effective project management.

This administrative structure was designed to enable Barr & Stroud to develop and introduce new products more effectively and efficiently, and to enlarge the market, particularly overseas, for existing lines. Effort was to continue to be concentrated on the integration of thermal imaging techniques with the tank gun sight and with the submarine periscope, both private ventures.

The prototypes held out the possibility that visual surveillance could be made round the clock during darkness and at times of poor visibility, except in the foulest weather conditions. For the naval and army commander this was a colossal advance, making submarine and tank operations at night practical. The first serial thermal scanner which gave higher resolution images was assembled in midsummer 1977 and the first fully operational infra-red submarine periscope module was completed by the autumn.[11] FVRDE invited Barr & Stroud, towards the close of the year, to demonstrate the capability of the tank laser sights in FV101 Scorpion armoured reconaissance vehicles and install one gun linkage mounting. Ten additional SHORTIE models were also contracted for.[12] To expedite these projects, more research staff were recruited and the company's electrical engineering facilities were reinforced by the takeover of A & S Engineering Designs (Edinburgh) Ltd.[13]

In the meantime the newly refashioned sales and marketing departments, under the commercial director, had been successful in securing very large orders from the government of the Shah of Iran for tracked Rapier SOGs and tank laser sights for the country's fleet of Chieftain tanks and the new FV 4030 Shir tanks. The contract was worth around £20 million, with the prospect of many more millions of pounds worth of work in the future.[14] Although only a small part of the Shah's total projected expenditure on new weapons, this business assured a large volume of work at Anniesland for several years. At home there were difficulties with the Ministry of Defence who questioned the mounting costs of developing the Improved Fire-Control System (IFCS) for use with the laser sights and thermal imaging equipment. Rather than place the all important IFCS contract in jeopardy, the company bore some additional development costs.[15]

More seriously, in December 1978, the Ministry claimed intellectual property rights in periscopes developed by Barr & Stroud for the Royal Navy. This was part of a further tightening of procurement procedure. Barr & Stroud strongly and successfully contested the Ministry's claim. Ever since the award of the first periscope contract during the First World War,

Barr & Stroud had undertaken, at the company's own expense, all subsequent development and enhancement. The board was, however, willing to transfer their rights to the MOD at a price and quoted a figure of several millions of pounds with the proviso that the Ministry should, as a result, have no right to a levy on sales to other friendly governments. This proposal was not adopted by the MOD.[16]

In common with other British defence contractors, the company was soon facing a serious crisis following the overthrow of the Shah of Iran in the spring of 1979. One of the first actions of the new government led by the Ayatollah Khomeni was to cancel all the orders for weapons placed by the Shah. Altogether, Barr & Stroud lost £14 million worth of orders in hand and the prospects of many more millions of pounds worth of business. The board was, however, successful in negotiating reasonable cancellation settlements.[17] With the British Labour government on the verge of collapse, there was little the Ministry of Defence could do in the short-term to soften the blow. The incoming Conservative administration of Mrs Margaret Thatcher, committed to cutting public expenditure, brought little comfort. As it turned out, even against a background of a reduced budget, the Ministry of Defence brought forward contracts already agreed to assist Barr & Stroud and other defence companies. Helpful as this action was, much equipment remained in the hands of arms manufacturers, including the tracked Rapier vehicles. As a result, cash-flow projections and profit forecasts were thrown into disarray and consequently, by the end of the financial year in March 1979, the company had sustained a net outflow of funds of £1.2 million.[18]

(a) The second and third generation laser rangefinders. On the right side is a Nd: YAG laser and on the left an advanced CO_2 laser.

(b) The Chieftain tank, alongside an armoured reconnaissance vehicle in the fields; Chieftains and Sorpions were fitted with laser rangefinders after 1974.

A group of products from the Vale of Leven factory, a lithium niobate boule at the back, a lithium niobate wafer on the left and on the right an integrated optics device with a fibre optic lead.

The Challenger tank fitted with TOGS. The Thermal Imaging Scanning Head (TISH) is fitted in the turret on the left with its door open.

To help solve these problems, Barr & Stroud again turned their attention to the civilian market, placing Bill Walker in charge of developing and marketing suitable products.[19] The PS5 automatic drafting projector, supplied to the Norwegian Kongsberg Vapenfabrikk, offered the most immediate possibilities at a time when much re-mapping work was in progress throughout the world. During the year the company negotiated an order for twelve PS5 projectors to be used in the new Kongsberg CAD/CAM computer controlled drafting system.[20] The development of the other new commercial products was centred around laser and fibre optic applications. Building on the previous experience of the dental flexible light guides, various computer card readers were designed and illuminated traffic signs. It had been found that the red and green 'walking men' and green arrows at traffic light systems gave false 'on' signals in certain light conditions, a problem that could be overcome by using fibre optic displays.[21] The company's Health Care Future Committee, which had taken over the duties of the Medical Development Group the year before, recommended the manufacture of a laser coagulator for the treatment of gastro-intestinal bleeding.[22] As a result of all these initiatives, for the first time, civilian business during 1979 - 80, exceeded £1 million, out of a total turnover of £18 million.[23] Although the company continued to be profitable, cash was very tight with the net outflow of funds for the year doubling to £2.5 million. In the midst of these problems, W. Guthrie Strang retired as chairman, remaining on the board as a non-executive director.[24] Gordon Morrison took his place and Tom Johnston became sole managing director.

Despite the setback of the loss of the Iranian orders, the outlook was promising. The Ministry of Defence placed production contracts during 1979 for the passive thermal imaging device for the Swingfire missile, to be manufactured in the United Kingdom. Launched from either an FV438 vehicle or the FV102 striker vehicle, this anti-tank missile was wire-guided, using a joystick and image intensified visual sight, situated either mounted on the vehicle's roof or in a forward position, linked by cable. By replacing the visual sight with a thermal imaging scanner, the daytime range was extended, allowing the operator to penetrate battlefield smoke, haze and light mist. Moreover, it was not affected by darkness, meeting the army commanders' urgent requirement to have the capability of holding an enemy attack at night. The only weather conditions which defeated the scanner were fog and rain where the size of the water droplets approached the far infra-red wavelengths, causing severe scattering, but the same problems would of necessity prevent enemy operations.[25] This was a major development for the deployment of conventional forces, holding out the possibility of orders for the prototype thermal imaging equipment installed in submarine attack periscopes and tank sights, which were performing well in trials.

There was also strong demand for Barr & Stroud's latest electro-optical material, lithium niobate, which had originally been developed as a laser 'Q' switching material, but was found to have much wider applications as wafers for surface accoustic wave delay line devices and for optical chips for a new generation of optical signal processors.[26] Work continued as fast as possible on the development of the Nd:YAG laser rangefinders. Two development models had been completed in 1977 and the first two prototypes fitted in tanks the following year. Further batches were assembled for the Ministry of Defence in 1978, while work went ahead on the design of the LF11 production model and a modified version for Jordanian Khalid tanks.[27] This advance in laser design was fundamental to the later evolution of the integrated Thermal Observation Gunnery Sighting System (TOGS).

As the world economy was forced into recession by the rise in oil prices consequent on the problems in the Middle East, the Ministry of Defence placed a moratorium on defence contracts in the summer of 1980 while the government considered future policy in the light of available resources.[28] Although Barr & Stroud were convinced that their new products would be assigned a high priority in such a review, this was a serious setback, coming so close after the cancellation of the Iranian contracts which were to be finally written off in the accounts for that year, hopefully reversing the outflow of funds. The moratorium was lifted in November, but the Ministry emphasised that a close check on all arms spending would continue.[29] In January 1981, Francis Pym, a moderate, who had served as Minister of Defence since Mrs Thatcher came to office, was replaced by John Nott, with a brief to conduct a much tougher inquiry into departmental expenditure.

Well before his recommendations were published in July, the Procurement Executive had begun to impose a much harder line on defence contractors. In April, Tom Johnston was summoned to a meeting with the Chief of Defence Procurement to be told that British government contract pricing conditions had to apply to all overseas contracts awarded on a government to government basis. This effectively meant that the majority of the company's defence contracts would be subject to the very tight profit margins and cost limits imposed by the Ministry of Defence and the Treasury, which left little room for modifications or the cost of future developments.[30] The company's natural reaction was to negotiate contracts directly with foreign governments. The Ministry acted quickly to prevent such unilateral action and, at the same time, made it clear that in the future all contracts for either development work or production would be awarded on the basis of competitive tender.[31] Although of concern, the financial regime imposed by Pilkington allowed the board to gauge the impact of the policy very rapidly. With turnover at a record £20 million in 1981 and the cash-flow projected to be in equilibrium, they were confident they could work within these rules.[32]

While Barr & Stroud were coming to terms with these new conditions, John Nott was engaged in an acrimonious dispute about his rumoured plans to reduce the Navy, which resulted in the dismissal of the Navy Minister, Keith Speed. Expecting the worst, the Barr & Stroud directors were relieved that the Minister's proposals allowed for modest development to the equipment of the land forces in Europe and, despite cutting back the surface fleet, placed greater emphasis on submarines, advocating the construction of five additional nuclear-powered hunter killers. Barr & Stroud could expect tenders to be issued regularly for the tank sights and periscopes.[33]

Barr & Stroud, by this time, were involved in another hard contest with among others the GEC subsidiary MSDS and the Philip's

The M578 tracked Rapier vehicle, originally ordered by the Shah of Iran, but acquired by the British Army, after he was deposed. The SOGS had to be redesigned to meet the more demanding conditions of a combined mobile system.

A Trafalgar class submarine with its two periscope masts and AJT communication aerial raised.

subsidiary MEL, for the full development contract for the Thermal Surveillance System and the Gun Sighting System which together formed the integrated Thermal Observation Gunnery Sighting System (TOGS) for the Chieftain tank and the new FV4030/4 Challenger tank, an improved version of the Iranian Shir tank. Barr & Stroud took the bold decision to develop a prototype system themselves as proof of the viability of their concept. With advice from a recently employed ex-Royal Armoured Corps officer, the system was designed to be as simple and elegant as possible. The Barr & Stroud submission to this tender was novel and as one option proposed a partial non-compliant solution. Following a very successful demonstration of their prototype system and much hard commercial bargaining, the company was awarded this significant contract.[34]

An aerial view of the Anniesland works, November 1987, showing the new periscope tower behind the high-rise block of flats. The old Maclehose factory, which was refurbished by Barr& Stroud between 1980 and 1982, is the large green-roofed building in the centre foreground. The building in the top right hand corner with the white roof is the North Works.

The TOGS contract was one of the earliest placed on an incentive basis for such a complex development project. This meant that a target cost figure was established which could be exceeded by only a very limited amount up to a fixed maximum sum. The penalty for being over the target cost was a reduced level of permissible profit. Conversely, the bonus for completing the work for less than target cost was a higher profit. Similarly there was an incentive bonus for achieving previously agreed technical milestones and pre-production model delivery forecasts.

The sums involved were many millions of

pounds and the outcome performance extremely important to the customer for what was an operational emergency requirement. The negotiations carried out by Charles Lindsay and his team with senior Ministry contract officers were arduous and complicated. For Barr & Stroud the contract was a watershed. It represented the fruits of a dedication to new and enabling technologies and carried the potential for winning large value and volume production work. It raised the company status from being a module supplier to the higher ranking and increased visibility of a system house.

Winning the contract presented a tremendous challenge to the company and also a very considerable risk both financially and for future credibility. The large amount of money involved meant that failure to meet target cost and delivery schedules would have serious financial repercussions which could affect future viability. If a fully satisfactory performance was not achieved, the directors were left in no doubt that future MOD business would almost certainly be affected. It was vital that the various technical assessments and estimates upon which commercial judgements had been founded and to which the company was now committed, were adhered to and improved upon if at all possible.

The implications extended well beyond development. Stemming from the contract, Barr & Stroud had to produce equipment which not only performed well to specification but did so at a value engineered competitive price for production. Otherwise, Barr & Stroud could not expect to win the production work so vital for its future. Accordingly, the board instituted various formal procedures to ensure that the monitoring and control of the work imposed the

discipline necessary for success. Various critical factors which had emerged during negotiations with MOD were spelled out at the board meeting in September 1981:

1. Cost and achievement targets must be maintained.

2. This meant rigid adherence to the specification on which estimates had been based unless formal contract amendments were made.

3. A formal risk approval procedure had to be established covering:
     - modifications requested by the customer
     - modifications requested by the Barr & Stroud project team.

The full implications of each such proposed modification would have to be considered covering the effect on costs, delivery and performance. This had to be notified in advance to the customer and could only be actioned when formal contract amendments confirming any relevant adjustments to price, delivery or performance were agreed. The MOD and company engineers were to be informed of the costs of such modifications as a way of ensuring mutual discipline.

[While the need for such control may seem obvious, in development contracts it had previously been understood by both sides that in an evolving situation, some flexibility was permissible. The difficulty was that for many years subsequent agreement of the result of such variations to price or delivery or performance had created considerable problems].

4. MOD had a budget for production equipment

which could not be exceeded. It also had a specific quantity requirement. It followed, therefore, that the unit value of each equipment had to match that need - which had to be the company target for a production price.

5. All future business with MOD would need to be on a similar disciplined and competitive basis and company systems and management must be structured accordingly.

The directors concluded that it was the government's intention to rationalise the defence industry, spreading the available business over fewer companies.[35] Taking heed of the warning, the board decided to call in consultants, Hay Management Services Ltd, to undertake an initial organisation study of the company aimed at improving the quality of all management and organisational aspects.[36]

Despite the concern over the direction of the Conservative government's policy on defence procurement, there was cause for optimism, not just because the TOGS contract had been won from some of the country's largest armaments firms, but also because British Aerospace had been informed in June that the British Army would purchase the tracked Rapier (M578) vehicles developed for the Shah. Before the details of the contract had been finalised, Barr & Stroud began, at their own expense, to manufacture fourteen SOGs and twelve collimators at an estimated cost of £260,000.[37] Another reason for confidence was the successful completion of the performance tests on the new design of attack and search periscopes for the Trafalgar class of hunter killer submarines. These were equipped with thermal imaging or image intensifying devices and the

search periscope was provided with electrical controls so that it could be operated remotely from a console within the control room. Sophisticated ESM aerials, covering the whole radar spectrum of frequencies, were fitted at the very top of the search periscope and ELINT directional analysis aerials replaced the radar ranging lens below the top window. Rotating joins and slip rings were contrived to accommodate the waveguides and coaxial cables that carried the signals from these aerials through the periscope to the control room. Orders began to be placed for these periscopes towards the close of 1981, both for the next generation of hunter killer submarines and for retrofitting in nuclear vessels already in service as part of a programme of mid-life improvement.[38] These contracts, along with the TOGS development work, were responsible for a rise in turnover of over 30 per cent in 1982 to £30 million.[39]

The volume of this defence work, along with further civilian contracts, notably for an additional ten PS5 projectors, made it essential to enlarge the factory space at Anniesland. In 1972 the directors of Robert MacLehose & Co, printers to the University of Glasgow, had told Barr & Stroud that their works opposite the main offices on the other side of Caxton Street, was now too large for their needs. They gave the company first refusal on the whole premises. Although this opportunity would have been welcome five years before when crystal and fibre optics production was moved to Strathleven, Barr & Stroud had little need for more space in 1972. Nevertheless, after long negotiations, Barr & Stroud purchased the factory, leasing half back to Robert MacLehose and part of the remainder to a motor distributor. In 1977

The laser coagulator Fibrelase 100 developed by
Barr & Stroud and later marketed by Pilkington
Medical Systems Ltd.

General Ghosh, chairman of Bharat Electronics, Bangalore, signing a laser rangefinder licence agreement with Tom Johnston, the managing director, on his right and Charles Lindsay, assistant managing director, on his left.

Robert MacLehose moved to Renfrew and Barr & Stroud took possession of the factory, using it as a store.[40] The board decided early in 1980, to occupy most of these South Works, as they were named, to create a unique manufacturing facility, embracing activities in visual, infra-red, and laser optics, together with a custom-built marketing conference room, fully equipped for audio/visual presentation. The building was re-roofed, incorporating modern standards of insulation, and a three-phase programme of refurbishment began. By midsummer 1981 phases I and II had been completed, with the installation of the high vacuum department and the optical assembly shop. Government grants were secured to help finance this investment.[41] The completed South Works were formally opened by the Secretary of State for Scotland, George Younger, on 5 April 1982.[42] His visit came at a time of crisis for the Conservative government, following the surrender three days before of the Governor of the Falkland Islands to the Argentinians.

During the next eight weeks, Britain launched one of the most difficult and expensive military operations since the Second World War to liberate the Islands. The conflict tested the resolve of Mrs Thatcher and her Ministers and reinforced the doubts of those who had questioned John Nott's defence review. Horrifying as the engagements were, they confirmed all too clearly the importance of investing in the most advanced conventional weapons, particularly infra-red systems that allowed operations to take place at night and in conditions of low light. Against this sombre background, Tom Johnston and his fellow directors conducted a wide ranging appraisal of the company's activities. In February 1982, Hay Management Services Ltd had finished their business analysis and output and organisational proposals recommending the formation of a Business Planning Group of senior executives to articulate a corporate strategy that would be enshrined in a business plan. Once their task had been completed, the group would continue to review and upgrade their projections in the light of actual results and the changing climate of the world economic and political structure. In a formal manner the board was collectively and consciously to consider the effect of external forces, like the Conservative government's procurement policy, on its fortunes and prospects. This was agreed and the group duly constituted.[43]

Towards the end of September 1982, the results of an in-depth investigation were presented to the board, proposing the internal reorganisation of the whole company under the supervision of an Organisational Planning Group. In concurring with this plan, the board emphasised that the 'over-riding priority for the company was to concentrate on its military business' and that 'the plans and actions to capitalise on that potential would be implemented and progressed urgently'.[44] Although considerable effort would continue to be devoted to the enlargement of the civilian business, it was felt that long-term planning had to be set in the context of Pilkington's broader objectives. Hay's chief criticism was that the Executive Board was still too involved in the day-to-day management of the company, telling the Business Planning Group that membership of the Management Committee should be

rethought.[45] It took several months of intense work by the Business Planning and Organisational Planning Groups to settle the details of future plans and the optimum corporate structure. This resulted in a further strengthening of the company's marketing methods, particularly for defence equipment. On 23 April 1983, Tom Johnston presented the final strategic document to his colleagues.[46]

The year-long discussion and deliberation to establish the framework for the future had not been without its events and problems. One of the casualties of the analysis of market trends was the decision in March 1982 to cease making the FT37 optical rangefinder, the successor of the product to which the company owed its origins almost a century earlier.[47] Within four months of this announcement, Barr & Stroud were dealt a heavy blow when British Aerospace made it known that they intended to design and manufacture the new thermal imaging electro-optical Rapier tracker system themselves.[48] This improvement on the earlier Rapier, which had done sterling service in the Falklands notably at the San Carlos beachhead, was badly needed to extend its operational use into the hours of darkness.

Just as the news broke, Gordon Morrison stood down as chairman and was replaced by Sir Richard Worsley, who had recently retired as Quartermaster General of the Army. This was the first time that the chairman of the company had been drawn from outside the ranks of long-serving senior executive directors. At the same time Trefor Jones joined the board from Pilkington, becoming assistant managing director a year later.[49] These appointments, however, were not intended to bring the company further under the control of the

Pilkington Group. On the contrary, their purpose was to increase Barr & Stroud's autonomy under strong leadership, as a component in a strategy of greater devolution introduced by Antony Pilkington on becoming Group chairman the year before. Sir Richard was quick to show his mettle, writing at once to the Under Secretary of State (Defence Procurement) setting out the company's case for retaining future Rapier development work. After lengthy discussions, British Aerospace conceded, subcontracting the development of a part of the thermally enhanced tracker (TOTE) involving further strengthening of the existing servo-optical group (SOG) to carry the addition of the thermal module.[50] Although this fell far short of the volume of work the board had anticipated, it retained Barr & Stroud's foothold in missile technology.

The disappointment at losing this segment of the Rapier business was counterbalanced by advances in civilian products, particularly in sales of lithium niobate for surface accoustic wave devices in radar and television circuits and for new applications for signal processing in optical communications systems which were becoming increasingly popular internationally. There was encouraging progress in the medical field. The laser coagulator, named Fiberlase100, had been well received in clinical trials and was being evaluated in acceptance tests in hospitals in the United Kingdom, the United States, Sweden and Japan. A distribution network covering Europe and the Far East was established and negotiations were in progress to extend coverage to the Middle East, the United States and Australasia.[51] Towards the end of 1981 a joint venture company, Minvade Ltd, had been established with Elven Precision Ltd of Crawley

to manufacture and sell medical endoscopes and related equipment. The launch of the Minvade range was planned for the autumn of 1983. The architect of these commercial achievements, Bill Walker, died in September 1983,[52] just as Minvade, of which he had recently become chairman, was poised to come to the market. Since the spring of the year he had also held the post of new business director of the Electro-Optical Division of Pilkington.[53]

Following the re-election of Mrs Thatcher's Conservative government in May 1983 and the appointment of Michael Hesseltine as Minister of Defence, there was a yet further tighening of procurement policy to make contracts even more competitive. Although turnover was rising much faster than inflation, and profits were keeping pace, the Barr & Stroud board had cause for concern. Cash had once again started to flow out of the business in 1983 and there was a need for even stronger financial discipline to stem the flow. This was successful, with the best outcome since the Pilkington takeover being recorded in the next financial year.[54] Because of the way prices for defence orders were to be calculated and investigated, the Barr & Stroud board, in the spring of 1984, resolved that certain civilian activities should in future stand as autonomous self-accounting units. As a result of this conclusion, the interest of Elven Precision Ltd in Minvade Ltd was acquired by Pilkington and Minvade ceased to be associated with Barr & Stroud, becoming, in November 1984, Pilkington Medical Systems Ltd. The new company took over Fiberlase 100 from Barr & Stroud along with a recently signed cross licence agreement with the American medical company Lasers for Medicine Inc.[55]

This hiving off of medical products was in

(a) and (b) Two views of Barr & Stroud's machine shop at Anniesland with the new microcomputer controlled equipment which facilitates automatic machinery.

Aligning a large Barr & Stroud laser at Anniesland using a helium beam.

some ways a logical outcome of the deliberations of the Business Planning Group and did not mean that the company intended to close its eyes to civilian applications of technologies developed chiefly for defence applications. During 1984 more formal ties were forged with universities through the award of two EEC research contracts under the Joint Opto-Electronic Research Scheme and the European Strategic Programme of Research in Information Technology. Both of these initiatives were designed to generate major civilian products enabling EEC countries to compete with manufacturers in Japan and the United States.[56]

The main thrust, however, remained in the core defence business: the final development and production of the Thermal Observation Gunnery Sighting System (TOGS), the infra-red remote-controlled submarine periscope and optronic pod, opto-electronic masts, and other thermal imaging systems for missile applications. The marketing and commercial aspects of these products were receiving much greater attention in a more structured fashion. It was recognised in successive business plans that new business had to be sought and won in overseas markets. Sales offices abroad were strengthened and agency networks stimulated to greater effort. Marketing and engineering teams travelled extensively, mounting equipment demonstrations, giving presentations and attending exhibitions. Much endeavour was put into areas where the company already had some credibility, such as in India where Barr & Stroud were fortunate in having a long established relationship going back to sales of the original optical rangefinders after Independence. Marketing effort was

concentrated on a requirement to update existing tank fleets of friendly powers with laser rangefinders initially, gradually extending to fully integrated thermal fire control-systems.

For some time it had been acknowledged by Barr & Stroud that sales to many friendly countries had to be much more than merely a straightforward customer/supplier relationship; rather it had to be a real partnership with shared benefits for both parties. Developing countries needed and were entitled to participate in some form of work sharing. In some cases it might be simply to provide employment; in others a desire and need for some assistance in transferring technological capability. India was such a country and from the beginning of the more recent negotiations both parties strove to satisfy this requirement. Initially, production would be from Barr & Stroud, but linked to a licence allowing the designated India company Bharat Electronics to take up manufacture itself in India by progressive stages on a realistic timetable. This joint effort was crowned with success early in 1986 with the placing of an initial contract for laser rangefinders and the signing of the related licence agreement. This partnership arrangement continues to evolve, with each company learning from the other and many friendly personal relationships developing as a bonus. It is this pattern of sharing and mutual benefits that business will follow in the foreseeable future.

Similar positive and successful partnerships have been established with Leitz in the Federal Republic of Germany, with Magnavox in the USA, with Nikon in Japan, and with Fairey in Australia. For a UK company, based in Scotland, it is particularly encouraging for Barr & Stroud to be in a position to license advanced technology to developed countries. Credit for this achievement is due not to any one individual or group of people, but to the outlook and culture of the enterprise which enables concepts quickly to become realities. Sometimes, in this process, decisions are arrived at not in any formal way, but through a dogged perseverence to overcome obstacles and objections whether financial or technical. When Charles Lindsay was interviewed on television after the signing of one licence deal, he was asked if such agreements would take work away from Anniesland — his answer, which is still applicable, was that such partnerships must stimulate work for both parties.[57]

In winning overseas business against strong competition, the Barr & Stroud Organisational Group had to redouble its determination to achieve even greater efficiency, borrowing management techniques from countries like America and Japan where it hoped to win custom. During 1984 a Product Support Group was established to provide improved after-sales service and the ARTEMIS system for project management introduced.[58] Early in the following year a computer-aided design system (CAD/CAM) was installed at a cost of £350,000 to keep the company's design capability abreast of the latest technology.[59] This concern with management performance led the board to commission further consultancy reports, this time from PA Management Consultants. Their report early in 1986 resulted in a project on Total Quality Management (TQM) which was fully implemented in December 1987.[60]

As this next stage in sharpening and refining all aspects of the company's activities was advancing, David Ritchie retired in June 1985, but continued actively to maintain contacts with colleges and universities, both locally and nationally. He was invited to become a visiting professor in the management of technical innovation at the University of Strathclyde. His responsibilities as technical director, which had greatly increased since 1970, were divided between Dr Arthur Slight, who became responsible for research and development, and Martin I. Bell, who became engineering director. At the same time Michael J. Holmes was recruited to join the board as civilian director.[61] On his appointment as deputy chief executive of the Pilkington Electro-Optical Division in July 1985, Trefor Jones stood down as deputy managing director, but continued as a non-executive director. The following year, Charles Lindsay and Martin Bell became assistant managing directors and to fill their previous posts Charles Berry was appointed marketing director and Gordon R. Smith, engineering director.[62] Sir Richard Worsely retired as chairman at the end of March 1986 and was replaced by Sir Robin Nicholson, who had recently joined Pilkington after serving as chief scientific adviser in the Cabinet Office. The outlook of the enlarged board was conditioned by the changes that Antony Pilkington was making in the objectives and organisation of the Group as a whole.[63]

Pilkington had suffered badly in the recession of the early 1980s which hit the construction industry more severely than any other sector. With a surplus of glass-making capacity world-wide, prices slumped and dumping became commonplace. In the United Kingdom, Pilkington, in just four years, saw its market share plummet from 80 per cent to 50 per cent. One of Antony Pilkington's first actions as chairman was

A simulation of a submarine control room showing a search periscope and the remote console and displays.

Reach for the sky! The new periscope test tower at Anniesland in the West Works completed in 1987. An advanced periscope under test.

to close plant and slash the workforce by some 36 per cent, incurring huge redundancy costs. When the immediate crisis was over, he began to push more executive responsibility down into the divisions and subsidiaries. This reinforced the steps Barr & Stroud had already taken to raise efficiency to meet the exacting demands of their principal customer, the Ministry of Defence. Antony Pilkington was also willing to learn from the experience of the subsidiaries who, having been encouraged to pay more attention to marketing, had become better at it than their parent. He confessed in 1986 that the Group had become 'too much distributors of a product and not very good marketers'.   With Sir Robin Nicholson, he took a fresh look at the Group's research and development programme, endorsing Barr & Stroud's strategy of focusing on designing new products to fill gaps in the market rather than devoting resources entirely to enhancing existing products and processes. By 1986 his efforts were beginning to be translated into profits as the world economy began to recover from the recession.[64] At the very moment when he was confident that the future was assured, Sir Owen Green, the formidable chairman of the conglomerate BTR, unveiled a bid on 20 November 1986 for Pilkington.   Sir Owen Green, who was not accustomed to losing such battles, criticised Pilkington's management style and its failure to make the most of its opportunities.[65]

From the outset, Antony Pilkington was determined that his family-founded enterprise, with its roots firmly in the north of Britain, would not be taken over by a London-based group, whose motives, he believed, were solely governed by short-term considerations. He hit back hard, concentrating on BTR's lack of commitment to research and development, quoting a reported statement of Sir Owen Green in October 1985: 'We have never seen the ethical need or the material reward for placing research and development to the forefront of our activities.'[66] In emphasising Pilkington's research and development, Antony Pilkington naturally singled out Barr & Stroud as a shining example of such Group endeavour at the boundaries of new technology. Consequently, Tom Johnston, as managing director, was called on to play an important role in the defence campaign, especially in lobbying the larger Scottish institutional shareholders, the Bank of Scotland, Standard Life, Murray Johnstone, and Scottish Amicable Assurance. After a hard battle, BTR was forced to withdraw. Undoubtedly, Pilkington was lucky to retain its independence. The bid came in the aftermath of the bitter struggle between Guinness and Argyll Foods for Distillers Company Ltd, which momentarily had made takeovers unfashionable. Well aware of his good fortune, Antony Pilkington and his senior executives knew that their victory would be short-lived if the Group did not return the profits forecast in the defence documents.[67] Although these predictions were supported by independent professional opinion, everyone in the Group knew that, for there to be no room for failure, further tuning of the management process would be necessary. As it turned out, the results more than matched expectations.

In the wake of the bid, Barr & Stroud redoubled its efforts to win contracts for its advanced defence equipment. The Ministry of Defence had instructed Barr & Stroud, between 1982 and 1984, to develop the latest opto-electronic periscopes for the new Vanguard class of four nuclear submarines. The production contract was placed in 1986. To accommodate these, a new periscope testing tower was built in the West Works later in the year. Orders for development and supply of thermal imaging modules for fitting in periscopes followed in 1986 from Japan. In November 1987 Barr & Stroud secured a £5 million contract to supply thermal imaging equipment for the United States Army's Pedestal Mounted Stinger (PMS) defence systems for rear areas of armoured and mechanised divisions. This business was won through the American licensee of Barr & Stroud's thermal imaging technology, Magnavox Electronic Systems, who had been selected by Boeing Aerospace to develop the forward-looking infra-red (FLIR) for the PMS system. In conjunction with Pilkington PE Ltd, Barr & Stroud will also supply fully assembled zoom infra-red telescopes for the front end optics of the FLIR system.[68]

One outcome of the takeover bid was the promotion of Sir Robin Nicholson within the Group and his resignation as chairman of Barr & Stroud. Trefor Jones was appointed chairman to lead the company into its centenary year. After a hundred years in business, Barr & Stroud continues to operate in 1988 at the forefront of technology, upholding the precepts of the founders. The company's research and scientific staff now number over 300 and the total workforce is 2,300 strong. The company has welded the latest management methods to its technical expertise and, in keeping with the Pilkington philosophy, is always on the lookout for new products that will fill gaps in the market. The management's approach, within tight financial discipline, is flexible, able to change the course of the business strategy quickly to back new opportunities as they emerge from the company's research and development. The future is by no means assured. Defence budgets in the western alliance and in friendly countries elsewhere in the world are under pressure. To maintain its presence in this market, Barr & Stroud will have to continue to refine its products and its management technique. There are exciting opportunities in the defence and civilian markets for opto-electronics and in the next generation of communication systems, but the competition will be severe. The company is already developing new products for these markets. Research is well advanced into the application of multi-sensor combinations for submarines which will survey the scene and the radiation above the surface under remote control, possibly replacing one of the two traditional periscopes with a single Electro-Optical-Non-Hull Penetrating Mast or EONHPM. Investigations are being made into new substances that can be used for more efficient signal processing for optical communications. In cases where more conventional optical systems are still appropriate, there is an ongoing programme of research into new coatings that can enhance or modify surface characteristics and which can withstand the most demanding environmental conditions. Barr & Stroud's performance in the next century will depend on its success in the complex and difficult task of managing this research and development, more and more of which will have to be financed as private ventures.

The decade since the merger with Pilkington has been one of great change and importance for Barr & Stroud. The international standing of Pilkington and its commitment to modern management methods and attributes has opened new opportunities for Barr & Stroud. Internally, organisational change has been effected through the establishment of a number of forums for the exchange of ideas and articulation of policy, such as the Pilkington Electro-Optical Division, Joint Marketing

The Prime Minister, the Rt Hon Mrs Margaret Thatcher, receives instructions on the use of a periscope in a Valiant class submarine and gets a clearer view of things.

Committee, Technical Steering Group, and the Business and Organisational Planning Groups. These have helped Barr & Stroud respond quickly to the further tightening of MOD procurement procedures by the Conservative government. The combined effect has been to make the company leaner and more efficient, better able to compete both in the domestic and overseas market.   In keeping with Barr & Stroud's long involvement in the local community and the great store Pilkington sets by such relationships, the directors have strengthened their external links. The company is now represented on various policy bodies of universities and institutions, with which it maintains close links. Tom Johnston is a past president of the Scottish Engineering Employers' Association, a member of the Scottish Industrial Development Advisory Board, and of the Scottish Council of the CBI. Charles Lindsay is immediate past chairman of the Defence Manufacturers' Association, represents the company on the Scottish Council, and is on the Executive Council of Scottish Business in the Community. All of these strands, and many more, help to forge the

communication links with the wider world, which companies must foster.   The newer, younger directors bring fresh strength and vigour, as well as a wealth of experience, to their task of taking the company forward.[69]

The first century draws to a close on a buoyant note. In the last few months the company has succeeded in winning several important overseas contracts from Asia, Australia and the USA, all against intense international competition. December 1987 saw the launch of an ambitious and imaginitive programme of Total Quality Management which is geared to the constant satisfaction of customer requirements. TQM involves each person in the company and will be achieved by harnessing everyone's complete commitment to the corporate objectives.   The whole staff and

Charles Lindsay, the assistant managing director, speaking to Peter Levine, the Chief of Defence Procurement.

Tom Johnston, the managing director, launching the Total Quality Management Project at the Scottish Exhibition and Conference Centre on 1 December 1987.

workforce of 2,300 people were present at the launch on 1 December 1987 against only two at the inauguration of the business ninety-nine years before. That fact alone says a lot about the development of the company after a century of enterprise.

Only time will tell if the first hundred years are the best.

APPENDICES

Current and Some Recent Directors
of Barr & Stroud, 1988

Tom O'Neil, Financial Director

Dr Arthur Slight, Research Director

Tom Johnston, Managing Director

David Ritchie, Technical Director (recently retired)

Martin Bell, Assistant Managing Director (Operations)

Trefor Jones, current Chairman

Hugh Kelly, Financial Director (recently retired)

Charles Lindsay, Assistant Managing Director (Marketing)

Gordon Smith, Engineering Director

Charles Berry, Marketing Director

Sir Richard Worsley (past Chairman)

Harold Brown, Production Director

NOTES

In researching this book, we have been able to delve into the extensive archives of Barr & Stroud. While we cannot pretend to have read through every one of the thousands of letter-books preserved by the firm, we have attempted to make full use of the facility in the time available to us. Letters cited without a catalogue number come from the volumes of the main series of general correspondence, and those from other series are identified by their catalogue numbers. Lest the reader be led to believe that we have scoured the pages of journals as diverse as the *South Australian Motor, Revista Maritima* and *Gas World,* we should confess that Barr & Stroud have preserved four volumes of press cuttings relating to their business and their fields of commercial interests, 1895-1945, and the majority of references taken from journals and newspapers were taken by us from this useful source.

CHAPTER 1

1. Glasgow University (GU) Matriculation Albums, 1873-74, held in Glasgow University Archives (GUA).
2. JBN (ed) *Fortuna Domus* (Glasgow University 1952), p.351.
3. GU Matriculation Albums, 1873-74.
4. *Engineering*, 6 September 1901, p.330.
5. Obituary, by J W French, in *Proceeding of Royal Philosophical Society of Glasgow*, LX, 1931-32, p.78.
6. GU Class Catalogue, 1873-77 in GUA.
7. GU Senate Minutes, 16 April 1877.
8. GU Matriculation Albums, 1876-77; GU Court Minutes, 3 January and 7 March 1877. Both in GUA.
9. GU General Council Register in GUA.
10. For details of Lord Kelvin's academic and business career, and his association with James White, see JBN *op.cit*, pp.321-8, Silvanus P Thomson *The Life of William Thomson* (London 1910) and C A Oakley *History of a Faculty* (Glasgow 1973).
11. From Dr Barr's speech on presentation of his portrait by GU, reprinted in Dr J Martin Strang *Barr & Stroud Limited: A History* (unpublished manuscript 1969), p.2.
12. Sidney Checkland and Anthony Slaven *The Dictionary of Scottish Business Biography*, Vol. 1, (Aberdeen University Press 1986), p.190.
13. *Bristol Trade Directory*.
14. Information in Dr Stroud's early life taken from his autobiographical essay *Apologia Pro Vita Mea* (published privately *c.* 1935) and his letters to his daughter Violet and to his granddaughter, Mrs Harper.
15. Edward Hilliard (ed) *Bristol College Register* (Oxford 1914). Interview with Mrs Harper, February 1986.
16. Interview with Mrs Harper. Dr Stroud's modest and unassuming manner was commented upon by many of Barr & Stroud's employees in later years.
17. Mary Stroud's private accounts are contained in a journal now in the possession of Mrs Harper.
18. Stroud *Apologia*. Testimonial written by Prof. Kohlransch, 1885, now in the possession of Mrs Harper. Information supplied by Simon Bailey, Archivist of University of London.
19. The testimonial is now in the possession of Mrs Harper.
20. Stroud *Apologia*, and *Early Reminiscences of the Barr & Stroud Rangefinders* (*c.* 1937), p.3.
21. Stroud *Apologia* and *Early Reminiscences*.
22. See Stroud's description of the Mekometer in his address to the British Association, recorded in the *Bradford Observer,* 11 September 1900.
23. Ibid. Sir Charles Caldwell and Sir John Headlam describe other rangefinders, and the problems involved in using them in action, in *History of the Royal Artillery 1860-99*, Vols 1-3, (1937-40).
24. For descriptions of the failings of British marksmanship see *Naval and Military Record*, 20 January 1915; *Outlook*, 8 December 1900; *Glasgow Evening News*, 9 February 1900; *English Mechanic and World of Science*, 28 April 1899, p.4; *Liverpool Weekly Post*, 27 June 1896; *The Globe*, 6 December 1899.
25. *Engineering*, 25 May 1888, p.12.
26. For Adie's and other early one-observer rangefinders, see Charles Darling 'Optical Appliances in Warfare', *Journal of Royal Society of Arts*, 10 March 1916; *Engineering Magazine*, February 1902; *Engineering*, 16 October 1891, p.457, and 17 February 1893, p.188.
27. Stroud *Early Reminiscences*, p.6.
28. Ibid. Lord Kelvin to Barr, 8 March 1889, in B & S Archive.
29. For further details of the rangefinder, see Archibald Barr and William Stroud 'Telemeters and Rangefinders for Naval Purposes', *Proceedings of the Institute of Mechanical Engineers*, 1896, parts 1-2, p.499. Strang op.cit. p.9.
30. Archibald Barr's inaugural address to GU Engineering Society, January 1892.
31. Stroud *Early Reminiscences* and *Apologia*.
32. Barr & Stroud Cash Book No. 1. Letter, 2nd Brigade Office to Dr Stroud, 10 March 1889, in B & S Archive.
33. Stroud *Early Reminiscences*. Letter, Dr Barr to Ordnance Committee, 18 May 1889, in Dr Barr's Private Papers.
34. Ibid. Cash Book No.1.
35. Archibald Barr and William Stroud 'On Some New Telemeters or Rangefinders', *Report of the British Association* 1890, p.499.
36. Cash Book No.1.
37. Barr's appointment is recorded in GU Senate Minutes. The cost of building the engineering laboratory in Leeds is mentioned by French in *Proceedings*, op.cit.
38. Stroud *Early Reminiscences*.
39. 'The Naval Gun in Action', *Cassiers Engineering Monthly*, December 1914.
40. Strang op.cit. p.13.
41. Stroud *Early Reminiscences*.
42. Ibid. Barr and Stroud 'Telemeters ...' op.cit.
43. Ibid.
44. Strang op.cit. p.13.
45. Ibid. p.18.
46. Letters, Director Navy Contracts to Drs Barr and Stroud, 10 June 1892 and 10 January 1893 in B & S Archive. Jackson to Cowan, Clapperton & Barclay, 20 October 1913, in BS4/2.
47. Strang op.cit. pp.13, 18.
48. Stroud *Early Reminiscences*. Cash Book No.1.
49. Stroud *Early Reminiscences*.
50. Ibid.
51. Cash Book No.1.
52. Strang op.cit. p.16. GU Matriculation Albums.
53. Harold Jackson's Personal Letter-book, 1893-99.
54. Strang op.cit. p.16.
55. Ibid. p.21.

56. Undated letter, Stroud to French, in the possession of Mrs Harper. For an account of the disaster, see Charles Hocking *Dictionary of Disasters at Sea During the Age of Steam,* Vol. 2, (Lloyds Register of Shipping 1969).
57. Cash Book No.1.
58. Strang op.cit. p.25.
59. Jackson to Armstrong Mitchell, 23 January 1896.
60. Strang op.cit. p.25.
61. *Janes Fighting Ships,* 1899.
62. Cash Book No.1. Strang op.cit. p.25. Jackson to Staats-Sekretar des Reichs-Marine-Amts, 4 October 1895, to Armstrong Mitchell, 2 January 1896, and to *Engineering,* 16 March 1896.
63. Strang op.cit. p.27.
64. Stroud *Early Reminiscences.*
65. Strang op.cit. p.29.
66. Strang op.cit. pp.28 and 29.
67. Ibid. p.32. Cash Book No.1. GU Matriculation Albums.
68. Jackson to Baird Thompson, 18 September and 23 October 1895, and to Sloanes & Mitchell, 6 and 27 September 1895.
69. *Glasgow Herald,* 16 April 1898.
70. Dr McKinnon 'When we were young', *Barr & Stroud Magazine,* 1-2, p.21.
71. Orders List, compiled by Dr J M Strang.
72. Cash Book No. 1.
73. Jackson to Lieut. Arthur Limpus RN, 22 November 1895.
74. Barr and Stroud, 'Telemeters and Rangefinders', op.cit.
75. Jackson to Armstrong Mitchell, 5 December 1895.
76. Strang's Orders List.
77. Jackson to Armstrong Mitchell, 20 January 1896.
78. Strang op.cit. p.35. Jackson to Glasgow District Subway Co, 6 November 1897.
79. Jackson to Armstrong Whitworth, 23 March 1898.
80. Jackson to Armstrong Whitworth, 21 May 1898.
81. Jackson to Armstrong Whitworth, 1 February 1899, 26 April and 7 September 1900, and to Captain Ijichi IJN, 21 May, 14 and 19 June, 17 July, 17 August and 31 October 1900.
82. Jackson to Captain Fitz-Graham, Royal Swedish Navy, 4 February 1901.
83. Jackson to Captain Ijichi, 18 June 1900.
84. Strang op.cit. p.22. Stroud to Barr, 16 May 1894.
85. Jackson to Armstrong Whitworth, 20 July 1898.
86. Jackson to Armstrong Whitworth, 1 August 1898 and to Director of Naval Ordnance (DNO), 10 March 1900.
87. *Electricity,* 9 August 1901. Strang op.cit. p.23.
88. Jackson to Clydebank Shipbuilding Co, 2 May 1899.
89. Jackson to DNO, 10 March 1900, and to Captain Fitz-Graham, 4 February 1901.
90. Jackson to Armstrong Whitworth, 29 June 1899, and to Bolling and Lowe, 3 November 1903.
91. Jackson to Admiral Thomson, Imperial German Navy, 16 May 1898, and to Armstrong Whitworth, 19 February and 9 April 1901.
92. Jackson to Dollond & Co, 21 April 1898 and to Armstrong Whitworth, 4 June, 17 Aug 1898 and 5 December 1901.
93. Letters to B N Napier, 17 October 1898, and to N F Stanley, 19 June 1900. The Fiske rangefinder is described in detail in *Engineering,* 17 October 1896.

94. Cash Book No.1.
95. Barr to William Taylor, 3 June 1903. *Archibald Barr 1855-1931,* printed privately by the firm in 1931, records that Dr Barr brought the first American milling machine to Scotland in 1898.
96. Jackson to 5 June 1899.
97. Strang op.cit. p.35.
98. Strang op.cit. p.35.
99. Jackson to Glasgow District Subway Co, 21 January 1899 and 18 February 1901, and to Clydesdale Bank, 31 January 1901.
100. Jackson to C P Watson, 16 December 1895. Strang op.cit. p. 33.
101. Dr McKinnon 'When we were young', *Barr & Stroud Magazine,* 1.4,p.12. Barr to Lord Kelvin, 24 October 1902.
102. Jackson to Porter, 22 March 1901. Porter's salary was £120.
103. Oakley op.cit. p.23. Strang op.cit. p.56. Barr to C P Goerz, 4 March 1898.
104. *Who's Who* 1929. Barr to Henderson, 16 March 1898. Henderson's salary was £225.
105. Jackson to N V Nimmo, 13 February 1904.
106. Jackson to Hilger & Co, 27 November 1908.
107. Jackson to Maurice Loir, French agent, 11 December 1907.
108. Jackson to Carlo Basso, Italian agent, 15 November 1907.
109. Jackson to Keuffel & Esser, 9 November 1908.

CHAPTER 2

1. Jackson to Artillerie Pruefugs Kommission, 8 November 1895, L U Kinkler, 15 November 1897, and Armstrong & Co, 8 December 1897.
2. Jackson to J Bolton, 21 July 1898. *Nature,* 25 October 1900.
3. Jackson to C P Goerz, 12 May 1899.
4. Strang op.cit. p.56. Jackson to Goerz, 1 May 1903.
5. Jackson to Goerz, 12 May 1899, and Armstrong Whitworth, 17 April 1900.
6. Jackson to Topographical Bureau, Switzerland, 9 and 24 July 1900, Armstrong Whitworth, 25 September 1900, Captain Ekeloff RSN, 30 September 1907, Captain M R Carr RN, 23 December 1908.
7. *Outlook,* 8 December 1900.
8. *World's Work,* April 1903, p.573.
9. Stroud *Early Reminiscences.*
10. Ibid. *Naval and Military Record,* 20 January 1915. Jackson to Major Guiness, 28 and 30 December 1899.
11. *Bradford Observer,* 11 September 1900.
12. Jackson to Major Hervey Scott, 30 March 1900 and Armstrong Whitworth, 17 April and 5 August 1901.
13. *Nature,* 17 October 1901. *Engineering Magazine,* February 1902. *Engineering,* 3 October 1902. *The Times,* 17 September 1903.
14. Stroud to Barr, 25 September 1901 and 8 February 1902.
15. Strang's Orders List.
16. Stroud to Barr, 16 March 1899.
17. Strang op.cit. p.40. Jackson to De Leval Electric Lamp Co, 25 October 1900 and J T Bottomley, 31 March 1903.
18. Strang op.cit. p.43. *Engineering,* 26 July 1901, p.117.
19. Strang op.cit. p.44.
20. *Glasgow Evening News,* 21 March 1904. Jackson to Caledonian Railway Co, 29 November 1905.
21. Jackson to Mr Lockie, 18 November 1902 and International Time Recorder Co, 25 March 1903.

22. Jackson to Bottomley & Liddle, 12 August 1896, re map carrier, 21 November 1898, re Stroud's Kinematograph, 26 June 1901, re Barr's internal combustion engine.
23. Strang's Order List.
24. Jackson to Inspector General of Fortifications, 10 September 1896, Under Secretary of State at War Office, 6 November 1897, C P Goerz, 12 May 1899. Strang's Order List.
25. Jackson to Director Navy Contracts (DNC), 10 July 1901.
26. Strang's Order List. Jackson to Lieut. Lynes RN, 9 Jan 1904.
27. Jackson to Armstrong Whitworth, 8 and 24 July 1903.
28. Jackson to Lieut. Crooke RN, 27 July 1903.
29. Jackson to Lieut. Lynes, 9 January and Strang, 29 April 1904.
30. Cash Book No.1.
31. Jackson to Cowan, Clapperton & Barclay, 30 May 1903.
32. Cash Book No. 2.
33. Ibid.
34. Jackson to Cowan, Clapperton & Barclay, 13 February 1901, 8 January 1902.
35. Jackson to Barr, 27 August 1903.
36. Ian Garvie to Dr J M Strang, 11 July 1969. Strang op.cit. p.57.
37. Garvie to Strang, 11 July 1969. Jackson to E Walker & Co, 7 August 1905. 'Our Company — its Development and Maintenance', *Barr & Stroud Magazine*, 2.3.
38. Jackson to John Paterson & Son, 17 August 1904.
39. Garvie to Strang, 11 July 1969. Strang op.cit. p.57.
40. *Engineering*, 4 May 1906, p.580.
41. Ibid. 1 August 1919, p.133.
42. Mackinnon op.cit. p.21. Strang op.cit. p.63.
43. Strang op.cit. p.36. *Iron and Coal Trades Review*, 27 March 1903. *Gas World*, 28 March 1903. Jackson to G Baldoff, 3 May 1906.
44. Jackson to DNC, 4 November 1905.
45. Strang op.cit. p.71.
46. Barr to editor of *Engineering*, 7 June 1907.
47. Oliver Porter to various parents, 19 and 20 February 1908.
48. Jackson to Mr Ralston, 14 September 1908.
49. Jackson to Campbell McDonald, 19 January 1915.
50. Jackson to Andrew Robertson, 11 January 1906. See Barr's reference for Blair sent to Williams & Robinson, 24 January 1902.
51. GU Matriculation Albums. Strang op.cit. p.60. Barr to Secretary of University Court, 3 January 1904, notes that McLean worked for a short time as his assistant in the Engineering Department.
52. Jackson to Barr, 27 August 1903.
53. Cash Book No.1.
54. Jackson to Armstrong Whitworth, 23 January and 19 July, and US Naval Attaché, London, 8 June 1899.
55. Jackson to Captain C H Stockton USN, 28 October 1903.
56. Jackson to Armstrong Whitworth, 17 April 1900, 19 July and 20 and 23 December 1901, 16 May 1902, and to Captain Ouspensky IRN, 19 July 1901.
57. Jackson to Takata & Co, 23 October 1903, 'our experience of exclusive dealing (with a sole agent) has been somewhat unsatisfactory' and to Armstrong Whitworth, 18 September 1903 and 23 November 1904.
58. Jackson to Takata & Co, 11 January 1904.
59. See David Walder *The Short Victorious War* (London 1973).
60. Jackson to Captain Bostroem IRN, 15 September 1902, and Admiral Wilson RN, 23 August 1904. *The Scotsman*, 12 April 1904. Cover illustration, *Warship* No 6.
61. Jackson to Takata & Co, 14 January 1905.
62. Philip Towle 'Battleship Sales During the Russo-Japanese War', *Warship International*, 4, 1986, p.402. Dr Oscar Parkes *British Battleships* (Seeley Service 1956), p.461.
63. J N Westwood *Witnesses of Tsu-shima* (Tokyo 1970), p.85.
64. Ibid. p.182. Jackson to Captain Ouspensky, 19 July 1901.
65. Westwood op.cit. and John Campbell 'The Battle of Tsu-shima', *Warship*, 5-8,1978, provide the best accounts of the battle.
66. Westwood op.cit. pp.182, 184, 214.
67. *Revista Maritima*, 19 June 1908.
68. The short-based rangefinders were not delivered until July 1905, too late to be used in action against the Japanese — see Jackson to Basil Zaharoff, 7 July 1905.
69. Jackson to Zaharoff, 28 April, 30 June, 11 August, 23 September 1904. Jackson told Keuffel & Esser, 3 December 1908, that a fast destroyer had been detached from 'another Government's fleet to collect rangefinders in the past'.
70. Jackson to Zaharoff, 21 October 1904 and 17 February 1905, and Wm Mitchell, 29 October 1904.
71. West op.cit. p.175, gives the initial range as 7,600 yards, while *Brassey's Naval Annual*, 1906, p.106, records that the Russians opened fire at between 8,000 and 9,500 yards. Westwood op.cit and William McElwee *The Art of War* (Indiana University 1974), p.295, describe the effects of Russian fire on the Japanese ships.
72. Oliver Warner *Great Sea Battles* (London 1963), p.248.
73. Westwood op.cit. pp.184, 214.
74. Ibid pp.181, 184, 214.
75. Jackson to J P Segg & Co, 26 September 1905. The battleships were the *Mikasa, Shikishima* and *Asahi*, the armoured cruisers the *Asama, Tokiwa, Idzumo, Iwate* and *Yakumo*. In a letter to W H Martin, Dutch agent, 29 September 1905, Jackson noted that the armoured cruiser *Nisshin* was equipped with another firm's range and order instruments — probably Vickers, but the instruments 'did not stand the shock of firing'.
76. *Evening News*, 15 June 1905.
77. Jackson to W H Martin, 29 September 1905.
78. Jackson to C P Goerz, 12 May 1906.
79. Strang's Orders List. Jackson to Ministero della Marine, Italy, 19 October, and Lieut-Commander Americo Silvado, 25 October 1905, and Maurice Loir, 26 January 1906. The revival of interest in Germany was short-lived. Jackson told Goerz on 16 August 1906 that Barr & Stroud had decided to give up their efforts to market rangefinders in Germany.
80. Strang op.cit. p.60.
81. Jackson to A F Yarrow, 8 September 1903, Table of results, Jackson, Barr and Captain John R Jellicoe taking readings using the 9-foot FQ at Anniesland, 7 September 1906 (in Private Papers, BS4/24).
82. Patent No. 1462, 21 January 1903. Strang op.cit. p.75.
83. Jackson to R H Parsons, 16 May 1906. The price rose to £357 in 1907, when a 4-foot 6-inch FA cost £238 and a 2-metre FQ, favoured by the French Navy, cost £335. The standard magnification of the naval FQ rangefinder was originally 30 diameters.
84. Jackson to A F Yarrow, 8 September 1903, mentions that Barr &

Stroud were making a 9-foot rangefinder for a Japanese firm, and to Basil Zaharoff, 21 December 1905, re a similar instrument for Russia. On 3 February 1906, Jackson told the Secretary of State of the War Office that two 9-foot rangefinders had been sent to the USA, and one each to the Royal Navy, Austria-Hungary and Russia. A letter to Schwanenflugel on 19 April 1906 mentions that the Royal and Italian Navies had adopted the 9-foot instrument, and another to Lieut. Bianchi, Royal Italian Navy, 28 December 1906, records that the Royal Navy had forty, Japan ten, Russia one, the USA two, Italy twenty-five and Austria one 9-foot FQ on order or already delivered.

85. Strang's Order List.
86. Ibid. Jackson to Maurice Loir, 28 November 1905.
87. For descriptions of early Zeiss rangefinders, see *Nature*, 18 October 1900, p. 608, and *Engineering*, 10 March 1916.
88. *Inventions*, 28 December 1898. Jackson to Major H de B Hovel, 19 August 1902.
89. See The *Windsor Magazine*, July 1918, p.146, for outline of Zeiss's history. Also Alexander Gleichen *The Theory of Modern Optical Instruments*, (English translation HMSO 1919).
90. Jackson to Armstrong Whitworth, 5 August 1902. Stroud's lecture to the British Association, quoted in the *Bradford Observer*, 11 September 1900.
91. Jackson to Keuffel & Esser, 3 December 1908.
92. Stroud to Barr, 27 July and Jackson to Armstrong Whitworth, 5 August 1902.
93. Jackson to Major H de B Hovel, 19 August 1902.
94. Jackson to Maurice Loir, 17 October, and Keuffel & Esser, 3 December 1908.
95. Jackson to Armstrong Whitworth, 30 July 1902.
96. Jackson to Major H de B Hovel, 13 October 1902, and Captain H N Price USN, 27 October, and Captain J E Drummond RN, 6 November 1908.
97. Jackson to Armstrong Whitworth, 30 December 1907, Maurice Loir, 2 May and 19 November 1908. Strang op.cit. p.89.
98. Stroud to Barr, 23 May 1908. Jackson to G R Seibert, Austrian agent, 11 June 1912, re duralumin.
99. Jackson to Captain J E Drummond RN, 6 November 1908.
100. Ibid. The FT field rangefinder of O.66metres was accurate to 5 yards at 1,000, the FT of 1metre to 2 yards at 1,000.
101. Ibid. Hahn became a partner in C P Georz in 1907.
102. Ibid. Adam Hilger & Co asked Barr & Stroud to participate in a joint venture to manufacture Maridin rangefinders, in 1907, but Barr & Stroud decided against it.
103. Strang's Order List.
104. Jackson to Bolling & Lowe, 30 November 1906.
105. Jackson to Maurice Loir, 20 July 1912.
106. Jackson to Porter, 12 March 1910. Interestingly, Jackson told Stroud on 20 July that the Zeiss was considered better than the Barr & Stroud field rangefinder at trials in Britain that year.
107. Jackson to Lieut-Col. W C Brown, US Cavalry, 7 August 1912.
108. Letters and memoranda relating to the patent action are contained in a special file, BS4/17, in the Barr & Stroud Archive. Barr & Stroud had taken out patents in Britain, France, Austria-Hungary, Japan, the USA, Norway and Sweden by March 1912.
109. Jackson to Strang, 8 March, and to C P Goerz, 22 March 1912. The court's decision is preserved in BS4/17.
110. Jackson Memo, undated, BS4/17.
111. Ibid.
112. Mackinnon Memo and Jackson Memo, both undated, BS4/17.
113. Jackson Memo, BS4/17.
114. Jackson to Zeiss, 20 January 1913.
115. The decision of the German High Court, 4 August 1913, is preserved in BS4/17.
116. *United Services Gazette*, 13 April 1911. Strang's Orders List. The Marindin rangefinder was manufactured by Barr & Stroud's suppliers of optical parts, Adam Hilger & Co. Hilger made over 200 instruments, but Jackson told Cowan, Clapperton & Barclay on 18 December 1913 that the rangefinder was a 'ghastly failure'.
117. Jackson to Cowan, Clapperton & Barclay, 1 December 1913 and 13 February 1914. War Office to Ashurst, Morris & Crisp & Co, 11 February 1914. In BS4/2.
118. Jackson to Prof. Gerschun, 26 November 1912.
119. Jackson to Satolias & Co, 2 March 1914.
120. Jackson to G R Seibert, 23 July 1914.
121. Jackson to Satolias & Co, 2 March 1914.
122. Jackson to Lieutenant Schwanenflugel, Danish agent, 2 January 1907.
123. Jackson to Maurice Loir, 20 July 1912.
124. Barr to Jackson, 9 May 1907, in BS4/24. By this date, Zeiss had works in Vienna and proposed to open others in St Petersburg and Paris. The Germans had an office in London.
125. The company was Société Barr et Stroud. See Jackson to Barr & Stroud, 7 June 1911, in BS4/29.
126. Strang op.cit. p 79. The French subsidiary and workshops were closed down after the First World War.
127. Jackson to G R Seibert, 14 November 1912.
128. Jackson to James McFarlane, 27 April 1914. Strang op.cit. p.86.
129. Letters from John Dunn, written during the war, are preserved in the B & S Archive.
130. Jackson to Barr & Stroud, 9 June 1908, in BS4/27.
131. Draft agreement with Keuffel & Esser, 1923 in the Barr & Stroud Archive, Misc. Papers, Envelope No. 7.
132. Jackson to Barr & Stroud, 18 March 1914, in BS4/29.
133. Jackson to Obhoukoff, 16 September 1912. Prof. Gerschun to Barr & Stroud, 6 December 1913 in BS4/11.
134. Jackson to J M Strang, 29 February 1912. Strang op.cit.
135. Jackson to Barr & Stroud, 19 April 1912 and 17 December 1913 re Balinsky's business (and ethical!) failings. Jackson to Barr, 6 April 1914.
136. Barr & Stroud Minutes of Shareholders Meetings, 6 July 1914. 1,500 shares were purchased, each of 100 roubles.
137. Jackson to Zeiss, 7 August 1912 in BS4/17.
138. Strang's Orders List. Jackson to Maurice Loir, 7 November 1913.
139. See Jon Tetsuro Sumida's forthcoming book on the history of technical innovation in the Royal Navy, to be published by Allen & Unwin. See also his (as editor) *The Pollen Papers* (Allen & Unwin, for Navy Records Society), and 'British Capital Ship Design... ' in *Journal of Modern History*, Vol. 51, March 1979. Jackson to G R Seibert, 20 July 1912, and Sigismund Vronsky, Russian agent, 14 May 1914, refers to the drawbacks of the Pollen-Cooke rangefinders.

140. *Optical Equipment: Rangefinders USN* (US Department of Navy 1913), p.27.
141. Strang's Orders List.
142. Figures compiled by Mr Hugh Kelly, from Barr & Stroud's Private Ledgers and Journals.
143. Minutes of Shareholders Meetings, 10 and 26 March, 18 June, 16 June, 1913 and 21 January 1914.
144. Ledgers and Journals, 1913.
145. The Strouds moved from Leeds to Rupert Lodge, Headingley, during the 1890s, and to a villa in Ilkley in 1903. He rented a house in Bearsden in 1909 before moving to Bankell House near Milngavie.
146. The Barr's moved from Royston to their new home, Westerton of Mugdock, near Milngavie, in January 1908. Jackson joined the move to the suburbs later, when he bought Baldernock House nearby.
147. Oakley op.cit. notes that they worked, at first, in the same office at Caxton Street, sharing a large desk, although Dr Barr spent long hours in his own laboratory at the factory.
148. Jackson to Maurice Loir, 12 August 1914.

CHAPTER 3

1. Jackson to G R Siebert, 29 July and G B Satolias, 7 September 1914.
2. Roy and Kay MacLeod 'War and Economic Development ...' in J M Winter *War and Economic Development* (Cambridge University Press), p.173.
3. Strang's Orders List. Strang to Professor Gerschun, 14 August 1914.
4. Strang op.cit. pp.94, 117.
5. Jackson to Secretary of War Office, 13 August 1914.
6. Jackson to Army Service Corps, 4th Coy. HLI, 25 August and Lieut. Schwanenflugel, 10 November 1914.
7. Barr & Stroud Industrial Committee Minute Book. Jackson to A G Duffill, 2 July 1916, in B & S Admiralty Letter-book, A3.
8. Jackson to Secretary, Board of Trade, 16 December 1914, explains that Barr & Stroud had to decline an offer to send skilled Belgian refugees to Anniesland, as the Admiralty insisted that foreigners were not employed at the factory during the war.
9. See James Hinton *The First Shop Steward's Movement* (Allen & Unwin, 1973), pp.123, 131.
10. Charles Moore *Skill and the English Working Class 1870-1914* (Croom Helm 1980), p.32.
11. Strang op.cit. p,117.
12. Industrial Committee Minute Book, p.1.
13. Ibid. Hinton op.cit. p.158.
14. Industrial Committee Minutes, 28 March and 4 April 1916.
15. *Engineering*, 19 September 1919, p.363.
16. Jackson Memorandum, 2 July 1918, in B & S Archive Envelope 14. Industrial Committee Minute Book, 4 April 1916, notes that women were to be paid 6d per hour, rising to 8d after completing their training. Unskilled men earned a maximum of 10d.
17. Jackson to Maurice Loir, 17 December 1914.
18. Ibid. Garvie to Strang, undated, 1969, in B & S Archive.
19. Jackson to Maurice Loir, 17 December 1914.
20. Jackson to Hilger, 13 November 1914. Barr & Stroud required a minimum of 100 pentagonal prisms each week, but Chance were unable to supply sufficient quantities to Hilger & Co, who manufactured the prisms for Barr & Stroud, to meet the demand from Anniesland. Jackson to DNC, 22 March 1916, notes that Chance Bros. had fallen behind with orders placed by Barr & Stroud.
21. Strang op.cit. p.101.
22. Ibid. p.102.
23. Ibid. p.103, R W Whipple, in the *Daily News,* 19 January 1922, implies that a member of Barr & Stroud's scientific staff worked for a time as an artisan in some potteries to learn the art of making pots in which to melt glass.
24. Jackson to Lieut. H D Hamilton RN, 28 November 1906.
25. Strang's Orders List.
26. Article by J W French in *Nature,* 24 July 1919.
27. 'Fire-control on HM Ships, December 1919', in Naval Historical Library.
28. Strang's Orders List.
29. Ibid. Jackson to Armstrong Whitworth, 9 October 1914, and to Commander Cochrane RN, 1 May 1916.
30. Strang's Orders List.
31. See the humourous account of the *South Australian Motor's* correspondent, 25 October 1922.
32. Letters from R S Stewart, O J Riley, J W Riley, and Mrs J Scott in answer to my request for information in the *Scots Magazine,* April 1987.
33. French to Barr & Stroud, 20 October, 1920.
34. Barr & Stroud Symbols Book.
35. General Sir Martin Farndale. *History of the Royal Regiment of Artillery* (RAI 1986), p.364. Strang op. cit. p.114.
36. Memorandum, 10 September 1914. Letter to Prof. Gerschun, 6 February 1915.
37. Papers relating to development of UB heightfinders, in Barr & Stroud Library.
38. Strang's Order List.
39. Stroud to Alice Stroud, 22 July 1918, in the possession of Mrs Harper.
40. Jackson to L Y Spear, 16 May 1903.
41. Jackson to Lieut. Hamilton RN, 16 May 1907.
42. Notes in Barr & Stroud Library. David S Ritchie 'Submarine Periscopes for the Royal Navy' in *Journal of Naval Engineering,* Vol.30, No.1.
43. J M Strang was taught to compute lenses while in St Petersburg in 1912. Turret periscopes are referred to in Barr & Stroud to Jackson, 20 March 1914.
44. Dr Strang's list of periscope orders. Jackson to Cmdr Hall, 21 March 1916.
45. A Walker's notes, in B & S Library. One FY1 was sent to the USA.
46. Strang's Periscopes List. The French Navy ordered eight FY1 periscope rangefinders on 17 November 1920, and the Poles ordered nine FY2 instruments in March 1934.
47. Strang op.cit. p.106.
48. Ibid. p.107.
49. Strang's Periscopes List. The first CH1 was fitted to L71, at Scott's Greenock yard in October 1919. The first CH2 was shipped to Harwich, 1918.
50. Strang op.cit. p.94.

51. Ibid. pp.95-97.
52. For explanations of the complex problems of naval fire-control, see Sumida (ed) op.cit.
53. Ibid. p.3, and his 'British Capital Ship Design' op.cit. p.209.
54. Correspondence file, Mouton and Stroud, BS4/12.
55. Ibid.
56. Sumida 'British Capital Ship Design' op.cit. p.218.
57. Anthony Pollen *The Great Gunnery Scandal* (Collins 1980).
58. Correspondence file, Mouton and Stroud, BS4/12. Jackson to French, 16 November 1912, notes that the firm was manufacturing a plotting board for Brazil.
59. Strang op.cit. p.98. Jackson to G R Seibert, 20 July 1912, and to Secretary of Admiralty, 19 March 1913.
60. Jackson to John R Jellicoe, DNC, 22 November 1906, to G R Seibert, 22 May 1913. Jackson to Stroud, 21 July 1914, notes that naval rangefinders were to have been fitted with Pollen's Argo uniform range gear until the rupture with Pollen.
61. Jackson to Barr & Stroud, 2 August 1911, commented that the firm supplied almost all the Royal Navy's dial sights, as C P Goerz were 'unable to meet the design from Woolwich' (BS4/29). Barr & Stroud to DNC, 17 March 1916, mention that French's dial sight design will be submitted 'soon'.
62. Strang op.cit. p.116. French to Stroud, 21 August 1916, re the Admiralty's requirements.
63. The following account of the battle is based on John Campbell's definitive *Jutland: An Analysis of the Fighting* (Conway Maritime Press 1986), Arthur J Marder's *From the Dreadnought to Scapa Flow*, 2nd edition, Vol.3, (Oxford University Press 1978) and *The Battle of Jutland: Offical Despatches* (HMSO 1920).
64. Jackson to Cmdr Cochrane RN, 1 May 1916. The *Orion's* was a trial rangefinder, installed before the war.
65. Scheer's report, reprinted in the *Official Despatches*, p.590.
66. Campbell op.cit. gives the best account of the gunnery of, and the damages inflicted on, the ships of the two fleets. V E Tarrant *Battlecruiser Invincible* (Arms and Armour Press 1986) described the performance and the tragic end of Hood's flagship.
67. Marder op.cit. pp.82-196. Campbell op.cit. p.366.
68. Marder op.cit. p.80.
69. *Offical Despatches,* p.375. Campbell op.cit. pp.156, 159. Tarrant op.cit. p.106.
70. Marder op.cit. p.167, quoting Padfield.
71. *Handbook for Stereoscopic Rangefinders 1919* in PRO, ADM186/237, and *Progress in Naval Gunnery 1914-18*, ADM186/238. Jackson to Admiral N E Mason USN, 27 October 1908.
72. Contained in the Public Record Office (PRO), Kew, ADM/186/259.
73. *General Information Collected by Mr J W French ... from Various Sources ...*, PRO, ADM186/243.
74. Ibid.
75. Marder op.cit. p.197.
76. Strang's Order List.
77. The FX2 is described in *Barr & Stroud Rangefinders: Tables of Standard Types*, No.129, in Barr & Stroud Library.
78. *Fire-Control on HM Ships*, December 1919, p.33. See also *Handbook for Naval Rangefinders 1921*, PRO ADM186/253.
79. The problem had been recognised as particularly acute on

destroyers, but Jackson complained in a letter to Lieut. R Backhouse RN, 13 October 1908, that rangefinders in the fighting tops of other warships were affected by 'horrible' vibration. See also *Fire-Control on HM Ships*, December 1919, p.34.
80. *Progress in Gunnery Material 1922 and 1923*, pp.26-34, PRO ADM186/259.
81. Strang op.cit. p.110.
82. Ibid. p.111.
83. Barr to Alexander Gracie, 24 February 1915.
84. Jackson to Alfred Herbert Ltd, 4 March 1915.
85. Hinton op.cit. p.147. Iain McLean *The Legend of Red Clydeside* (John Donald 1983), p.76.
86. *Glasgow Herald*, 4, 8, 9 and 19 February, 1, 12, 14 April 1916.
87. Industrial Committee Minutes, 18 April 1916, in Barr & Stroud Archive.
88. Barr to Archibald Sharp, 14 May 1918, 'A very considerable ... number of our skilled men are joining or being called up.' Barr to S Z de Ferranti, 26 July 1918. Jackson to Investigation Officer, 11 July 1917.
89. Barr to Archibald Sharp, 14 May 1918. Jackson to W Brodie of the ASE, 30 July 1918.
90. Industrial Committee Minutes, 28 December 1917 and 15 January 1918.
91. Barr to Captain H R Sankey RE, 28 January 1918, Barr's Private Letter-book No.2.
92. Jackson to General Secretary of Bureau of State Research, USA, 14 October 1919.
93. Barr to H S Hele Shaw, 24 August 1915, in Barr's Private Letter-book No.2.
94. Strang to Barr & Stroud, 15 April 1913, 'I have learned some extremely interesting things about optical work', in BS4/10. Morrison to Barr, 12 October 1916, re Strang's camera obscura for trench warfare. French to Barr, 6 September 1919, re the employments of a lens computer. Jackson to Director of Optical Engineering Department, Imperial College of Science and Technology, re Miss Kennedy and Miss Gardner's attendance of lectures on computing and optical design there.
95. Barr to Secretary Carnegie Trust, 21 October 1908, in Barr's Private Letter-book No.2, outlines Morrison's career. Strang op.cit. p.83.
96. Minutes of shareholders, 1 February 1916, 1 March 1920. Jackson retained his post as Secretary.
97. Barr to Arthur J Balfour, First Lord of Admiralty, 14 July 1915, in Barr's Private Papers.
98. Barr to Capt. H R Sankey RE, 31 May 1918, Barr's Private Letter-book No.2.
99. Information supplied by Mrs Harper.
100. Barr to Col A C Williams RA, 14 May 1917, in Barr's Private Letter-book No.2. Stroud family papers, held by Mrs Harper.
101. Information supplied by Archie Walker and Mrs Harper.
102. Ledgers and Journals, 1914-18.
103. Ibid.
104. Papers relating to Admiralty Settlement, BS4/13. The orders included those for HMS *Anson, Howe*, and *Rodney*, three battle-cruisers in the *Hood* class which were cancelled at the end of the war. Letters in BS4/14 relate to the settlement of Barr & Stroud's

claims for 'broken' contracts — DNC to Barr & Stroud, 16 September 1925, notes that the firm accepted £356,808 in respect of all claims that year. The War Office settled claims for cancelled UB2 heightfinders in 1922.
105. Barr & Stroud Ledgers and Journals, 1918.
106. Strang's Orders List.
107. Barr to A.H. Hall, 30 October 1919, in Barr's Private Letter-book No.2.

CHAPTER 4
1. Jackson to Alliance Kinematograph Machine Co, 5 September, and French to Barr, 29 April, 6 and 9 September 1919, and B & S to Alfred Tongue & Co, 25 February 1921. For details of Stroud's own patented kinematograph, see Jackson to Bottomley & Liddle, 21 November 1898.
2. Barr to Lord Kelvin, 24 October 1902, in Barr's Private Letter-book, 1900-1901. Jackson to Major H de B Havel, 19 August 1902.
3. Strang op.cit. p.125.
4. William Reid 'Binoculars in the Army' in *Army Museum*, 1981.
5. Strang op.cit. p.117. B & S to Barr, 9 September 1919.
6. Barr & Stroud to British Impactors, 2 May 1919, and Alfred Tongue & Co, 25 February 1921.
7. *Sunday Mercury*, 9 March 1919.
8. Strang op.cit. p.136.
9. Information supplied by Archie Walker.
10. Barr to Professor J G McKendrick, 16 November 1921, to Royal Glasgow Asylum for the Blind, 13 February 1922, in which he records that Jameson could now read 60 words per minute using the optophone, and to William Wilmer, 17 June 1927, in which he notes his reading speed had increased to 100 words per minute. All in Barr's Private Letter-book No.2.
11. Strang op.cit. p.136. Barr to Thomas Jameson, 6 September 1922, in Barr's Private Letter-book No.2.
12. Barr to C P McCarthy, 15 December 1922, in Barr's Private Letter-book No.2. Jackson to C P McCarthy, 16 February 1921, noted that Barr & Stroud had spent 'several thousand pounds' developing the optophone.
13. *South Australian Motor*, 25 October 1922.
14. Barr & Stroud to Single Sleeve Valve Engine Co, 6 June 1919. *The Motor Cycle*, 20 November 1919. Minutes of shareholders, 2 December 1920.
15. Minutes of shareholders, 2 December 1920.
16. *The Englishman*, 18 February 1922. *The Motor World*, 27 January 1922. The firm manufactured single-cylinder engines of 349 cc, 500 cc, and a 1000 cc V twin engine.
17. *The Motor World*, 27 January 1922, *The Motor Cycle*, 28 December 1922, *Bicycling News and Motor Review*, 17 October 1923, *The Motor Cycle and Cycle Trader*, 27 January 1922, *The Scotsman*, 31 January 1922.
18. Various advertisements, preserved in Barr & Stroud Press Cuttings, Vol. 2.
19. Strang op.cit. p.119. Iain Russell *Sir Robert McAlpine & Sons: The Early Years* (Parthenon 1988), p.152.
20. Strang op.cit. p.120.
21. Ibid. p.120. Minutes of shareholders, 30 June 1926. Agreement, undated, in Barr & Stroud Library.
22. Strang op.cit. p.121. Austin Lighting Co to Morrison, 18 November 1927, in Barr & Stroud Library.
23. Ibid. Jackson had become concerned about the cost of the venture as early as 25 February 1921, when he wrote to Barr that the firm could not afford to spend more on tools and apparatus until profits from sales offset rising production costs. French and Stroud were also less than sanguine about the engine's prospects for commercial success.
24. Information supplied by Archie Walker.
25. Strang's Orders List. *Nautical Magazine*, June 1924, notes that nearly 200 liners, tankers, yachts, etc. now carried rangefinders.
26. PRO, ADM186/259, p.39. Because the FX contained larger optical parts, it gave better illumination than the FT, although there was a slight loss in accuracy.
27. Letter, DNC to Barr & Stroud, 27 March 1924, in BS4/13.
28. *Handbook for Naval Rangefinders*, PRO, ADM186/253. *Progress in Naval Gunnery 1914-18*, ADM186/238.
29. Strang's Orders List.
30. Strang op.cit. p.153.
31. Jackson to DNC, 23 June 1916, in A3. The Italians wanted FT25 rangefinders on triplex mountings similar to those supplied for the French battleship *Courbet*.
32. PRO, ADM186/259, p.26.
33. Strang's Orders List.
34. Barr & Stroud CO records.
35. Information supplied by Mari Williams. See OPL Memorandum, 12 July 1931, re progress of rangefinder manufacture in France.
36. Barr & Stroud Visitors' Book No.1.
37. Jackson to Japanese Imperial Navy, 20 January 1913, declining to accept Japanese workmen in the factory, 31 January 1914, stating that the firm's policy had changed, and 23 October 1914, noting that two more Japanese workmen had arrived at Anniesland to learn how to repair rangefinders.
38. Strang's Orders List.
39. Strang op.cit. p.138. Yamada studied Engineering at Glasgow University during the war, and spent some of his holidays working for Barr & Stroud.
40. Barr & Stroud Visitors' Book No.2.
41. Strang op.cit. p.138.
42. Ibid. p.112. Barr & Stroud to French, 3 March 1921, noted that the price of the rangefinder, complete with mounting, transmission gear, etc. was approximately £10,000.
43. Ritchie op.cit. p.134, Strang op.cit. p.139.
44. Periscope Orders List.
45. Notes supplied by Archie Walker.
46. Strang op.cit. p.142. The patent was not published until 1950, as the Admiralty asked that details of the binocular periscope be kept secret.
47. Ledgers and Journals, 1919-24.
48. Garvie to Strang, undated, 1969.
49. Strang op.cit. p.121.
50. Information supplied by Archie Walker.
51. Ibid. Strang op.cit. p.93. Minutes of shareholders, 25 January 1922, re discussions on sale of West Works.
52. Ledgers and Journals, 1925-28.
53. Minutes of shareholders, 17 January 1928.

54. Most of Jackson's letters from abroad are contained in BS4/27 and 29.

55. Jackson to C P MCarthy, 16 February 1921, re the optophone project. His role in tempering the enthusiasm of others is clear in the letter to Barr, 25 February 1921.

56. Marginal note on letter, Stroud to Barr, 29 September 1901, in BS4/21.

57. Stroud to Barr, 16 February 1895, 'I don't quite know how you will keep a man and boy busy in the new workshop.' Stroud to Barr, 18 April 1895, querying need and cost to install a telephone at the Byres Road workshop. Both in Barr's personal papers. Stroud to Jackson, 31 July 1838, 'You don't mean to say you have 100 Rfs in process of construction. Well, of all the rash proceedings of the firm this is the rashest.... Then talk of building a place 6 times as big as at present, that is unmitigated imbecility.... Why, you two are worse than Hooley ...', in 'Papers of Historical Interest' catalogued by French.

58. Jackson to C P McCarthy, 16 February 1921.

59. Minutes of shareholders meetings, 4 August 1927.

60. See letters in BS4/21-23.

61. See letters in Barr's Private Letter-book No.2 — including letter to C P McCarthy, 15 December 1922, re his visit to Egypt in 1920, to Professor A V Hill, 16 January 1923, re his trip to Aswan from January until April that year, and to Alec Davidson, 20 January 1927. Letters in BS4/21-23 reveal that both Barr and Stroud felt that their health suffered from the pressures of working for the firm while fulfilling their duties at their respective universities.

62. The directors' duties were not sharply delineated — for example, Strang continued to contribute a great deal to the development of submarine periscope lens systems, and French, while ultimately subordinate to Barr in matters of technical development, took on many of Jackson's responsibilities in the day-to-day management of the different departments.

63. Strang op.cit. p.146.

64. Ibid. p.147.

65. Ibid. p.147. Barr & Stroud to John Bell, 18 December 1939. 'The original photonymograph and other kindred instruments for the Geographical Department of the WO were designed by ... [Dr] Barr .... In collaboration with Dr H G Fourcade [of South Africa] Barr & Stroud designed and delivered a Stereogoniometer ...'.

66. Information supplied by Archie Walker.

67. Ibid. Strang op.cit. p.126.

68. Strang op.cit. p.127.

69. Strang to J B Brown, 31 December 1931.

70. Ibid. Barr & Stroud to Commander of Lady Denison-Parker, 5 June 1932. The CF15 could be purchased from Barr & Stroud for £17, including post and packing.

71. Periscope Orders List.

72. Strang op.cit. p.145. 15 Year Agreement with SFIO, 1 October 1923, in Barr & Stroud Library. Strang to B S Clapperton & Co, 20 and 27 May 1931 re dispute with SFIO. Daily Record and Mail, 13 October 1931, reported on an order for periscopes from the USN, and the Daily Telegraph, 12 October 1931, claimed that all Japanese submarines were equipped with Barr & Stroud periscopes.

73. Strang's Orders Lists.

74. Strang op.cit. p.145.

75. Ibid. p.155.

76. Strang's Orders List.

77. Strang op.cit. p.160.

78. Ibid.

79. Barr & Stroud to DNC, 8 February 1929.

80. Strang op.cit. p.161.

81. Ledgers and Journals, 1928-33.

82. Morrison to Percy Gray, 11 August 1931. Barr & Stroud to H G Fourcade, 30 June 1931, notes that Barr had been ill for three months.

83. Obituary in Engineering, 14 August 1931.

84. Oakley op.cit. Obituary in Glasgow Herald, 6 August 1931.

85. Oakley op.cit. Obituary in Proceedings Royal Philosophical Society of Glasgow, LX, 1931-32, p.78.

86. Barr to General Manager, Corporation Tramways, 18 August 1901, re Pinkston. See Barr's Private Letter-book, 1900-01, re consultancy work on electrical power, and 1899-1900 re the electrical light installations in Waverley Station, the offices and hotel. Also his University Engineering Department letter-book, 1899-1903. Barr to John Young, 22 September 1903, notes that Barr was to conduct trials of the engines at Pinkston the following day. John Young, manager of Glasgow Tramways, was Barr's brother-in-law.

87. Barr to J S Napier, 19 August 1908, Albion Motor Car Co, 5 May 1911. J Croall & Sons, 14 April 1914, all in Barr's Private Letter-book No.2.

88. Strang op.cit p.57a.

89. Proceedings RPS, Glasgow, LX, 1931-2, p.78.

90. Ibid. Obituary in Engineering, 14 August 1931.

91. Barr to J C Mitchell, 13 September 1917. 'Royston' was left to Glasgow University in Barr's will. Westerton-of-Mugdock was left to charity, and became the Scottish Convalescent Home for Children.

92. Archie Walker recalls that Barr would often do small machinery jobs in his lab himself. Barr's formidable appearance cloaked a kindly nature, revealed by his chairmanship, 1921-31, of the Governors of the Royal Scottish National Institution for the care of mental defectives, and his donation of £8,000 to Paisley Abbey, in 1928, to defray the cost of a new organ.

93. Minutes of shareholders, 29 October 1931.

94. Strang op.cit. p.164.

95. Barr to G T Beilby, 28 July 1915, in Barr's Private Letterbook No.2. Morrison to Jackson, 14 November 1916.

96. Strang op.cit. p.164.

97. Ibid. p.150. R Wallace Clarke 'Drawing a Bead' Aeroplane Monthly, parts 1-4, February-May 1983; see February, p.102.

98. Strang op.cit. p.152.

99. Ibid. p.151.

100. Clarke op.cit. March, p.125. Strang to Ross Whistler, 22 September 1969.

101. Strang op.cit. p.162. Several thousand UB7 instruments were manufactured at Anniesland during the war.

102. Barr & Stroud to G R Seibert, 10 July 1931. A sound-locator was put on the roof of the factory during the war.

103. Ledgers and Journals, 1934-37.

104. Strang op.cit. p.165.
105. See his obituary in *Nature,* 18 June 1938.
106. Manuscript autobiography of Violet Murray, in the possession of her daughter Mrs Harper.
107. Stroud to Barr, 16 April 1909, in BS4/23. The family stayed in Rupert Lodge, Headingley, before the move to Ilkley.
108. Oakley op.cit. The office was often very smoky — Stroud calculated in 1936 that he had smoked 110,000 cigars during his life. He jokingly ranked his conversion of his colleague to the evil weed — Barr began to smoke a pipe in 1908 — as one of the great achievments of his life.
109. 'Professor Stroud: an Appreciation' in *The Gryphon,* XII. No.4, March 1909, p.55
110. Ibid. Stroud *Apologia.*
111. Violet Murray's autobiography.
112. Information supplied by Mrs Harper. Various letters in BS4/21-23.
113. Ibid.
114. Ibid.
115. Barr to Henderson, 16 March 1898. He later used 'Wyschoff's expression' when referring to his association with Stroud.
116. The ways in which Barr, Stroud and Jackson made decisions on business policy emerge from their detailed correspondence in B54/21-23 and in Barr's Private Letter-books.

CHAPTER 5
1. Strang op.cit. p.169.
2. Ibid.
3. Ibid. Information supplied by Archie Walker.
4. The firm began to recruit substantial numbers of women during the early 1930s, when binoculars production increased. Five hundred women went on strike at the factory in 1937, demanding an extra penny per hour. (*Daily Worker,* 7 April 1937). Information on women at Barr & Stroud supplied by Archie Walker and Alan Mackinlay.
5. Strang op.cit. p.166. Envelope No.12, Barr & Stroud Library.
6. Information supplied by Archie Walker.
7. Strang op.cit. p.178. French to Morrison, 23 September 1940, Envelope No 13, Barr & Stroud Library — doubted that rumours concerning Dr Gregor, once German Consul in Glasgow and later a high-ranking officer in the Luftwaffe, having specially singled out Barr & Stroud for attack.
8. French to Ministry of Home Security, 13 December 1940. No sooner had the roofs been painted over on official instructions, than a Factory Inspector told Barr & Stroud they must remove the paint because the men must not work in artificial light! French also complained that the nightshift continually opened the factory windows, and the firm had to employ men to go round closing them again.
9. Information supplied by Archie Walker. French to DNC, 10 April 1940 (in Envelope 13), claiming that all the firm's employees could get down to the shelter in just ten minutes.
10. French to Vice-Admiral B A Fraser RN, 14 March 1941, in Envelope 11.
11. French to Secretary of the Admiralty, 1 July 1940, in Envelope 11.
12. French to Ministry of Supply, 24 May 1940, in Envelope 11. The rifle club men had ten .22 rifles, accurate only to about 200 yards.
13. French to Ministry of Aircraft Production, 15 June 1940, in Envelope 11.
14. Ibid.
15. Eric Brash *Random Reflections* (unpublished 1975), held in B & S Library.
16. French to Ministry of Aircraft Production, 19 and 22 July 1940. In August the firm was still awaiting a promised delivery of revolvers, grenades, shotguns and an anti-aircraft machine-gun. Although they had nearly 5,000 rounds of 303 ammunition for their Bren gun, in September they had no bullets to replace the fifty rounds fired in practice.
17. Brash op.cit.
18. Ibid.
19. Ian Mackenzie to Strang, 15 July 1969, in Envelope 76. Strang op.cit. p.89 notes that the firm had made over 47,000 FT field rangefinders by 1969.
20. 'Adjuster', 'The Manufacture of Rangefinders' in *Barr & Stroud Magazine,* 1.12, p.7.
21. Barr & Stroud Library, Envelope 7. Correspondence relating to licensing arrangements in Canada and USA. Strang op.cit. p.172.
22. Unsigned letter to Strang, 3 December 1969. Barr & Stroud Symbols Book. Robin Cross *The Bombers* (Bantam 1987), p.121.
23. Clarke op.cit. March, p.127. Strang to Ross Whistler, 22 September 1969.
24. Clarke op.cit. March, p.124. 'W P' to Strang, 10 December 1969.
25. A E Neumann to Air Ministry, 26 April 1938, in notes supplied by R W Clarke.
26. Clarke op.cit. April, p.200. Strang op.cit. p.176. Mackenzie to Strang, 12 December 1969.
27. Alan Raven and John Roberts *British Battleships of World War Two* (Conway Maritime Press 1985), p.8.
28. See Raven and Roberts op.cit, p.349, and S W Roskill *History of the Second World War: The War at Sea,* Vol.1, (HMSO 1954), p.404.
29. Raven and Roberts op.cit. pp.171-184, 354.
30. John Winton The Death of the Scharnhorst (Grenada 1983).
31. Strang op.cit. p.171.
32. Ibid. p.155. Montague Timbury to Strang, 25 November 1969, in Barr & Stroud Library.
33. See Barr & Stroud's records of naval instruments carried on British warships, 1939-45, in jotters marked RF and RN, Barr & Stroud Archives.
34. Information supplied by David Ritchie.
35. Timbury to Strang, 25 November 1969.
36. Strang op.cit. pp.128-130.
37. Ibid. p.128
38. Marder op.cit. p.198.
39. Ibid.
40. Paul J Kemp *British Submarines in World War Two* (Arms and Armour Press 1987), p.5.
41. Strang op.cit. p.174.
42. Ibid. p.175.
43. Ritchie op.cit. p.135. Minutes of meeting held at Northways, 1 July 1943, in Barr & Stroud Library, Envelope 70.
44. Kemp op.cit. p.5.
45. Strang op.cit. p.175. Stephen Roskill *The Navy at War 1939-45*

(London 1960), p.317.

46. Rear-Admiral C B Barry to Barr & Stroud, 9 October 1943.

47. French's energetic direction of the defence of the factory from air and ground attack emerge from his letters in Barr & Stroud Library, Envelope 11. See also Strang op.cit. p.32 and the obituary in *Nature*, 15 February 1953.

48. The story may well be apocryphal!

49. House of Commons Committee of Public Accounts, 1941-42, No.127, 28 April 1942, and the evidence of French and Morrison given on 19 May 1942.

50. *Glasgow Herald*, 4 December 1943, p.4.

51. Strang op.cit. pp.90 and 128. About 75,000 Barr & Stroud binoculars were delivered to the Royal Navy during the war.

52. C S Goyder, Department of Scientific Research and Experiment to Morrison, 23 February 1944. Chance Bros were the leading suppliers of optical glass to the armed forces.

53. Ledgers and Journals 1939-45.

54. Ibid.

55. Brash op.cit.

56. Strang op.cit. p.179. The firm also manufactured hundreds of thousands of details for the Parker 51 fountain pen.

57. Ibid. p.197. Information supplied by David Ritchie.

58. Ibid. p.205. F C Hammel to Barr & Stroud, 24 August 1947.

59. Strang op.cit. p.217.

60. *Scottish Daily Mail*, 3 May 1947. *Barr & Stroud Magazine*, 2.9.

61. Strang op.cit. p.183.

62. Ibid. p.186.

63. Ibid. p.185. Information supplied by Robert Bell. Campbell *Naval Weapons*, pp.15-21. Ross Walton *The Cruiser Belfast* (Conway Maritime, 1985), pp.14 and 98. Strang notes that John Davy attended special intensive courses in electronics technology at HMS *Collingwood* after the war, to ensure that the firm was well informed of the latest developments in the field.

64. Ledgers and Journals 1946-50.

65. Memorandum in Barr & Stroud Library, Envelope 47.

66. Strang op.cit. p.186. Notes by Strang in 'Navy Centenary Papers' in Barr & Stroud Library, Envelope 14.

67. Strang op.cit. p.181.

68. Minutes of shareholders, 23 March and 6 July 1949 and 22 March 1950. Andrew Alison succeeded Strang as secretary in June 1954.

69. Strang op.cit. p.61. Barr & Stroud's football club was formed in 1905, but initial attempts by the firm to rent ground near Temple Gasworks for a football pitch were unsuccessful. The team probably played on hired pitches prior to Mr Maclean's gift of the playing fields.

70. Information supplied by David Ritchie.

71. The existing preference shares were of 10 per cent, having been increased from 6 per cent at a meeting of the shareholders on 1 July 1928.

72. Articles of Association are contained in the minutes of shareholders, 1954.

CHAPTER 6

1. See for example C J Bartlett *The Long Retreat — A Short History of British Defence Policy, 1945-70*, (Macmillan, 1972), Chapter 3.

2. Strang op.cit. p.188 and Annual Report (AR) No.42, 1954.

3. AR No.43, 1955.

4. Ritchie op.cit. and Dr J M Strang op.cit. p.187.

5. Ritchie op.cit. p.136.

6. M Critchley *British Warships since 1945* (Maritime Books 1981), p.34.

7. Ritchie op.cit. pp.136-7 and Strang op.cit. p.242.

8. Ritchie op.cit. pp.137-9.

9. Ibid. pp.140-141.

10. Strang op.cit. pp.202-4.

11. Ibid. p.242.

12. Ibid. p.242, and D S Ritchie op.cit. p.140.

13. Ibid. p.243.

14. *Navy Estimators, 1954-55*, (HMSO 1954), cmd 9079.

15. Critchley op.cit. p.62.

16. Ritchie op.cit. pp.142-3.

17. E J Grove *Vanguard to Trident — British Naval Policy since World War II* (The Bodley Head 1987), pp.229-33.

18. Interview with D S Ritchie and Barr & Stroud Symbols Book.

19. Ritchie op.cit. p.143 and Strang op.cit. pp.207-8.

20. See for example *Statement on Defence 1955*, (HMSO London) cmd 9391, paras 7.6 and 7.7.

21. W N Arnquist 'Section 2. Survey of Early Infra-red Developments', *Proceedings of the RE*, September 1959, pp.420-7.

22. Strang op.cit. p. 220.

23. M C Timbury, typescript notes on Dr J M Strang's unpublished History of Barr & Stroud, notes on Infra-Red Instruments p.1.

24. Strang op.cit. pp.221-2 and Timbury op.cit. pp.1-2.

25. Strang op.cit. p.187 and Paul Beaver and Terry Gander *Modern British Military Missiles*, (Patrick Stephens Limited 1986), p.59.

26. Strang op. cit. p.187.

27. Ibid. p.187 and Terry Gander *Royal Airforce Aircraft* (Patrick Stephens Limited 1987), pp.19-20.

28. See for example AR No 44, 1956.

29. Strang op.cit. pp.209-10 and pamphlet No.H1578-0368 'Integrated Microdensitometer'.

30. Dr Alex Hope unpublished 'Colour Television Lecture Notes', nd.

31. Strang op.cit. p.191.

32. Strang op.cit. p.192-6.

33. AR Nos.42 and 46, 1954, 1958.

34. Strang op.cit. p.212 and information supplied by the company.

35. Interviews with present and former directors.

36. F A Johnson, *Defence by Ministry —The British Ministry of Defence 1944-1974* (Duckworth 1980), pp. 54-56.

37. AR No.46, 1958.

38. *Defence — Outline of Future Policy* (HMSO 1957), cmd 124, para 58.

39. *Report on Defence1960*, (HMSO 1960), cmd 952, para 23.

40. AR No.48, 1960.

41. Strang op.cit. pp.209-10.

42. Minute Book (MB), No.4, meeting of 1 December 1959.

43. Strang op.cit. p.211.

44. MB No.4, meeting of 27 July 1960.

45. MB No.4, meeting of 31 January 1961.

46. AR No.49, 1961.

47. MB No.4, meeting of 17 February 1961.

48. MB No.4, meeting of 30 October 1961.

49. MB No.4, meeting of 29 November 1961.
50. MB No.4, meeting of 29 November 1961.
51. AR No.49, 1961.
52. AR No.49, 1961.
53. Strang op.cit. p.235.
54. MB No.4, meeting of 4 September 1962.
55. AR No.50, 1962 and M C Timbury op.cit. notes on Medical Instruments.
56. MB No.4, meeting of 4 September 1962.
57. *Explanatory Statements on the Navy Estimates 1960-61* and *1961-62*, (HMSO 1961 and 1962), cmd 1282 and 948.
58. Judy Allen *Lasers and Holograms*, (Pepper Press 1983), pp.28-29.
59. Strang op.cit. pp.256-7 and AR No.50, 1982.
60. Strang op.cit. pp.256-7.
61. MB No.4, meetings of 25 February, 16 May and 1, 4, and 5 July 1963.
62. MB No.4, meeting of 7 November 1963.
63. Information supplied by D S Ritchie and The Royal Armoured Corps Museum, Bovington Camp, Dorset.
64. Barr & Stroud Symbols Book and MB No.4, meeting of 16 June 1964.
65. Information supplied by Dr Alex Hope.
66. Beaver and Gander op.cit. pp.54-55 and Strang op.cit. pp.251-2.
67. Timbury op.cit. note on Computers.
68. Barr & Stroud Symbols Book and Strang op.cit. pp.215-17.
69. MB No.4, meeting of 22 April 1964.
70. MB No.4, meeting of 11 January 1963.
71. MB No.4, meeting of 4 July 1963.
72. Annual Meetings Minute Book No.1, meeting of 13 May 1964.

CHAPTER 7
1. F A Johnson *Defence by Ministry —The British Ministry of Defence 1944-1974*, (Duckworth 1980), Chapter 6.
2. Ibid. pp.128-38.
3. C J Bartlett *The Long Retreat — Short History of British Defence Policy 1945-70* (Macmillan 1972), pp.195-6.
4. Strang op.cit. pp.257-8 and Barr & Stroud (B & S) Symbols Book.
5. Strang op.cit. pp.259-60 and Minute Book (MB) No.4, meetings of 21 October and 12 November 1964.
6. A L Rodgers et al *Surveillance & Target Acquisition Systems Brassey's Battlefield Weapons Systems & Technology*, Vol.VII, pp.107-110 and Annual Report (AR) No.57, 1969.
7. Paul Beaver and Terry Gander *Modern British Military Missiles* (Patrick Stephens 1986), p.55.
8. Strang op. cit. p.251 and *Janes Weapon Systems 1969-70* (London), pp.49-50.
9. Beaver and Gander op.cit. p.56.
10. Strang op.cit. p.222.
11. MB No.4, meetings of 27 July and 21 September 1965.
12. E B Brash op.cit. chapter on 'The Evolution of Optical Computing'.
13. Ritchie op.cit.
14. Ibid. pp.147-8.
15. M C Timbury, typescript notes on Dr J M Strang's unpublished History of Barr & Stroud, notes on Infra-Red Instruments, pp.2-3.
16. Strang op.cit. p.221.
17. Timbury op.cit. notes on Infra-Red Instruments, p.3 and B & S Symbols Book.
18. Strang op.cit. pp.229-30.
19. MB No.4, meeting of 3 April 1964.
20. AR No.54, 1966 and Strang op.cit. p.231.
21. Typescript 'Survey of Barr & Stroud activity in the field of medical instruments' (Med. instr.), 1977, section B4.
22. Strang op.cit. p.260 and manuscript note.
23. Med. instr. op.cit. section B3.
24. Barr & Stroud PS5 Systems and Kongsberg Drafting Systems publicity leaflets.
25. MB No.4, meeting of 13 May 1964.
26. Strang op.cit. p.231.
27. AR No.55, 1967.
28. AR No.56, 1968 and Strang op.cit. pp.239-40.
29. AR No.54, 1966.
30. AR No.56, 1968.
31. MB No.4, meeting of 29 March 1968.
32. MB No.4, meeting of 4 June 1968.
33. Strang op.cit. pp.245-6.
34. MB No.4, meeting of 17 February 1969.
35. AR No.57, 1969.
36. Strang op.cit. p.248.
37. Ibid. p.249 and AR No.56, 1968.
38. MB No.4, meeting of 23 September 1969.
39. Strang op.cit. pp.253-5 and MB No.4, meetings of 28 February and 11 March 1969.
40. AR No.53, 1965, and No.56, 1968.
41. Annual Meetings Minute Book No.1, meeting of 18 May 1970.
42. AR No.57, 1969.
44. MB No.4, meeting of 11 March 1969.
45. MB No.4, meeting of 5 June 1970.
46. Timbury op.cit. notes on Directors.
47. Interviews with T Johnston and D S Ritchie.
48. MB No.4, meeting of 16 October 1970.
49. AR No.58, 1970.
50. AR No.59, 1971.
51. *Government Organization for Defence Procurement and Civil Aerospace* (HMSO 1971), cmd 4641.
52. AR No.59, 1971 and Timbury op.cit. notes on Optical Glass.
53. MB No.4, meeting of 27 April 1971 and John Marriott *Submarine —The Capital Ship of Today* (Ian Allan Ltd 1986), pp.67-8.
54. Timbury op.cit. notes on Rapier and Beaver and Gander op.cit. pp.56-7.
55. MB No.4, meetings of 28-29 January 1971 and interview with D S Ritchie.
56. MB No.4, meeting of 7 December 1971.
58. AR No.60, 1972.
59. Ritchie op.cit. pp.147-8.
60. Ibid. pp.149-50, Marriott op.cit. pp.65-67 and notes supplied by S J Pratt.
61. T Gander *Modern British Armoured Fighting Vehicles* (Patrick Stephens 1986), pp.20 and 22.
62. Timbury op.cit. notes on Neodymium Rangefinders and A L Rodgers et al, op.cit. p.110.
63. Unpublished typescript 'Thermal Imaging Systems' 1979, p.82.

64. Ibid. p.84, and Ritchie op.cit. p.150.
65. Ibid. p.83 and Beaver and Gander, p.98.
66. Med. instr. op.cit. sections A1 and A2.
67. Ibid. A3.
68. Ibid. A4.
69. Ibid. A4, A5.
70. Ibid. A4.
71. Ibid. B3.
72. Ibid. B5.
73. Ibid. C6.
74. Ibid. C3, C4.
75. Ibid. B1, B2.
76. Timbury op.cit. notes on Medical Instruments.
77. AR No.63, 1975 and Timbury op.cit. notes on The Merger with Pilkington Brothers Limited.
78. MB No.4, meeting of 22 August 1973 and interview with T Johnston.
79. Timbury, loc.cit.
80. Ibid.
81. MB No.4, meeting of 21 March 1977 and Press Release by Gordon Morrison, 22 March 1977.
82. Timbury, loc.cit.
83. Letter Sir Alastair Pilkington to Gordon M Morrison, 22 March 1977.

CHAPTER 8

1. T Barker *The Glassmakers: Pilkington — The Rise of an Industrial Glass Company* (Weidefield & Nicolson 1977), p.29.
2. Ibid. pp.416-20.
3. *Pilkington Brothers Limited and UKO International Limited - A Report on the proposed merger* (HMSO 1977), cmd 267, pp.14-19.
4. Ibid. pp.35-42.
5. Ibid. pp.51-62.
6. Minute Book (MB) No.5, meetings of 17 June and 5 October 1977.
7. MB No.5, meeting of 27 October 1977.
8. M C Timbury, typescript notes on Dr J M Strang's unpublished History of Barr & Stroud, notes on Additional Space, p.3.
9. MB No.5, meeting of 27 October 1977.
10. Interview with Hugh Kelly.
11. Information supplied by Gordon Hamilton.
12. MB No.5, meeting of 14 December 1977.
13. MB No.5, meeting of 8 November 1977.
14. Timbury op.cit. notes on Revolution in Iran and interview with C G Lindsay.
15. MB No.5, meeting of 7 November, 1978.
16. MB No.5, meeting of 12 December 1978 and interview with T Johnston and C G Lindsay.
17. AR No.66, 1978, and M C Timbury loc.cit.
18. AR No.66, 1978.
19. MB No.5, meeting of 6 March 1979.
20. Barr & Stroud (B & S) Symbols Book and Kongsberg Drafting Systems publicity leaflet.
21. Timbury op.cit. notes on Commercial Products.
22. Timbury op.cit. notes on Medical Products.
23. AR No.67, 1979.

24. MB No.5, meeting of 12 December 1978.
25. Terry Gander, *Modern British Armoured Fighting Vehicles* (Patrick Stephens 1986), pp.39-41 and 77.
26. AR No.65, 1977.
27. B & S Symbols Book.
28. E J Grove *Vanguard to Trident — British Naval Policy since World War II* (The Bodley Head 1987), pp.343-4.
29. MB No.5, meeting of 11 November 1980.
30. MB No.5, meeting of 28 April 1981.
31. MB No.6, meeting of 30 September 1981.
32. AR No.69, 1981.
33. Grove op.cit. pp.345-353.
34. MB No.6 meeting of 26 August 1981 and Pamphlet 500/12 and 9 J1888A 'Thermal Imaging for Chieftain'.
35. MB No.6, meeting of 30 September 1981.
36. Ibid.
37. MB No.5, meeting of 29 June 1981 and MB No.6, meeting of 30 September 1981.
38. Notes supplied by S J Pratt.
39. AR No.70, 1982.
40. Timbury op.cit. notes on Additional Space.
41. AR No.68, 1980 and AR No.69, 1981.
42. AR No.70, 1982.
43. MB No.6, meeting of 2 February 1982.
44. MB No.6, meetings of 29 September and 23 November 1982.
45. MB No.6, meeting of 23 January 1983.
46. MB No.6, meetings of 19 and 27 April 1983.
47. MB No.6, meeting of 24 March 1982.
48. MB No.6, meeting of 20 July 1982.
49. MB No.6, meeting of 20 July 1982.
50. MB No.6, meetings of 29 September 1982 and 22 March 1983.
51. AR No.71, 1983 and MB No.6, meeting of 16 February 1983.
52. AR No.71, 1983.
53. MB No.6, meeting of 26 October 1983.
54. AR No.71, 1983, and AR No.72, 1984.
55. MB No.6, meeting of 26 September 1984.
56. AR No.72, 1984.
57. Interview with T Johnston and C G Lindsay.
58. AR No.72, 1984.
59. AR No.73, 1985.
60. MB No.6, meeting of 20 March 1986 and TQM information literature.
61. MB No.6, meeting of 23 April 1985.
62. AR No.74, 1986.
63. Jules Ambrose 'Why once-dingy Pilkington now has that certain sparkle' *International Management*, August 1986, pp.44-48.
64. Ibid.
65. *Pilkington News Bid Fight Special*, 28 November 1986.
66. Pamphlet 'Why you should reject BTR', Pilkington, 10 December 1986.
67. John Manley 'Pilkington: No longer just a local hero' *Financial Weekly*, No.409, 5-11 February 1987, and interview with T Johnston.
68. *Pilkington News*, 11 November 1981, p.1.
69. Interviews with T Johnston and C G Lindsay.

BIBLIOGRAPHY

Allen, J, *Lasers and Holograms*, Pepper Press, London, 1983

Beaver, P, and Gardner, T, *Modern British Military Missiles*, Patrick Stephens, Wellingborough, 1986

Bartlett, C J, *The Long Retreat — A Short History of British Defence Policy, 1945-70*, Macmillan, London, 1972

Bayliss, J, (ed), *Alternative Approaches to British Defence Policy*, Macmillan, London, 1983

Caldwell, Sir Charles, and Headlam, Sir John, *History of the Royal Artillery 1860-99*, Vols 1-3, London, 1937-40

Campbell, John, 'The Battle of Tsu-Shima', *Warship*, Nos 5-8, 1978

Campbell, John, *Jutland: An Analysis of the Fighting*, Conway Maritime Press, London, 1986

Campbell, John, *Naval Weapons of World War Two*, Conway Maritime Press, London, 1985

Clarke, R Wallace, 'Drawing a Bead', *Aeroplane Monthly*, February-June, 1983

Council for Science and Society, *UK Military R & D*, Oxford University Press, Oxford, 1986

Critchley, M, *British Warships & Auxiliaries*, Maritime Books, Cornwall, 1987/8 edition

Critchley, M, *British Warships Since 1945*, Maritime Books, Cornwall, 1981

Farndale, General Sir Martin, *History of the Royal Regiment of Artillery, Western Front 1914-18*, RAI, London, 1986

Gardner, T, *Modern British Armoured Fighting Vehicles*, Patrick Stephens, Wellingborough, 1986

Gardner, T, *Modern Royal Air Force Aircraft*, Patrick Stephens, Wellingborough, 1987

Gleichen, Alexander, *The Theory of Modern Optical Instruments*, HMSO, London, 1921, 2nd Edition, with appendix by H H Emsley and W Swaine

Grove, E J, *Vanguard to Trident. British Naval Policy since World War II*, The Bodley Head, London, 1987

Johnson, F A, *Defence by Ministry —The British Ministry of Defence 1944-1974*, Duckworth, London, 1980

Kemp, Paul J, *British Submarine in World War Two*, Arms and Armour Press, Poole, 1987

MacLeod, Roy and Kay, 'War and Economic Development: Government and the Optical Industry in Britain, 1914-18' in J M Winter (ed), *War and Economic Development*, Cambridge University Press, 1975

McLean, Iain, *The Legend of Red Clydeside*, John Donald, Edinburgh, 1983

Marder, Arthur J, *From the Dreadnought to Scapa Flow*, Vol. 3, 2nd Edition, Oxford University Press, 1978

Marriott, J, *Submarine —The Capital Ship of Today*, Ian Allan, London, 1986

More, Charles, *Skill and the English Working Class 1876-1914*, Croom Helm, London, 1980

Northcott, Maurice, *Hood Design and Construction*, Bivouac Books, London, 1975

Raven, Alan, and Roberts, John, *British Battleships of World War Two*, Arms and Armour Press, Poole, 1976

Reid, William, 'Binoculars in the Army', *Army Museum*, 1981-84

Rodgers, A L, et al, *Brassey's Battlefield Weapons Systems and Technology Vol VII - Surveillance and Target Acquisition Systems*, Brassey's Defence Publishers, 1983

Roskill, S W, *The Navy at War 1939-45*, Collins, London, 1960

Rosecronce, R N, *Defence of the Realm —British Strategy in the Nuclear Epoch*, Columbia University Press, New York and London, 1968

Sked, A, and Cook, C, *Post-war Britain — A Political History*, Penguin Books, London, 1984

Sumida, Jon T, 'British Capital Ship Design and Fire-Control in the Dreadnought Era', *Journal of Modern History*, Vol 51, March 1979

Sumida, Jon T, (ed), *The Pollen Papers*, Allen & Unwin, London, 1984

Watton, Ross, *The Cruiser Belfast*, Conway Maritime Press, London, 1985

Index

Aberdeen University, 98, 168
Adie, Patrick, 19, 20
Admiralty Compass Observatory, 190
    Fire Control Clock, 123
    Gunnery Establishment, 165
    Research Laboratory, 170
    Signals Establishment, 154
Alison, Andrew, 157, 172, 175
Allan Glen's School, 32, 38
Alliance Cinematograph Co, 103, *103*
Anniesland Works, opens 45
    aerial photos, *104, 131, 136, 159, 217*
    electronic lab, *162*
    environmental testing, *193-4*
    gear cutting dept, 171, 180
    North West Works, *101*, 114
    quality control dept, *193*, 196-7
    South Works, 221
    West Works, 115, *131, 134, 138*, 171, 192, *229*, 230
Anti-vibration mountings, 95
Apnoea radar, 204
Apprentices, 48, *50*, 112
Armstrong, Mitchell & Co, 30, 33
Armstrong, Whitworth & Co, 34, 50
Arrol & Co, Sir William, 43
Arrol-Johnston Motor Car Works, 49
Arsenic trisulphide, 168
ARTEMIS, 227
A & S Engineering Design (Edinburgh), 211
Ashton Lane workshops, *36*, 37, *38, 39, 44*
Associated Industrial Consultants, 175, 183
Atomic Energy Authority, 170-1, 173, 175, 182
Atomic Weapons Research Establishment, 204
Auden, A C, 45
Austenitic stainless steel, 163
Austin Lighting Co, 107
Austin Motor Co, 107
Auto Club, Scottish, 124

Babcock & Wilcox, 114
Baird, John Logie, 176
Balinsky, Pierre, 68
Ballantyne, Archibald, 138
Balliol College, Oxford, 15
Bank of Scotland, 230
Barclays Nominees, 183
Barclay nuclear power station, *183*
Barr, Archibald, early life, 13
    Young Assistant, 14, 15
    Professor of Engineering, Yorkshire College of Science, 15
    first rangefinder, 22
    Professor of Civil Engineering and Mechanics, Glasgow University, 24
    on efficiency, 46
    FT1, 58
    Barr & Stroud Ltd, 71
    retires from chair, 72
    glassworks, 77
    depth and roll Recorders, 84
    strike 1917, 97
    WW1, 99
    semi-retirement, 116
    death, 123
Barr & Stroud Ltd, 69
    Amateur Athletic Association, 158
    public coy, 159
Barr & Stroud's Patents, 31 *et seq*
Barr, Douglas, 99, 106
Barr es Stroud es Tarsa, 67
Barr, Gordon, 99
Barr, Isabella, 17, 24, 32
Barr, Lieut Jack, 99
Barr und Stroud GmbH, 67
Bausch & Lomb, 67-9, 110
Beatty, Vice Admiral Sir David, 89
Becker, Professor Ludwig, 43
Bell, Robert, 196
Berry, Charles, 227
Bharat Electronics, *221*, 226
Binoculars, 104, 120, *121*, 145-6, *146*, 150, 199
Blair, George, 37, 49
Blindfire radar *see* Rapier missile
Blue Study, 169
Boer War, 41
Bomb Sights, 126, 139
Boeing Aerospace, 230
Brash, Eric, 194, 197
British Aerospace, 203, 219, 222-3
British Aircraft Corporation (BAC), 181, 188
BTR, 229
Buccaneer aircraft, 169
Burt and McCollum, 106
Butter dishes, 120
Byres Road workshops, 31, 33, 36

Cail, D, 208
Calcium Aluminate, 168
Camera, high speed, *169*, 170-1
Camera Obscura, Edinburgh, 154, *155*
Cape Matapan 1942, Battle of, 146
Caro, Dr C G, 204
Caxton Street, 45
Central Station Instrument Board, 122, *122*
Chance Brothers & Co, 78, 206-7
Clifton College, Bristol, 15
Close Range Blind Fire, 156
Clyde Workers Committee, 75
Colidar, 178-9
Collier Associates, Thomas, 204
Coopers & Lybrand, 206
Craig & Co, A F, 13
Christie, W H M, 20

Conscription, 73, 96
Cooke-Pollen rangefinder, 108
Cook, R W, 176
Cooke & Sons, Thomas, 22, 41

Davy, John R, 146, 157, 171, *175*, 176, 179, 195
De Gaulle, General, 149
de Grousilliers, A H, 56
Defence Research Policy Committee, 185
Dendrometer, 153, *153*, 170
Depth and Roll Recorders, Torpedo, 84, *87*
Dial Sight, GB, 88
Dichroic coatings, 170, *180*, 178
Dilution of labour, 75, 77
Dobbie, W H McInnes (Electronics) Ltd, 173-4
Dogger Bank Incident 1904, 51
Dounreay nuclear power station, 182
'Dragon' reactor, 182
Dreyer Fire Control Table, 86
Driver's sight *see* tanks
Dumaresq calculator, 86
Dunn, John, 67

Edison Swan Electric Co, 43
EEC research contract, 226
ELINT aerial, 219
Elven Precision, 223
EMI, 189
Emett, Louisa, *see* Stroud
Endoscopes, 191, 204, 223
Environmental Test Laboratory, 207
EONHPM Mast, 231
Epidiascope, mapping, 119, *119*
ESM mast, *194*, 219
ET 316, *see* Rapier

Falklands War 1982, 221-2
Ferranti, 140, 157, 169, 189, *196*
Fibrelase100, *220*, 223
Fibre optics, 176, 191-2, *193*, 195-7, 204, 214
Fighting Vehicle Research and Development Establishment (FVRDE), 179, 186-7, 210-11
Firestreak missile, 167, 168-9, *177*
Fiske, Lieut Bradley A, 36, 40
Fleming & Co, Robert, 206
Float Glass Process, 199, 207
Forbes, Professor George, 42
French, (Sir) James Weir
        joins Barr & Stroud, 32
        in Germany, 37
        chief scientific assistant, 45
        commission, 50
        design department, 71
        glassworks, 77
        periscopes, 83
        GB dial sight, 88

Inter-Allied Commission of Control, 94
        technical director, 118
        deputy chairman, 125
        chairman, 131
        WW2, 135-7
        knighthood, 148
        retires, 157

Garvie, Ian, 150, 157, 172, 201
Genito Urinary Manufacturing Co, 191
GEC, 202-3, 215
Germanium, 168, 190, 202
Gerschun, Professor A, 67
Gerstenberg, Frank, 122, 157, 172, 194
Ghosh, General, *221*
Glasgow, University of, 13, 14, 38, 97, 124, 172-3, 189, 192, 219
Glassworks, Anniesland, 78, 199
Goerz AG, CP, 37, 54, 60, 65, *66*, 68, 104, 139
Grant, Roy, *111*
Green, Sir Owen, 229-30
Grubb, Howard, 83
Guided missiles, 162, 167, 179, 181, 185, *187*, *197*, 203, *208*, 214
Gunn, John C, 175, 201, 208
Gunsight, reflector, GD5, 126
                GJ3, 16, *126*, 139
                GM, 127, *127*, 139
                Mark III, 140
Gyro Angle Re-Transmission Unit (GARTU), 165, *166*
Gyro Gun Sight, 140

Hahn, Friedrich, 60, *66*
Hailsham, Lord, 174
Hall, Commodore S S, 83
Haw-Haw, Lord, 135
Hay Management Services, 219, 222
Healey, Denis, 185
Health, Ministry of, 176, 191
Health and Social Security, Department of, 204
Height and stagger gauge, *179*
Heightfinders, *81*, 82, 121, 127, *130*, 138, 143, *145*, *151*
Henderson, James Blacklock, 38, 45
'Hero' reactor, 182
Heseltine, Michael, 223
High Angle Control Towers, 143
Hilger & Co, Adam, 26, 27, 39
Holland Torpedo Boat Co, 82
Holmes, Michael J, 229
Home Guard, 136
Hope, Dr A, 170
Hughes Aircraft Corporation, 178-9, 186
Hughes International, 178, 187, 189

Impactor golf machine, 103
Imperial Chemical Industries (ICI), 171
Improved Fire Control System, 203, 211
Inclinometer, S F, *88*, 89

Industrial Committee 1916, 77, 96
Integrated Optics, *213*
Infra-red, 162, 167, 168, *173*, *176*, *177*, 189, 195-6, 202, *208*, 230
    IR4 *see* SHORTIE
    IR18, *196*, 203, *209*
International Telephone and Telecommunications Corporation, 198
Iran, Shah of, 201, 211, 219

Jackson, Harold Drinkwater
    joins Barr and Stroud, 29
    office manager, 32 *et seq*
    de facto commercial manager, 38
    at Anniesland, 48
    at Tsushima, 54
    on FT, rangefinder, 59
    Austro-Hungary, 65
    Barr & Stroud Ltd, 71
    dealings with unions, 75-8
    administration during WW1, 79, 96
    at Muir's trial, 96
    managing director, 99
    death, 115
Jameson, Margaret, 105
Japanese Navy, Imperial, 31, 33, 42, 50 *et seq*, 108, 110
Jellicoe, Admiral John R, 79, 90
Johnston, Thomas, 158, 194, 198-9, 204, 210, 214-5, *221*, 222, 230, 232, *234*
Jones, Trefor, 222, 227, 230
Jones, Professor R V, 168
Jutland 1916, Battle of, 89-95

Kelly, Hugh, 208, 210
Kelvin, Bottomley & Baird, 83
Kelvin, Lord, 14-15, 18
Keuffel & Esser, 67
Khomeni, Ayatollah, 211
Kollmorgen, 167
Kongsberg Vapenfabrik, 192, 214
Korean War, 156

Lancaster, University of, 204
Lane, R.N., Commander, 165
Lane Roundabout, 165
Lantern-slide camera, 17

Lasers, 178, 195, 202, 214, *225*
    CO_2, *212*
    Nd:YAG, 203, *212*, 214-5
    Ruby, 178, 202-3
Lasers for Medicine Inc, 223
Levine, Peter, *232*
Leitz, 226
Lindsay, Charles, 210, 218, *221*, 227, 232, *232*
Lister Auto Truck, 174
Lithium niobate, *213*, 214, 223
LOFTIE thermal imager, 203

London office, 98
London University, 15, 16

M578, *see*, Rapier missile, tracked
McCann, John, *111*
McFarlane, James, 67
Macgill, Charles, 49, 95
Mackenzie, Ian, 150, *153*, 171, *175*, 179, *188*, 188-9, 198
Maclean, Neil J, 49, 71, 75, 77, 96, 118, 135, *135*, 157
MacLehose, Robert, 29, 45, 135, *217*, 219-21
McNab, Robert, 32, 66
Magnavox, 226, *230*
Magnetic Compass Test Table, 191
Majuba Hill, Battle of, 18
Mallock, Arnulf, 20, 26
Marconi Wireless Telegraph Co, 107, 170
Marindin, Captain A H, 60, 64
Mauler missile, 181, 188
Maydon, RN, Lieut, 147
Medical Instrument Development Group, 204-5
Medical Supply Association, 204
Mekometer, Watkin, 18, *19*, 23, 26, 41, 60
Microdensitometer, *168*, 170, 173, 175, 192, 204
Middlemiss, W, *17*
Milne, A J, 208
Minvade, 223
Monopolies Commission, 206, 208
Morrison, Francis, 97, 105, 107, 118, 157, 161, *161*, 172, 176, 184, 194
Morrison, Gordon, 176, 183, 194, 199, 205-6, 208, 214, 222
Morrison, John Donald, 32
Mountbatten, Lord Louis, 186
Mouton, Admiral, 87
Monte Casino 1944, Battle of, 138
Muir, John, 75, 77, 96
Munitions, Ministry of, 73, 77, 96
Murray Johnstone, 230

NATO, 174, 179, 185, 188
Negretti and Zambra, 205
Nicholason, Sir Robin, 227, 230
Nikon, 226
Nord Deutscher Lloyd Co, 43
Nott, John, 215, 221
Nuclear weapons, 161, 178, 185
Nuclear power, 170, 175, 183

O'Beirne, T H, 182
Obhoukhoff Steel Works, 67, 97
Officer of Fair Trading, 206
Oliver, Admiral Sir Geoffrey, 146
Optique et Precision de Levallois, 110
Optophone, *104*, 105
Owen's College, Manchester, 15

PA Management Consultants, 227
Paris workshop, 66

Parra-Mantois, 73
Parson, Sir Charles, 105
Patent disputes, 1911-12, 60-5
Paterson, Alexander, 45
Peat Technologies, 204
Periscopes, submarine, 82-4, 85, 112-4, 121, *123*, 146-8, *161*, 162-4, *163-4*, 167, *181*, 182, 183, 189-90, *190*, *194*, 198, 201-2, 204, 210-11, 219, 226, *228*, *229*, 230, *231*
        see also sextant, rangefinders, submarines and Atomic
          Energy Authority
Park & Elmer Co, 209
Philips, 215, 217
Photonymograph, 119, *120*
Pickering, R & Y, 169
Pilkington Bros plc, 205-7, 215, 222-3, 227, 229, 231-2
        Medical Systems, *220*, 223
        PE, 207-8, 230
Pilkington, Sir Alastair, 206-7
Pilkington, Antony, 223, 227, 229-30
Pilkington, Dr Lawrence, 209
Pinkston Power Station, 124
Plessey, 179
Plotting tables, 119, 183
Polaris missile, 185, 202
Pollen, Arthur H, 69, 87
Porter, Oliver, 37, 45, 50, 67
Prices and Consumer Protection, Department of, 206, 208
Procurement Executive, 215
PS5 mapping systems, 192-3, 214, 219
Public Accounts, House of Commons Committee of, 149
Pym, Francis, 215

RADAR, 140-4
        Navigational Chart Comparison Unit, 182
        Research Establishment (RRE), 167-8
Range and Order Indicators, 34, *35*, 38, *69*
Rangefinders, laser, 178-9, *184*, 186-7, 204, *212*
        LF1, 179, *185*
        LF2, 186-8
Rangefinders, optical, Barr & Stroud

first infantry model:	19 *et seq*	
Aldershot trials 1889:	23	
first naval model, FA1:	24 *et seq*	
FA2:	33 *et seq*	
first artillery model:	42	
FA3:	43 *et seq*	
FQ2:	55 *et seq*	
FT1:	58	
FR:	79	
15 foot FT:	79	
FT 17 and 27:	80	
FT 24:	90	
FT 32:	108	
FX:	108	
FM:	110	
FZ:	112	
FT 37:	138, 150, 168, 222	

Rangefinders, optical, Carl Zeiss of Jena, 42, 56 *et seq*, 60, 65, 68, 92-5, 108, 110
Rangefinders, periscope, 83
Rapid cassette changer, 178, 204
Rapier missile, 181, *187*, 188, 197, 200-1, 204, 222-3
        Tracked, 201, 211, *216*, 219
Rayner, Derek, 199-200
Red Top missile, 169
Research Enterprises, 138
Reid, Sinclair, 26, 32, 37, 77, *111*, *128*
Ritchie, David S, 158, 171-2, 174, 194-5, 198-9, 202, 227
ROCORD, 88
Rowan & Co, D, 48
Rowan System, 48
Royal Aircraft Establishment, 140, 182
Royal Armament Research and Development Establishment (RARDE), 190
'Royston', Dowanhill, 26, *27*
Rozhestvensky, Rear-Admiral Zinovy Petrovich, 50 *et seq*
Russian Society for Optical and Mechanical Industry, 68
Russo-Japanese War 1904-5, 50 *et seq*

Sandys, Duncan, 172-3
Schnorkel, 163
Schott, Otto, 56
Scorpion armoured reconaissence vehicle, *188*
Scott, Sir Giles Gilbert, 153
Scott, R.N., Captain Percy, 86
Seacat Dark Fire missiles, 182, *192*
Seaslug missile, 156
Second Pacific Fleet, IRN, 51 *et seq*
Sextant, periscope, 164-5, *164-5*
Ships: *Amazon*, 122
         Ambuscade, 122
         Arethusa, 26
         Asahi, 33
         Asama, 33
         Askold, 51
         Aurora, 52
         Azuma, 33
         Barham, 90
         Belfast, 156
         Bismarck, 141-3
         Blanco Encelada, 31
         Blenheim, *29*
         Borodino, 53
         Buenos Aires, 31
         Camperdown, 30
         Canopus, 35
         Courbet, *94*
         Diana, 50, 51
         Dreadnought, 55
         Dreadnought (nuclear submarine), 166
         Duke of York, 143
         Excalibur, 166
         Excellent, 26

Extant, 149
Hatsuse, 33
Hood, 109, *109*, 141-3
Indefatiguable, 89
Inflexible, 92
Iron Duke, 92
Invincible, 55, 91
Iwate, 33
Izumo, 33
Kelly, 145
King George V, 143, *144*
Kniaz Suvaroff, 52
Konig, 92
Lutzow, 91, (WW2), 148
Malaya, 90
Mikasa, 33, 52
Nelson, 109
Orel, 53, 54
Orion, 90
Oslyaba, 54, 54
Pallada, 51
Prince of Wales, 141-3
Prinz Eugen, 141-3
Queen Mary, 90
Revenge, 90
Rodney, 109
Royal Oak, 90
Royal Sovereign, *31*
Scharnhorst, 143, 148
Sheffield, *142*, *143*
Shikishima, 33
Taciturn, 165
Takasaga, 33
Thunderer, 92
Tirpitz, 148
Tokiwa, 33
U-1407, 166
Umbra, 147
Undaunted, 82
Valiant, 90
Variag, 51
Victoria, 2
Warspite, 90
Yakumo, 33
Yoshino, 31
SHORTIE (IR4), *189*, 211
Siebert, GRE, 67, 73
Singapore 1942, Fall of, 112
Single-sleeve valve motor cycle engine, 106, *106*, *107*
Sino-Japanese War, 31
Slight, Arthur, 227
Smith, Albert, 37
Smith Gordon R, 227
Smoke indicators, 153, 170
Societe d'Optique et de Mecanique, 110
Societe Francaise des Instruments d'Optique, 121

SOLIDAC computer, 182
Sound locators, 127, *129*
Spanish-American War, 36
Squires, Rear-Admiral R R, 210
Standard Life, 230
Stereoscope, topographical, *118*, 119
Steward Telemeter, *19*,
Strang, John Martin, 62, 67, 97, 118, 120, 154, 157, 161, 171-2, 174, *175*, 179, 184, *191*, 193-4, 204
Strang, W Guthrie, 171-2, 175, 183, 194, 199, 208, 214
Strang, William G, 32, 38
Strathclyde University of, 227
Strathleven factory, *193*, 197, *213*, 219
Stroud, Bertie, 99
Stroud, Henry, 16
Stroud, Louisa, 17
Stroud, Mary, 16
Stroud, Reginald, 99
Stroud, William
    early life, 15
    studies in Germany, 16
    Professor of Physics, 16
    first rangefinder, 22
    range and order instruments, 38
    infantry rangefinders, 42
    FQ, 56, 95
    FT, 59
    Barr & Stroud Ltd, 71
    retires from chair, 72
    fire control, 87
    WW1, 99
    semi-retirement, 116
    death, 129
Submarines, 'A' class, 163
    'T' class, 163, 165, 178
    Oberon class, 166, 178, *181*, 182, 190, *194*
    Porpoise class, 166, 178, *194*
    Valiant class, *190*, *231*
    Trafalgar class, *216*, 219
    Resolution class, 190
    Vanguard class, 230
    'X' class, 182
    'X'-Craft, 148
Stinger missile (PMS), 230
Swingfire missile, *197*, 203, 214

Takata & Co, 50
Tanks, 186-7, 202-3
    Challenger, *213*
    Chieftain, 179, *184*, 185-6, *186*, 211, *212*, 217
    Churchill, 179, 182
    Conqueror, 179
    Khalid, 214
    Scorpion, 210-11, *212*
    Shir, 211
Television, colour, 170

Thatcher, Mrs Margaret, 211, 215, 221, 223, *231*
Thermal imaging, *189*, 190, 192, 195, *197*, 202-3, *209*, 210, *213*, 214, 219
Thermal Observation Gunnery Sighting System, (TOGS), *213*, 215, 217, 219, 226
Thomson, Professor James, 14, 15, 24
Thomson, Sir William *see* Kelvin
Thorneycroft, Peter, 185
Timbury, Montague C, 171-2, 183, 193, 196, 198-9
Togo, Admiral Count, 31, 51 *et seq*, 11
Torpedo Control Calculator (TCC), 165, *166*
Total Quality Management (TQM) Project, 227, 232, *234*
Trades Unions, 75, 96
Tryon, Vice-Admiral Sir Reginald, 29
Tsuboi, Rear-Admiral, 31
Tsushima 1905, Battle of, 51 *et seq*

UK Optical and Industrial Holdings, 207-8
Uniform scale gear, 88
United States National Defence Research Committee, 167

Vacuum pump, 43, *43*
Vale of Leven *see* Strathleven factory
Vickers clock, 86
Video Homer, 169
Video therm, 192, 204

Waddell, R S, 183
Walker, Archibald, *119*
Walker, William, 210, 214, 223
Washbourn, Rear-Admiral R E, 178
Washington Naval Treaty, 108
Watkinson, J, 23
Watt, R Watson, 140
Weapons Development Committee, 185
West of Scotland Neuro-surgical Unit, 178
Western Regional Hospital Board, Scotland, 204
Westerton-of-Mugdock, Milngavie, 125
White & Co, James, 15, 22, 25, *26*, 29, 31, 37, 82
Window, wire heated, 166-7, *177*
Wolverhampton Exhibition 1902, 43
Women workers, 77, 134
Worker, The, 96
World War, First, 73 *et seq*
World War, Second, 134 *et seq*
Worsley, Sir Richard, 222-3

Yalu, Battle of, 31
Yamada, Mr, 111, *111*
Yamamoto, Commander Isoroku, 111
Yorkshire College of Science, 15-17, 24, 38, 124
Young, Isabella, *see* Barr
Younger, George, 221

Zaharoff, Basil, 53
Zeiss of Jena, Carl (see also Rangefinders), *66*, 104, 120